The
Viagra
Ad Venture

PETER LANG
New York • Washington, D.C./Baltimore • Bern
Frankfurt am Main • Berlin • Brussels • Vienna • Oxford

Jay Baglia

The
Viagra
Ad Venture

Masculinity,
Media, and the
Performance
of Sexual Health

PETER LANG
New York • Washington, D.C./Baltimore • Bern
Frankfurt am Main • Berlin • Brussels • Vienna • Oxford

Library of Congress Cataloging-in-Publication Data

Baglia, Jay.
The Viagra ad venture: masculinity, media,
and the performance of sexual health / Jay Baglia.
p. cm.
Includes bibliographical references and index.
1. Sildenafil. 2. Impotence—Social aspects.
3. Enzyme inhibitors industry. I. Title.
RC889.B27 616.6'92061—dc22 2004020889
ISBN 0-8204-7489-4

Bibliographic information published by **Die Deutsche Bibliothek**.
Die Deutsche Bibliothek lists this publication in the "Deutsche
Nationalbibliografie"; detailed bibliographic data is available
on the Internet at http://dnb.ddb.de/.

Cover design Lisa Barfield

The paper in this book meets the guidelines for permanence and durability
of the Committee on Production Guidelines for Book Longevity
of the Council of Library Resources.

© 2005 Peter Lang Publishing, Inc., New York
275 Seventh Avenue, 28th Floor, New York, NY 10001
www.peterlangusa.com

Printed in the United States of America

To my uncle, John Alden (1928–2003),
who taught me the value of asking questions

Contents

Acknowledgments

This book would not have been possible (or nearly as much fun) without the treasured guidance and mentoring of Elizabeth Bell. The summer morning I walked into her class (ORI2000: Introduction to Communication as Performance) changed my life—all for the better. She is a marvelous thinker, a brilliant writer, and my very good friend.

At Peter Lang Publishing my heartfelt thanks to Damon Zucca, who believed in this project from the moment we met (his nonverbal response spoke volumes). I'm also thankful for the work of Lisa Dillon and Dan Geist at Peter Lang.

The very early days of this project were nurtured and stroked by Eric Eisenberg, Jane Jorgenson, Carolyn DiPalma, and Marilyn Myerson—I am deeply indebted to these scholars for the questions they asked. The Department of Communication at the University of South Florida is a special place and I'd particularly like to thank Michael Arrington, Christopher Carden, Angela Day, Bernard Downs, Kim Golombisky, Krista Hirschmann, Stacy Holman Jones, Dennis Leoutsakas, Daniel Makagon, David Payne, Gil Rodman, Larry Russell, G'han Singh, and Lisa Tillmann-Healy for their friendship and support while we shared space there. Many of my colleagues at Southwestern University read drafts of these chapters and heard presentations of this research in various stages: Hector Amaya, Teena Gabrielson, Dan Hilliard, Mary Grace Neville, Kathleen Juhl, Elizabeth Piedmont-Marton, and Sarah Walker. These multidisciplinary perspectives were of inestimable value. I'd also like to thank Joan Parks at the Frank Smith Library Center at Southwestern.

I attended the Summer Institute on the Study of Sexuality, Culture, and Society at the International School for Humanities and Social Sciences at the Universiteit van Amsterdam during the warm summer months of 2001.

While there I met Carole Vance and Stefan Dudink; these two scholar-activists proved to be sources of inspiration and I am grateful for the time spent in their classrooms. And I shared memorable conversations with Jessica Zucker, Leslie Gotlib, and Mirjam Schieveld.

Any study involving the body, communication, and sexuality inevitably propels the researcher to a deeper understanding of his/her own. And I acquired body knowledge as the result of the attention paid to me by Dale Morphew, Bonnie Tiemann, Margot Montemayor, Ken Blair, Meghan Lowery, Danise Rogers, and Christine Kiesinger—massage therapists, yoga instructors, reiki practitioners, and enlightened physicians.

I have been blessed by the presence in my life of four extraordinary brothers: Greg, Andy, Alan, and Joel. They are creative, loving, funny (!), and devilishly handsome. Similarly, the friendships I've enjoyed with Bill Barrett and Joe Conn have proved to be a lifelong exploration of masculinity and its fluidity. Mel's Hot Dogs live on! To Ron Olson, my high school creative writing teacher, who showed me (first) how rewarding this can be. To my father, the late Joseph Baglia, I owe my love of sports and feisty countenance. To Lynn and Vincent Nalbone, I am deeply grateful for all they have provided (and for finding each other). I must acknowledge my partner, Elissa Foster, for her kindness, her suggestions, her editing skills, her patience, and, above all, her love. Finally, I'd like to thank my students—for asking tough questions and exceeding expectations.

ntroduction
Erections, Normalcy, and Performance

Nearly every book about human sexuality will tell you that impotence is something all men experience at some time or another—that is, it's "normal." And if this is true then it helps explain the multitude of treatments, advice, and caution that have been recommended over the centuries: from the tiger penis and rhinoceros horn powder (and other natural "aphrodisiacs" like mandrake and yohimbine) to vacuum pumps, penile prostheses, and sex counseling and therapy.[1] But it wasn't until 1983 that pharmacology entered the market.

At the annual meeting of the American Urological Association, held that year in Las Vegas, British physiologist Giles Brindley took a gamble. He had been working on a treatment for impotence that required injecting a drug (phentolamine) directly into the shaft of the penis.[2] That Brindley had been experimenting on himself was not a big surprise (he was fifty-seven at the time and self-study seemed to satisfy the ethics committee); that he injected himself moments prior to his presentation and then pulled down his pants so that his colleagues could take a look—now that was a surprise. Thus the pharmacological era of treating impotence was born.

In March 1998, the Food and Drug Administration (FDA) approved the release of Viagra (sildenafil citrate)—a highly anticipated prescription medicine, manufactured by Pfizer Pharmaceuticals, to treat erectile impotence. In the first month of its release, nearly 600,000 prescriptions were filled; analysts predicted that Viagra would be a billion-dollar product. As a result, Pfizer's stock values soared, making Wall Street investors as excited as Viagra users.[3] By November 1998, however, the FDA confirmed that at least 130 deaths in the United States had resulted from taking Viagra. This news prompted changes in product labeling and calls for more careful screening by physicians, as well as raising suspicion over Viagra's rapid FDA approval.

Seven years later, curiosity about Viagra abounds. Its use is widespread among straight and gay men alike. Even as questions continue to be raised not only about the drug's safety, but also about its ability to improve the quality of erections, decrease the "wait time" after ejaculation, and increase libido, its use as a party drug (to counteract erection-debilitating recreational drugs like cocaine and ecstasy) has become sufficiently common to give rise to a street name: poke. Moreover, the overwhelming success of Viagra has spurred the development and release of at least two competing prescription medications here in the United States.[4] As a profeminist, I have been trained to be cautious, indeed skeptical, about how the marketing and mass media industry *language* claims, especially where gender, health, and the body are concerned. As a man rapidly approaching "a certain age" I was especially intrigued by the ways in which Pfizer Pharmaceuticals marketed Viagra, by how the news media seemed to uncritically embrace the arrival of "the potency pill," and by how everybody was talking about it.

As a commercial product, Viagra entered the American lexicon quickly and is now the most recognized brand name in the United States after Coca-Cola.[5] Considered as a word, Viagra evokes vitality, aggression, grace, and vigor (its phonemic resemblance to both Niagara and vagina underscores some of these connotations and encourages others).[6] The myriad ways in which we have come to equate Viagra with sexual performance aptitude are no less remarkable. Three examples: During the television broadcast of a Kiss concert, lead singer Paul Stanley becomes frustrated by the fact that his microphone repeatedly droops on its stand as the result of a loose screw. He looks out at the audience and remarks, "My microphone needs Viagra." When a technician runs onto the stage to tighten it, Stanley adds, "But that doesn't mean *I'm* not excited." A television commercial for Pennzoil motor oil begins with a white-haired gentleman rattling a medicine bottle labeled "Vigoroso." As he swings open the bedroom door his waiting (and apparently willing) wife unties the bow of her nightgown. The very next scene shows the same man swinging open the door to the garage where a classic sports car awaits. This time he is shaking a can of Pennzoil as the graphic reads, "Improve performance and engine reliability." And in Eddie Murphy's *Dr. Doolittle 2,* a pair of Galapagos tortoises who "haven't mated in a hundred years" are told by the famous veterinarian to crush up some pills and mix them in with their food. The next scene shows the male lasciviously (but with characteristic slowness) approaching his mate, warning her to "get ready." Taken together, these snippets from popular culture reinforce how Viagra—known as the "Pfizer Riser" in advertising circles—has significantly impacted attitudes and expectations about male sexual health, aging, erectile dysfunction, and, importantly, treatment options.[7]

In the process of becoming erect, the penis begins to expand and harden due to increased blood flow to the groin. Originally developed to relieve the chest pain occasioned by heart disease, Viagra works by dilating blood vessels, thus improving blood flow through the arteries. For most of the last century, researchers and therapists thought impotence was caused by psychological concerns; the fear of being unable to produce an erection (thereby perpetuating impotence) has been called "performance anxiety." Certain medical experts (including, in an institutional sense, Pfizer) claim damaged arteries at the base of the penis cause "erectile dysfunction," relegating impotence to a structural problem that Viagra can treat. Psychological and relational dynamics have been erased from the equation. The rhetorical change from the feminized, psychologically and relationally flaccid "impotence" to the masculinized, structurally based "erectile dysfunction" has contributed much to this erasure.[8] And by propping up the stumbling male libido through chemical means, Viagra perpetuates the towering illusion that is the male sex role. In so doing, I wonder if Viagra temporarily trumps a potentially transformative moment for masculine sexuality, a critical moment when male sexuality might consider pleasure as important as performance.

Twenty years prior to Viagra's well-promoted debut, James Harrison called attention to the physiological effects of sex roles in a paper titled "Warning: The Male Sex Role May Be Dangerous to Your Health." In this study, Harrison implicates some men's risk-taking behavior as the likely source for everything from automobile accidents to heart attacks.[9] Some (though not all) of the men who die after ingesting Viagra foolishly combine it with a form of nitrate—a chemical found in chest pain medication and in the recreational drugs known as "poppers"—despite awareness of the danger. The risk of such behavior is further amplified by a related psychological trait: in the quest to maintain the image of toughness, Harrison argues, men and boys deny pain and often fail to seek medical attention even when absolutely necessary.[10]

Even at the risk of death, how does the construction of erections persist in the performance of masculine sexuality? In other words, how is it that the erection—in the face of so many other changes on our sexual horizon in the past forty years—has maintained its position as the sine qua non of manliness and of male pleasure? I will consider these questions from a gender studies perspective. Gender studies dispute essentialist claims of masculinity and femininity, recognizing that the cultural characteristics of each are constructed and arbitrarily attributed.[11] An examination of how Viagra reifies the metonymy of erect penis and masculinity, of how it "accomplishes" the masculine, can tell us a great deal about how power is exerted and how social disparities are produced and maintained. In this book I argue that Viagra is manufactured to preserve a particular masculinity and to maintain a specific cultural order.

By taking a pill, men are discouraged from examining the incapacitating effects that stress, poor diet, and alcohol/drug abuse can have on their health generally and on the vascular system specifically.[12] Rather than exploring other possibilities for sexual fulfillment or reassessing their interpersonal relationships, men (and their partners) are instructed to "ask your doctor" and "see if a free sample of Viagra is right for you." Pfizer Pharmaceuticals, the manufacturer of Viagra, thwarts the possibilities for the improvisation of male sexuality at a time in our history when it is becoming more and more obvious that traditional performances of masculinity need desperately to be questioned even as they are revalorized. The raison d'être of most new technologies is to improve the status quo, rather than transform it. As a reinscription of heterotopia's penile-vaginal penetration, the arrival of Viagra may in fact be stalling the potential for new models of male sexuality. We tend to think that necessity is the mother of invention but, as evolutionary biologist Jared Diamond suggests, new technologies can create a society's need for them.[13]

Defining "Normalcy"

In his historical look at normalcy, Columbia University English professor Lennard Davis discusses how the concept of "normal" has shifted from meaning *average*—recognizing and incorporating anomaly—to meaning *ideal*—eradicating anomaly.[14] Recall the *Seinfeld* episode where we find George Costanza trying desperately to describe "shrinkage." After a swim, George is in the process of changing his clothes when a female friend catches sight of him naked. Worried that his penis size will be underestimated, George explains how the cold water impacts the male body, causing the genitals to retreat "like a frightened turtle." He feels "short changed" as he explains, "That was not me." George represents a version of masculinity terrified of being uncovered, of being assessed at less than capacity.[15] Susan Bordo, author of *The Male Body*, maintains that the nonerect penis suggests a delicacy—"a sleepy sweetness"—that renders it a physiological anomaly in its ability to occupy both sides of the hardness-softness continuum. "It's not just soft," Bordo reminds us, "it's *really* soft."[16] Why is it in this limp condition—this soft (not hard) state—that so many men feel vulnerable? Even when the "studliest" characters from our cultural imaginary can be summoned—*Boogie Nights'* Dirk Diggler springs to attention—we are still talking about penises that are languishing in detumescence most of the time. As a culture, why do we deny the penis its usual (normal) structure?[17]

Viagra is prescribed to remedy a perceived aberration—namely, the unresponsive penis.[18] Hardness—whether we're talking about the penis or the personality—has been described by sociobiologist Lionel Tiger as the essence of masculinity; the ability to become hard is thus a *mark* of masculinity.[19] So it seems that the nonerect penis creates two separate but related concerns for the performance of masculinity: it is not at its capacity and, regarding impotence specifically, it is not under control. These two concerns—capacity and control—are directly tied to notions of American masculinity.[20]

Historically, theories of sexuality have used dichotomies as a way to define normalcy. Psychoanalytic theorist Jacqueline Rose, however, has reminded us of how dangerous it is to generalize "male" and "female" when discussing sexuality.[21] Despite advances in our understanding of sexuality over the last forty years, the medical discourse of sexuality has continued to do exactly what Rose warned against by (1) defining physiology in terms of functional and dsyfunctional; (2) suggesting and producing correctives—like Viagra—that fail to take into account sexual variations and possibilities; and (3) maintaining a Cartesian separation of mind and body. Viagra, marketed as a tool to correct a supposed physiological dysfunction, is yet another example of how masculinism defines and controls what is normal.

In the discourse of normalcy, Sophie Freud differentiates among three definitions of "normal."[22] From a statistical perspective, the norm is what is *average* or typical—the normal in this regard is often viewed positively but with a suggestion of mediocrity. Another usage designates normal as *ideal;* the example of consummate good health (mental or physical) gives normal an above-average, aspirational, or potential quality. This definition becomes crucial in a study of how sexual health is assessed. The third definition attests to community standards of behavior. Here, normal is understood as that which is *acceptable and commonplace*—"He was a quiet neighbor. You know, normal." She contends that this third definition of normal is especially likely to reflect culturally specific conventions. With regard to sexuality, Freud gives the examples of homosexuality, masturbation, and oral sex as behaviors that, at one time or another, were viewed as psychologically abnormal and implicated in a host of societal ills.[23]

To Sophie Freud's definitions of normal, psychologist Leonore Tiefer adds two more: the subjective and the clinical.[24] The subjective defines normal from a personal perspective: if I view myself as normal and you are like me, then you are normal, too. Her definition of clinical normalcy shares aspects of both the statistical and the aspirational. In the clinical view of normalcy, if something demonstrates the capacity to exist, then it *should* exist. It is from these fictions of normalcy, suggests sociologist Erving Goffman, that we "impute a wide range of imperfections."[25] Whether or not we believe human sexuality is biologically "natural" or the result of socially constructed "scripted behavior," masculinity and sexual health are social performances enacted daily, with implications for both society's expectations and individual sense-making.[26]

Tiefer maintains that medical authorities—including physicians, health-care administrators, pharmaceutical companies, and insurance companies—provide the dominant ideology of sexuality. Her 1995 book, *Sex Is Not a Natural Act,* examines the power dynamics driving the "biological bedrock"—the overriding tendency to privilege anatomical and physiological domains in the discourse of human sexuality research and, more specifically, sexual health.

Until relatively recently, according to Tiefer, sexual norms came from religious authorities eager to maintain moral boundaries.[27] With regard to women's desire, Tiefer maintains that the Judeo-Christian tradition dominant in Western society has, to some extent, endorsed the "denial of fleshly interests," while for adolescent boys in particular, a high degree of interest and enjoyment in sex—that is, heterosexual sex—is required for our culture's approved performance of teenage masculinity. Now, owing to the statistical data collected in the past century by the likes of William Kraft-Ebbing, Havelock Ellis, Alfred Kinsey, William Masters and Virginia Johnson, and Shere Hite, the American public turns to "experts" for their definitions of sexual normalcy. With regard to sexual health, the biomedical model (drawing on presentations of anatomy and physiology as universal and innate) and the statistical "evidence" (establishing the means and modes of sexual variation) do not take into account the individual experiences of pleasure, fantasy, and sexual diversity.

This double dose of "hard" science, with the full endorsement of health-care's political economy, has resulted in the unquestioned authority with which the medical profession delimits, diagnoses, and doctors sexual dysfunction. What has happened with Viagra is that the very industry that produces a treatment also defines the condition it is meant to treat. In this sense, the medicalized discourse on sexual health is *performative* in Judith Butler's sense of the term, for it produces as an effect the very subject it names.[28]

Here I will introduce performance theory as a lens through which Viagra and related aspects of masculine identity—both individual and collective—can be fully examined. As an academic keyword, "performance" includes as much as it excludes. Feminist performance theorist Jill Dolan writes, "Performance happens all around us, if you look at it that way."[29]

Defining "Performance"

Drama professor Bert States demonstrates the slipperiness of "performance" as an academic keyword. For States, "Even the attempt to investigate the nature of performance turns out to be something of a performance."[30] Performance in its versatility and complexity can be both intentional and unintentional, both artistry and sham. As a method of inquiry, performance theory utilizes the theatrical metaphors of "role," "act," "script," "stage," "drama," and, most significantly, "audience," to account for the conscious and unconscious acts we perform as Donna Haraway's "material-semiotic actors." The way I interpret Haraway's phrase is that we are both material bodies (with biological parts and systems) and products of language, responding to cultural conventions and the myth of objectivity.[31] As a result, our actions illustrate various levels of consciousness. Performance theorist Dwight Conquergood illustrates these levels of consciousness as he describes performance as "faking," "making," and "breaking" and occurring across a range of human activity.[32] In Goffman's usage, performance is faking—our everyday performances highlight the ways in which we, as social actors, *manage impressions,* staging our worlds in a semiconscious way.[33] Goffman characterizes everyday life as rule bound, a structure of obligations and performative assumptions realized through communicative exchanges. We have motives for conforming to social expectations and our methods for controlling the impression others have of us are based in routine. This idea that we manage impressions suggests that our appearances are "faked" and that there is, instead, a real self that we go to great lengths to conceal. Goffman goes even further by saying that groups of individuals—"teams"—foster collective identities. These teams are carefully orchestrated so as to maintain the illusion of cohesion.

It is this aspect of performance that I find especially fruitful in analyzing masculinity. The performances of masculinity are collective ones in which members of *a* masculinity participate in an ongoing collusion that supports perceptions of an idealized masculine type. Goffman's definition of performance as the "activity of a given participant on a given occasion [serving] to influence [. . .] other participants" highlights the essential component of *audience* to our individual performances.[34]

But performance in the everyday-life sense is quite different from a performance in a ceremonial or theatrical sense where it also identifies a site for transformation.[35] For anthropologist Victor Turner, the conscious transition necessary for transformations to occur requires a ritual passage across a threshold. Weddings, baptisms, initiation rites all have to do with change taking place within a structured ceremony. The movement from one *stage* of life to the next results in the "making" of a new reality.[36] For boys interested in losing their virginity and, as a result, taking a step closer to manhood, the liminal act that marks that loss/transformation is vaginal penetration. There is no substitute. What Viagra does is maintain the importance of this act well past middle age. Performance, in these examples, is always about transformation through accomplishment (and rarely about competency).

To look at performance as a "breaking" points to the poststructuralist theorists who advocate an adjustment of the lens through which claims of truth and objectivity are perceived and distributed. To take advantage of multiple points of view—versus the hegemonic points of few—is to ask Jill Dolan's question, "How does it look from here?"[37] Breaking implies full consciousness and is, as a result, the most dangerous, the most accountable aspect of performance. In this book, I imagine the effects of Viagra from a number of perspectives. The metaphor of performance allows me to theorize discursively the materiality of existence. The satchel of performance studies— as critical lens, as embodied practice, and as theoretical framework—enables mobility in the exploration of men's sexual health and wonders its effects and meaning-shaping on bodies themselves. These mechanisms of "looking," "being," and "thinking" are what performance theorists utilize in the exploration of rhetorical motives and purposes.

By reporting that 30 million American men suffer from erectile dysfunction and by supplying a simple and easily accessible treatment, Pfizer Pharmaceuticals sponsors the belief held by American men that they maintain perpetual virility. Goffman's theory regarding the "performance of teams" accounts for the collective agreement with this belief; he argues that groups (men, for example) become invested in and *buoy up* a reality, rather than acknowledge the obvious flaws in its maintenance. As an integral part of a sexual performance, Viagra restores, or *reiterates,* the social role that men feel compelled to rehearse and replay their whole lives. For Richard Schechner, performances consist of "restored behaviors"—physical or verbal actions that are practiced and rehearsed.[38] Finally, the term "performance" is ubiquitous in the literature of sexual function (e.g., performance anxiety). Interestingly, "function" is derived from the Latin *fungi,* to perform.

British actor Fiona Shaw argues that both gender and performance are "metaphors for the unknown."[39] Rather than the unknown, I suggest both gender and performance are metaphors for the not-to-be-pinned-down; based in conscious and unconscious acts and affects, they are fluid and ambiguous. Gender both creates and subverts performances. And performances both create and subvert gender.

Gender is performative, then, when it constitutes as an effect the very subject it appears to express. As a performative mode, masculinity and femininity involve a stylized repetition of acts, culturally defined but ever changing—never fixed, but contingent.[40] Within a social structure, it is the individual agent/actor *watching him-/herself being watched* who is the contingent variable in the maintenance or elaboration of societal hierarchies, binaries, and expectations. A performance, therefore, assumes an audience. Elin Diamond observes, "Performance is the site in which performativity materializes in concentrated form, where the concealed or dissimulated conventions of which acts are mere repetitions might be investigated and reimagined."[41] As culminations of repeated acts, gendered performances are, according to Moya Lloyd, "produced through the reiteration of the discursive norms that precede, and are in excess of, her/him."[42] Our bodies perform, then, in concert with the discursive norms that stand outside them but to which we are beholden. Lynda Birke writes, "[P]rocesses involved in creating and continually recreating (sexed) bodies are partly material and partly social/experiential."[43] The medicalization of sexual dysfunction is such a process.

Nothing tells a man he is masculine—not muscles, intelligence, earning potential, an attractive partner, or even height—so much as his erection does. But as Denise Riley reminds us, "Only at times will the body impose itself or be arranged as that of a woman or a man."[44] What Riley's quotation demonstrates in relation to the absent erection is how—by virtue of the erection—men define themselves and their bodies by what is not female.

Erecting Viagra

In his cultural history of the penis, journalist David Friedman writes,

> The lucrative new therapies developed and marketed by Pfizer and others are covered by the media as a personal-hygiene *update* for the estimated 30 million Americans who struggle with erectile dysfunction, a number supplied (critics say fabricated) by the very erection industry that profits from identifying those men as patients [my emphasis].[45]

As a manufactured "update," Viagra is the reiteration and recreation of male sexuality writ large. This update is merely the latest test of endurance. Whether virtual reality or ritual virility, Pfizer's marketing of Viagra and the masculine imperative of erectile capability have performative functions. Even if enacted unconsciously (which I, for one, doubt they are) these functions are surely both politically and economically driven. By examining the discourses surrounding male sexuality and Viagra, this book seeks to locate a genealogy of factors that produce and maintain these assumptions of the sexualized male body.

Who and *how* "normal" is defined, then, delimits the space within which individuals (both professional and lay) investigate, perceive, and evaluate personal experiences and preferences. When norms are communicated by the health profession's experts, matters of individual predilection and satisfaction often take a backseat to cultural conventions.[46]

In the case of "arousal disorders," medical authorities (e.g., Pfizer Pharmaceuticals) begin with the assumption that the expectation is heterosexual intercourse. These expectations are then dictated via powerful and influential mediums such as news stories, television commercials, glossy magazine advertisements, and even online questionnaires. In this book I investigate various discourses of sexual normalcy and dysfunction, seek to bare the unexamined holes in sexual health discourses, posit claims about how those discourses define and delimit the scope of human sexuality, and provide a critical view of how Viagra has impacted our understanding of sexual health in the seven years since its well-promoted debut. I delve into the discourses of masculinity that frame, reflect, deflect, and insinuate expectations for and of sexual health. I explore men's sexual health as a social performance that is enabled by Viagra and the claims of Pfizer Pharmaceuticals. Specifically, I analyze news stories in the popular press as well as Pfizer Pharmaceutical's marketing materials. These two sets of "texts" reveal, in different ways, the arrival of Pfizer's Viagra as a mechanism for phallocentrism and patriarchy. As discourse, these texts contribute to how we have come to understand the meaning of Viagra.

The rhetoric of biomedicine—whether consumed in popular news outlets or through more authoritative medical journals—is a *discourse*. French historian and philosopher Michel Foucault defines a discourse as communication (whether written or spoken, text-based or symbolic) in an area of technical knowledge in which there are accredited specialists and a specialized vocabulary or jargon. According to Foucault, these technical fields are imbued with increasing control over people. As a result, these "discursive regimes" have a profound impact on individual agency and the social structures that shape society.[47] What is most powerful about these discursive formations is their ability to both advocate for specific social experiences *and* dismiss the possibility for options. British psychologist Lynne Segal suggests that discourse theorists

> emphasize that masculinity and femininity refer neither to any collection of traits, nor to some set of stereotypical roles, but rather to the effects of discursive practices—conventional ways of conceiving and representing reality which produce sexual difference in specific contexts of knowledge.[48]

In the texts that I investigate, I find both latent and manifest messages that are demonstrative of communication theorist Cheris Kramerae's muted group theory. Kramerae contends that cultures typically utilize discourses that do not include speakers equally because not all speakers participate in its creation. Because a discourse is created by the dominant group, other groups (women, for instance, and marginalized men) cannot express their experiences.[49] In the case of Pfizer's marketing, the messages about sexual normalcy and dysfunction characterized and maintained by the dominant group will define expectations for all groups. I find an expectation of heteronormativity in sexual practices, the maintenance of the mind/body split in sexual health messages, and the deep structure of our nation's political economy in healthcare.

The questions, hypotheses, and methods outlined in this introductory chapter continue to be explored in the remaining chapters of this book (for a particularization of my methodology, see Appendix A). To make the case outlined above, I begin by examining the role of social construction in the area of health, sexuality, and the body. The purpose of chapter 2, "Strange Bedfellows: Masculinity Studies and Sexology," is to unpack the keywords "masculinity" and "sexual health" and to establish the importance of troubling these terms. According to Raymond Williams, the meanings of keywords are "inextricably bound up with the problems being used to discuss them."[50] As a result, keywords are "messy" and subject to multiple readings and interpretations. This chapter clarifies my usage of these terms and previews my assumptions of their interplay. I also provide a historical overview of sexual health's political economy as examined by cultural critics who utilize feminist theory as their primary method of investigating issues related to the body. In this overview, I discuss how this book will add to the feminist conversation of the politicized body in contemporary culture. Finally, I should add that throughout this book, I employ architectural metaphors—sometimes overtly and often subtly—in order to demonstrate how Viagra is not only a localized treatment for erectile dysfunction but also an example of how bodies are politicized to serve powerful social constructions.

Chapter 3, "Blueprints: Viagra in the Media," is the first of two chapters in which I analyze a particular set of texts. Here I will examine over six years of news stories covering Viagra—from its auspicious debut to the introduction of two competing erectile dysfunction drugs: Levitra and Cialis. In this chapter, I chronicle the Viagra stories of the popular press, specifically those articles appearing in the *New York Times, Newsweek,* and *U.S. News & World Report.* These sources maintained extensive coverage before, during, and some five years after the product's release to the public and, as a result represent the (re)education of the public's understanding of erectile dysfunction. These popular press reports expose the ways in which the medical discourse of sexual health maintains dominant ideologies. Furthermore, popular press reports provide the larger American society (and perhaps, the world) that is *not* a target user of Viagra with information about sexual dysfunction in ways that produce and maintain social stock knowledge.

Next, I analyze how Viagra has been promoted. Chapter 4, "Shims and Shills: Viagra and the Marketing of Transcendence," interprets Pfizer's program of action as evidenced by its advertising and marketing campaign. I explore the ways in which Pfizer creates its target market of erectile dysfunction sufferers through print, television, and direct-to-consumer advertising, including informational videos. How this consumer is "drawn" reveals Pfizer's expectations about male sexuality.[51] In addition, I explore a particular piece of promotional material—a "premium"—provided to physicians and healthcare providers.[52] This information reveals the rhetorical strategies developed to answer the legitimate concerns of the Viagra user. These concerns, once extrapolated, are likely to provide the greatest clues to the possibilities for transcending dominant beliefs about sexuality. Sociologists Adele Clarke and Virginia Oleson write, "[Spaces] where discourses meet agentic actors can be important sites for diffraction and revision."[53]

These chapters set the groundwork for chapter 5, "Bare Necessities: Masculinity, Sexuality, and Architecture." This chapter synthesizes the previous chapters and identifies the implications of perpetuating heteronormative and hegemonic expectations for male sexuality. This final chapter also offers a new metaphor: "horizontal architecture." As a corrective, this chapter invites possibilities for future scholarship in this area.

trange Bedfellows
Masculinity Studies and Sexology

Never waste jealousy on a real man;
it is the imaginary hero that
supplants us all in the long run.
—GEORGE BERNARD SHAW, *HEARTBREAK HOUSE* (1919)

In the exploration of masculinity, sexuality, and health, social construction is an important theoretical foundation. The proponents of social construction theory maintain that aspects of our social reality are constructed through human interaction and communication in specific contexts.[1] From a communication perspective, advocates for a theory of social construction recognize the role of *language as discourse* in the formation of societies and their corresponding systems of power.[2] Communication and its components—language, symbols, and significant social performances and actions—create the norms, regularities, and expectations that move a society from discursive to practical consciousness, allowing that society to *go on*.[3] In so doing, communication—as *the* social construction of reality—also produces exceptions, peculiarities, and pariahs.

To understand masculinity, sexuality, and health as socially constructed is to recognize the power of a society's values in the formulation of discursive regimes and the resulting fictions of normalcy. Because the biomedical model has defined the unresponsive penis as a problem to be solved, the development of Viagra not only defines the solution to a condition, but discursively defines normal as well.[4]

Over forty years ago, Erving Goffman wrote:

> [In] an important sense there is only one complete unblushing male in America: a young, married, urban, northern, heterosexual Protestant father of college education, fully employed, of good complexion, weight and height, and a recent record in sports. . . . Any male who fails to qualify in any of these ways is likely to view himself—during moments at least—as unworthy, incomplete, and inferior; at times he is likely to pass and times he is likely to find himself being apologetic or aggressive concerning known about aspects of himself he knows are probably seen as undesirable.[5]

Goffman's list implicitly names all other "incomplete" men. And even while we pay attention to this list of credentials attributed to our "unblushing" male, we see him surrounded with other bits of information that will, eventually, question his claims to masculinity.

In the last twenty years, an explosion of books and articles—in both the popular and academic press—have addressed the issue of masculinity. This emergence can be seen as (1) a legitimate response to the critique of women's roles in feminist theory and criticism; (2) a part of the postmodern project of deconstructing societal hegemonies; and (3) a better account of both the privileges and oppressions of masculine roles and performances. Robert Connell's *Masculinities* (1995) extends the framework he suggests earlier in *Gender and Power* (1987) and that is echoed by Harry Brod in *The Making of Masculinities* (1987)—that there are *masculinities*.[6]

In *The Male Experience* (1983), James Doyle identifies themes similar to those developed earlier by Robert Brannon (1976) and implied in Goffman's list of complete men above. Brannon's four "types" are the "Big Wheel," the "Sturdy Oak," "Give 'em Hell," and "No Sissy Stuff." Doyle asserts that there are five things expected, required, of American men, four of which match Brannon's labels precisely. They are "Be successful," "Be independent," "Be aggressive," and "Don't be feminine." The fifth is "Be sexual." A successful man (the Big Wheel) in the United States today is largely defined by his ability to make money. The masculine ideal as successful provider is evident in this requirement. Success is not defined by being liked, but by being envied.[7] Independence (the Sturdy Oak) is demonstrated by self-reliance. The appearance of being able to take care of oneself in all circumstances and the tendency to avoid requests for assistance are commonly assumed masculine traits (e.g., don't ask for directions!). Self-reliance is also exhibited through confidence and autonomy. Aggression (Give 'em Hell) is operationalized not only as a willingness to stand and fight or never give up, but also as a willingness to engage in risk-taking behaviors. Frequently, risk-taking behavior is sex-specific as evidenced in the expression "That takes balls!" Don't be feminine (No Sissy Stuff) refers indirectly to psychodynamic theories of family relations.[8] A boy learns how to be a man not through the observance of his father (who is absent), but by *not* doing what his mother does. Furthermore, in the quest to achieve a version of masculinity, anything considered feminine becomes devalued. Later these stereotypes of "not woman" emerge in a variety of contexts. To show sensitivity or vulnerability is to open oneself up to ridicule. Not showing or displaying "feminine" emotions is one way to perform masculinity.

To these, Doyle adds his fifth requirement: "Be sexual." To be masculine, a man must establish an ability to consistently demonstrate sexual prowess through multiple female partners. Leonore Tiefer concurs, "Sexual virility— the ability to fulfill the conjugal duty, the ability to procreate, sexual power, potency—is everywhere a requirement of the male role, and thus 'impotence' is everywhere a matter of concern."[9] But "Be sexual" really means "Be *het-ero*sexual," with even Tiefer's definition revealing exclusionary language codes such as "conjugal" and "procreate."

I maintain that all of these requirements for building the American man are undergirded by an unstated sixth requirement: "Be healthy." Illness threatens the fulfillment of every one of the preceding requirements, so good health becomes a mandatory component in the performance of hegemonic masculinity. To better account for cultural performances of masculinity, Robert Connell developed a four-pronged approach to describe relationships *among* Western masculinities.[10] He is clear in his acknowledgment that these divisions are not everywhere fixed but contingent. He labels these divisions *hegemonic, complicit, subordinate,* and *marginalized.* Hegemonic masculinity refers to a culture's preferred performance of masculinity. By "preferred," I mean rewarded or held up as the model to be emulated. According to Ernesto Laclau, hegemony defines the terrain of political relations.[11] In the United States that terrain is occupied by a corporate display of masculinity epitomized by big business and political influence.

Complicit masculinity is that which upholds notions of hegemonic masculinity. Connell falls just short of referring to complicit performances as "slacker" versions of hegemony, but instead teases out the complexities of a group that realizes a dividend (i.e., male privilege) without the risk. Hegemony relies on complicity's silence to maintain its illusory standards of normalcy and acceptance. Subordinate masculinities might include gay and bisexual men but, more specifically, refer to masculinities that are, from a hegemonic perspective, aligned with femininity. As such, they are *abject* masculinities. Overtly emotional men, male ballet dancers, male nurses, or men who teach elementary school are, in certain circles, considered subordinate.[12] To the categories hegemonic, complicit, and subordinate, Connell offers that of marginalized masculinities, an admittedly unsatisfactory distinction that adds the effects of race and class to those divisions previously mentioned.

All these examples, in turn, point out how gendered stereotypes are reinscribed even by those intent on deconstructing them. In the index to Michael Messner's *Politics of Masculinity,* for example, "aggression" is listed along with a page number, while under "crying" the reader is directed to "see *emo-*

tions," as if aggression were not an emotion, too. To theorize masculinity is to, at times, reinscribe admitted stereotypes.[13]

Connell does not position "physical disability" in his framework, although Kathy Charmaz suggests that a chronic illness—like impotence—will marginalize a particular masculinity among masculinities.[14] Perceptions of physical ability—whether marginalized, subordinated, or both—are produced *situationally*. As there are "masculinities," there are corresponding performances of them—social performances, institutional performances, relational performances, and sexual performances. Judith Butler's concept of performativity suggests that we perform gender through a stylized repetition of acts. Furthermore, she argues, gender is most often framed as a hierarchy (with the masculine superior to the feminine), as a binary (with masculine defined as what is not feminine), and as "compulsory heterosexuality" (with transgressions and subversions carrying punishments and penalties). For Butler, the most important corrective is to recognize that gender—masculinity and femininity—is a cultural performance and not something "natural."

In "Social Construction of Sexuality," anthropologist Carole Vance points out how "identical sexual acts may have varying social significance and subjective meaning" depending upon spatially and temporally bound cultural definitions.[15] Sexuality, like gender, is situational. In other words, culture plays a significant role in how sexual behavior and attitudes about that behavior are produced and maintained. In our society, according to Vance, reproductive heterosexual intercourse is served as the "meat and potatoes" on the Euro-American sexual menu, while variations—oral sex, anal sex, and S/M, whether homosexual or heterosexual—are labeled appetizers, side dishes, and desserts. For Vance, the possibilities for a culture are expanded when the natural, biological, and essentialist status of sexuality is questioned.

Sexuality necessarily involves power and its production. In this analysis, the construction of erections constitutes an effort to sustain a specific male sexuality and the power that that sexuality *preserves*. In *Discipline and Punish,* Michel Foucault examines how power and resistance are organized through the body.[16] Here, Foucault argues, power is produced and normalized discursively; he theorizes that localized terminology, interpretation schemes, and classificatory systems goad human behavior and physical experience.[17] A sexual "act" between two men in ancient Rome, for example, was interpreted as something much different than the same act would be today, when the behavior becomes the determining factor in how an identity is assessed and interpreted.[18] In the analysis of Viagra, what becomes particularly important in approaching sexuality is the social construction of desire. Through the societal control of a gender binary and through codes and regulations about sexual practices, desire itself is created, distributed, and policed; what is enjoyable as "sex" is given to discursive formations of privilege, adherence, and taboo. In the West, erections are inextricably linked to desire.

Sociologists Pepper Schwartz and Virginia Rutter ask, "How might an erection be socially constructed?"[19] They begin to answer this question by acknowledging specific cultural perceptions about the causes of impotence: the man isn't "man enough" or the partner isn't attractive enough. The "macho male myth" requires that a penis always be hard and interest in (hetero)sexual opportunity always apparent. Schwartz and Rutter suggest that the theory of social constructionism becomes a more powerful tool when it takes the biological or evolutionary views of essentialism into account. Their *integrative* view of desire makes sense of how bodies, environments, relationships, and institutions link to determine the boundaries of human sexual possibility. They write:

> Erections are not always evidence of romantic interest, though our culture interprets them as such. But their absence or presence, which is a physical phenomenon, takes on great meaning thanks to Western culture's prevailing beliefs and norms. . . . Growing up in a culture that considers erectile unpredictability a problem influences the way men in that culture feel about themselves and about their sexual partners, and the way sexual partners feel about them.[20]

This fear of unpredictability spurs most of the medicalization of sexuality. Moreover, the erect penis is firmly connected to issues of power, control, and immortality. As a result—and consistent with Western culture's embrace of binaries—the erect penis is synonymous with masculine virility while the nonerect penis is a harbinger of weakness and effeminacy.[21] It is the erect penis, rather than its flaccid counterpart, that signals phallic power. The flaccid penis is perceived as feminine precisely because it is not a firm structure; it does not take up the space that it is *capable* of taking. In chapter 4, I will address medical science's inability (or unwillingness) to differentiate *capacity* from *normalcy* regarding sexual dysfunction. Here I'll turn to a discussion of the way sexology has responded to the limp, albeit willing, penis.

Because Western notions of heterosexuality equate the occasion of an erection with the possibility of sexual intercourse, its absence represents the erosion of masculinity and, as a result, a crisis to be confronted for Western science. Before looking specifically at penises, however, it is important to review the history of modern sexology. I'll do so by examining two works that examine the development and impact of modern sexology.

Janice Irvine traces the history of contemporary sexology in *Disorders of Desire*.[22] Beginning with the reports published by Alfred Kinsey, Irvine examines the evolution of sexual discourse around issues of normalcy and deviance. Despite unveiling the sexual variety apparent in the lives of mid-twentieth-century Americans, Kinsey's quantitative report sanctioned that which many already believed to be unalienable: that marital coitus was "[s]ocially the most important of all sexual activities because of its significance in the origin and maintenance of the home."[23]

Irvine describes how social scientists criticized Kinsey's work for dismissing ethical, emotional, and contextual interpretations of sex. By concentrating on the functional elements of sex to the exclusion of the relational, Kinsey fortified the position of science as the arbiter of issues pertaining to sex and sexuality. With regard to issues of national identity, Kinsey's claims of a universal "capacity" for homosexuality, "fueled the cultural panic of the early 1950s."[24] At this time in American history, homosexuality was often conflated with communism in its supposed ability to undermine the family.

In large part because of the work of Masters and Johnson in the mid-1960s through the early 1970s, Irvine pinpoints the emergence of sexology's status as a legitimate—albeit divided—profession. Beginning with *Human Sexual Response* in 1965 and continuing with *Human Sexual Inadequacy* in 1970, William Masters and Virginia Johnson established the "mechanics" of sexual normalcy in a way that America's technologically focused citizenry was conditioned to accept. Corroborated by their "white coats" of officialdom in the pages of *Newsweek,* the duo of dysfunction established the field's credibility in the eyes of a public that, more and more, seemed to embrace "rigid scientism" as the method par excellence. Irvine explains how "a profession is most successful when it can reflect the dominant values of a society while simultaneously addressing public concerns"[25] and that a market is established "only with the promise of simple and effective techniques and commodities that will ameliorate, if not solve, the presenting dilemma."[26] This emphasis on professionalism is important because it establishes how we come to accept knowledge. To rely on a sanctioned profession is to rely on its methods and techniques and, as a result, to become beholden to them. With Viagra (an accidental cure), Pfizer Pharmaceuticals has fulfilled—or has claimed to fulfill—these criteria of "simple and effective."

While Irvine acknowledges the significant impact the work of Masters and Johnson had on the burgeoning field of sexology, she explains how this impact was soon divided between two camps of sexologists: humanist and scientific. Humanist sexologists claimed—as social scientists had in their critique of Kinsey—that scientific sexologists omitted the capacities for variety in human expression and relationship in their development of methods to regularize human sexual response. Meanwhile, scientific sexologists were quick to criticize the experimental therapeutic techniques inherent in humanist sexology—techniques that reflected a commitment to the philosophies of America's counterculture but were clearly unprofessional from the scientific perspective. What followed was a sort of territory war that is personified at annual conventions of sexologists even today. As Irvine describes it, "The patchwork of programs and lifestyles at sex conferences reflects the dilemma of contemporary sexology: how to consolidate and establish legitimacy as a profession, yet retain diversity and flexibility."[27] This dilemma, Irvine makes clear, was further problematized by the simultaneity of the feminist and gay rights movements of the 1970s. Both movements were loath to accept not only scientific sexology's bias for gender stereotyping and traditional expectations of marriage and family, but also humanist sexology's tendency to equate "sexual liberation" with "women's liberation," as if women's interests inhered in male-prescribed notions of sexual freedom.[28]

So Irvine leaves us in what seems like an untenable position of endorsing neither a scientific nor a humanist approach to sexology.[29] As for erectile dysfunction, my question is not whether a scientific approach or a humanist approach is more effective, but whether or not the erection is a necessity for male sexual fulfillment. Feminism and the gay rights movements, argues Irvine, "*politicized* sexuality" (emphasis original).[30] They challenged "the intellectual power of sexology to define the normative parameters of sex and gender,"[31] as well as the "principle of consistency,"[32] our culture's prescribed system of norms binding biological sex to gender and sexual orientation.

Unfortunately, Irvine also reports that sexual science has been, for the most part, "impermeable" to important aspects of feminist and gay theory. Sexology remains a science of expertise with sexologists clinging to both a "myth of objectivity" and an agenda they perceive as apolitical. The male-dominated field continues to "valorize" heterosexuality and marriage at the expense of marginalized sexualities and relationships. And finally, sexology remains essentialist, with a "more sex the better" ideology apparent at multiple levels of the field's discourse.

Nonetheless, feminism's entrance into sexology has helped raise important questions about power, gender roles, marriage, and the family. "By formulating a political analysis of sex, gender, and marriage," writes Irvine, "the feminist and gay movements underscored the hollowness of solutions based on technique."[33]

Irvine identifies the research of Shere Hite as an indispensable investigation into the *meanings* attributed to specific aspects of sex. Whereas other quantitative research denies a political slant, Hite's work exposes the social pressures and power structures that dictate conformity. Specifically, *The Hite Report* unveils the cultural adherence to the "goals" of vaginal orgasm and male sexual socialization.

These goals are, of course, interrelated. Judith Butler writes, "[M]asculine and feminine are . . . accomplishments, ones that emerge in tandem with the achievement of heterosexuality."[34] For heterosexual American boys, the loss of virginity—narrowly defined as vaginal penetration—is a defining moment in the accomplishment of masculinity. This particular masculinity, however, is something that—through the life course—must be continuously accomplished in different ways. It is in this sense, I believe, that masculine sexuality is *endured*.

From the Latin *indurare,* "endurance" connotes perseverance. The Latin term has its etymological roots in the Sanskrit word *daru,* meaning "wood"

(!). American masculine sexuality, as a state to be endured, gives rise to the need for different types of performances. Sexuality, contends Leonore Tiefer, is situational and contingent, rather than a universal drive.[35] For Tiefer, to describe sex as "natural" implies a particular way or style that is accepted as the natural way or style to perform it.

While Irvine's critique focuses the issues around the scientific and humanist branches of sexology, Tiefer seeks to explain the stranglehold (and resulting legitimacy) the biomedical model has had on the study of sexuality to the detriment of a social constructionist model. This biomedical model— which naturalizes sexuality by presuming sex differences, evolutionary theories of species reproduction, and heterosexuality—maintains a "monolithic professional culture,"[36] thereby impeding cultural improvisation.

To engage a discussion of how the biomedical model has maintained this legitimacy requires the acknowledgment that scientists are authorized with the interpretation of nature, which has historically worked for men at the expense of women.[37] In contrast, feminist scholarship endeavors to question claims of normalcy, legitimacy, and methodological rigor to redress the imbalance of power imposed by the legitimacy of scientism.[38]

According to Tiefer, prefeminist sex research is identified by its (1) implications of sexuality as universal and innate; (2) mechanization of body parts as disconnected components in need of high-tech evaluation and repair; (3) obsessive focus on genitals and the concomitant sex/gender correlation grounded in biology; and (4) validation of perceived normative heterosexual intercourse.[39] What Tiefer imagines for a feminist re-vision of sex research is a focus on the "politics of pleasure," and not the impairment of plumbing.

Contrasting Hite's research on the *meaning* of sexual experience,[40] Tiefer demonstrates how, for the most part, sex therapy's limited focus on *sensory* experience perpetuates sexual "scripts of foreplay-to-intercourse-to-orgasm" and lacks emotional or relational dimensions that might include communication, comfort, and connectedness.[41]

As a psychologist working in hospital urology departments, Tiefer is intimately connected to the psychophysiological aspect of male sexuality and has witnessed—step-by-step—the "medicalization of men's sexuality."[42] She confesses surprise at the reemergence of the penis as the predominant area of interest in sexology after the advancements made by women throughout the 1970s and early 1980s. Tiefer suggests that the authority of patriarchal structures and the political economy of contemporary medicine function as Foucault's "prevailing sociopolitical winds."[43] These are the forces behind the mounting interest in medical management. It is not the sexual satisfaction of women that drives the research in erectile repair, but yet another crisis in masculinity.

"A feminist vision of sexuality," imagines Tiefer, ". . . would focus on sexuality as it occurs within cultures and relationships."[44] This view requires a radical rethinking of the supposed either/or choice between humanist and biologically based sex research and would relegate the *hydraulics* of sexual expression to the periphery. While Tiefer emphasizes the way women's sexuality is harnessed by power structures that dictate norms, notions of "proper," "acceptable," and "exemplary" sexual behavior are everywhere manifestations of an anxiety of male attitudes and expectations about sex.

Tiefer's comprehensive book predates the advent of Viagra by several years, so her review of biomedical approaches to male sexual problems is concerned with what are generally perceived as overtly invasive techniques of repair: specifically, penile prosthesis implantation and pharmaceutical injection. In addition, Tiefer highlights the use of the term "impotent"—often used to describes the individual sufferer as well as his unresponsive penis—as "stigmatizing and stress-inducing."[45] For Tiefer, "*impotent* reflects a significant moment in the social construction of male sexuality" (emphasis original).[46] This is important because in its literature Pfizer Pharmaceuticals has all but replaced this label with the more medically sensitive "erectile dysfunction" (or ED). Thus, the need to understand male sexuality as both medically and semantically constructed has never been more apparent.

According to Tiefer, there are no proven methods for distinguishing between organic (physical) and nonorganic (psychological or relational) causes for erection problems.[47] For those interested in reestablishing a psychological approach to sexuality, the term "erectile dysfunction" obfuscates the significance of nonorganic causes to male sexual difficulties. And although male patients are more willing than ever before to discuss their sexual histories and habits, a biomedical solution (whether prosthetic, hypodermic, or pharmaceutical) seems to be preferred by physicians. Communication in the doctor—patient relationship is best explained here as a means to an end: namely, a *medical* diagnosis and solution. Regardless of the cause of erectile dysfunction, however, Tiefer observes that the solution is always grounded in the assumption that the erectile function of the penis *must* be repaired. This performance of *active* concern ratifies a commitment to masculinity that a *passive* acceptance does not. For Teifer, this erection *requirement* for male sexuality accentuates the importance of male gender role confirmation as much as it emphasizes intimacy and pleasure.[48] Tiefer writes, "[S]exual health for men has been reduced to the erectile functioning of the penis."[49]

Citing a number of authorities, Tiefer examines how many men's *beliefs* around sexuality in general, and sexual performances in particular, are genitally centered. These beliefs include (1) men are always (or should be) willing to participate in sexual activity and are responsible for initiating, teaching, and satisfying both partners and themselves; (2) women prefer intercourse to any other kind of sexual activity; (3) all good sex culminates with intercourse; and (4) sex is serious (not play)—the ability to satisfy a woman depends on a "proper" erection and ejaculation and is something that must be proven on each occasion.[50] The inflexible male sex role relies on the potency (both material and imagined) that comes with a hard penis. It is an essential part of the script. These beliefs point to a desire for the continuous performance of sexual health that itself suggests a construction of "normalcy." And, suggests Tiefer, it is the taken-for-grantedness of that construction—a blueprint, a script—that makes the medicalization of sexuality so palatable to men in particular.

These reviews of "dysfunction construction" by Irvine, a feminist historian, and Tiefer, a feminist psychologist, reveal some of the underlying complexities inherent in the splintered field of sexology. In its many costumes, American sexology simultaneously pursues both scientific legitimacy and a larger audience for its services. Dangerous assumptions perpetuate the former and inhibit the latter of these two objectives.

Essentializing occurs when a single aspect of biological sex is called upon as the definitive—or, perhaps, vital—aspect of that sex. With regard to sexuality in particular, female sexuality has withstood decades (if not centuries) of speculation regarding the source of pleasure.[51] What has remained unexamined is the source of pleasure in men. In a discussion of masculinity and sexuality, Andreas Philaretou and Katherine Allen maintain that "contemporary men need to negotiate a reconstruction of their sexuality."[52]

For the vast majority of men in the United States there is no question that it is the erect penis that provides the agency to their sexual pleasure. What is more, many men believe the erection is essential—heterosexually speaking—in order to provide pleasure for women. Lynne Segal writes, "[Western] culture has increasingly impressed upon men the importance of female orgasm—a man must, as it were, stand firm as the instrument of repeated female orgasm."[53] Because masculinity is so closely aligned with sexual adequacy and sexual adequacy with erectile capability, suggests Segal, there is no "room for maneuver," either in creating a masculine identity or in experiencing the pleasurable aspects of the male body without the promise of an erection.[54] Essentializing is dangerous.

A coalition of healthcare-industry institutions—pharmaceutical companies, insurance companies, the American Medical Association, medical technology manufacturers—are economically driven to expand both their authority of diagnosis and treatment *and* the quantity of services available. Speaking on behalf of what Irvine would call humanist sexology, Tiefer claims that changing sexual scripts is one feature of a therapeutic approach. Through this approach,

> Sexuality can be transformed from a rigid standard for masculine adequacy to a way of being, a way of communicating, a hobby, a way of being in one's body—

and *being* one's body—that does not impose control but rather affirms pleasure, movement, sensation, cooperation, playfulness, relating [emphasis original].[55]

This is a worthy goal. What needs to be evaluated and critiqued, however, is the continued separation of mind and body that seems to drive the discourse of sexology in general. In fact, the implied bifurcation of humanist as "mind" and scientific as "body" is, in itself, a perpetuation of this Cartesian philosophy.

It has become a sort of cultural joke that men don't go to the doctor. But the reason behind this conscious decision is more than a bit baffling. Or is it? Doctors, we are led to believe, are rational. Science, we are led to believe, is objective. What could be more appealing to men—the rational, objective gender—than the promise of empiricism? Thomas Mann's *The Magic Mountain* provides a hint at the subordinate position the privileged male (Hans Castorp) might be avoiding in an encounter with the gaze of a domineering physician:

> [The doctor] gripped Hans Castorp on the upper arm with his mighty hand, pushed him away, and looked at him sharply—not in the face, as one man looks at another, but at his body; turned him around, as one would turn an inanimate object, and looked at his back.[56]

There are, it seems, contradictory allegiances at work when it comes to men and health—producing what Janice Radway calls an *ideological seam*. Somewhere between idealized roles of American masculinity and the practices of the health-conscious virile male is a fault line that disallows an intersection. Masculinity abounds with the "conflicts, slippages, and imperfect joinings" that characterize Radway's seams.[57] For many men, the strategies for performing hegemonic masculinity coincide with tactics for avoiding the objectifying scrutiny of the penetrating gaze of the powerful medical eye/I. Furthermore, Sander Gilman has pointed out how the category of disease contributes to the boundary creation between the "healthy observer" (whether physician, nurse, or layperson) and the "patient." As a result, this constructed image of patient is "always a playing out of the desire for a demarcation between ourselves and the chaos represented in culture by disease."[58]

As mentioned earlier, cultural expectations for masculinity are inextricably bound to self-imposed expectations for a healthy body. According to Donald Sabo and David Gordon, the development of a sociocultural model in the 1960s helped identify gender (along with race and socioeconomic status) as a significant variable in health and illness.[59] In the 1970s, feminist theory not only revealed the ways in which gender affects societal perceptions of health and illness, but also the ways in which the field of medicine has been corrupted by centuries of masculinist partiality.[60]

   Profeminist men's studies willingly examine and critique the privileges and limitations of hegemonic masculine roles.[61] Both Lynne Segal and Robert Connell have suggested that the study of masculinities needs to be aimed at the body but not by lapsing into essentialism.[62] In the early years of the field, men's studies were already examining the body as a site for the manifestation of society's expectations for masculine models, although the majority of these studies focused around the role of sports in the organization of masculinity.[63] Nonetheless, researchers were not quick to make the links between gender (as a cultural performance), bodies, and men's health.[64] Events in the 1990s have changed that.

   Around the close of the millennium, an assortment of well-publicized events further challenged the precarious solidity of men's health. When NBA star Ervin "Magic" Johnson revealed his HIV-positive status in 1991, the threat of AIDS to heterosexual men could no longer be denied. The late actor and activist Christopher Reeve's paralysis was the result of risk-taking behavior—participation in an equestrian event (a sport that is arguably inseparable from money and the masculine directive of success). Even John F. Kennedy Jr.'s tragic plane crash can be seen as epitomizing the consequences of the supposed masculine predilection for self-reliance. In a complementary way, the increased publicity (and resulting public awareness) surrounding prostate and testicular cancer (and the attendant threats to potency and fertility) reinscribes the links between expectations for maleness in our society and the contingencies of masculine mortality. Indeed, it is likely that some forms of heart disease can be attributed to male modes of aggression and independence. Thus, society's prescription for traditional masculinity often results in medical prescriptions for chronic illness as well.

   Donald Sabo and David Gordon assert that feminist theory and research catalyzed the need for research that drew connections between gendered behavior and men's health and illness.[65] Acknowledging Robert Connell's concept of competing "masculinities," Sabo and Gordon cite a concomitant hierarchical system that privileges men over women as well as a second hierarchical system of *intermale* dominance. These two systems fuel each other, resulting in an advantaged subgroup operating at the expense of lesser-status subgroups, economically, politically, and culturally.

   Each of James Doyle's five requirements for successfully performing the male sex role—success, independence, aggression, aversion to all things feminine, and incessant interest in (hetero)sex—necessitate a narrowly defined healthy body in order to be enacted convincingly. At the same time, it is exactly these stipulations that may contribute to a less-than-efficacious result: a body made susceptible to illness due to mitigating circumstances.[66]

   Elianne Riska points out how the medical diagnostic category of "hardiness" that emerged in the late 1970s "demedicalized and legitimized" the values attributed previously to the 1950s candidate (the "Type A man") for coronary heart disease.[67] Through "control, commitment, and acceptance of change," the hardy man becomes a personality characteristic that overcomes the "executive disease"—coronary heart disease—rather than a character type that brings it on. Riska points out how the test for "hardiness" relied on a sample of mid-to-upper-level executive males between the ages of forty and forty-nine, married with two children, and the wife not working outside the home.[68] Thus, the medical discourse was able to integrate the growing concerns of modern stress-related illness to a "challenge" by which *real* men (traditional men conforming to American ideals) could exhibit their requisite combative arsenal.

Performing hegemonic masculinity requires resources not available to all men. Those seeking to affirm masculinity where social and economic challenges—race, sexual preference, and class—do not conform to the hegemonic model turn to risk-taking behaviors, physical toughness, aggression, violence, and sexual prowess as avenues for avoiding a subordinate status within their social group.[69]

Among male bodies, the universality of sexual prowess as a desired aspect of masculinity warrants an examination of certain cultural influences working to sustain its prominence. In the early twenty-first century, Viagra must be implicated. By looking at the maintenance of the penis/phallus and its role in the construction of masculinity, we may come to understand the relationships of power among American masculinities and the influence of this power on the contemporary political economy.

In addition to the healthcare industry, Leonore Tiefer adds that mass media also advocates for the medicalization of sexuality.[70] The language of science sells sexual health subject matter in a way that legitimates the *newsworthiness* of newspaper and magazine articles and television and radio news reports.

It is not necessary to argue that the United States is an advocate for the continued medicalization of sexual health. The ongoing struggle for universalized medical care in the United States presupposes that our current system is working for the stakeholders for whom power means more than consistent erections. Rather, I argue that the medicalization of men's sexual health—and, in particular the production of Viagra—preserves a privileged masculinity. Lynne Segal writes, "However familiar we may be with competing biological and clinical narratives of male impotence and sexual dysfunction, it is these myths of penile prowess which we need relentlessly to expose in our rethinking of heterosexuality."[71]

In Louis Althusser's parlance, the U.S. medical system is an ideological state apparatus (ISA)—a structure—that interpellates the citizen.[72] When the ISA calls out "Hey you!" the citizen knows that he/she is being summoned and turns to acknowledge the source. Moya Lloyd writes,

> From the day we are born we are interpellated as gendered beings, and we con-
> tinue to be gendered throughout our lives in a variety of ways. Moreover, we
> understand ourselves as gendered beings. Filling in forms, reacting to wolf whis-
> tles in the street: in a multiplicity of ways gender impinges upon us and encodes
> us.[73]

In Foucauldian terms, our turning around to meet the voice signifies the way
in which we police ourselves. Gender and, more specifically, masculinity are
frequently overlooked variables in how the complex U.S. healthcare system is
made more complex by relationships of power. For many men, health and
sexuality are properties of a privileged masculinity that must be endured over
the life course. As a result, the deconstruction of phallocentrism is delayed.
When Pfizer Pharmaceuticals tells us that erectile dysfunction is physiological
(rather than relational or psychological), there is something in the male psyche that is counted on to turn around without exercising the power of agency
that might otherwise question the summons. But I *must* question it *and* risk
being accused of violating the complicity that maintains the power structure.
To question the ideology beneath Pfizer's marketing—that men must have
erections and penetrative sex to be men—is to be caught in one of Radway's
ideological seams. Men must balance the agency that comes with choice.
Complicity with Pfizer's agenda/ideology purchases the possibility for erectile control and traditional definitions of what it is to be a man. Questioning
the benefits of Viagra requires the exercising of individual agency and creates
the possibility of structural improvisation—that is, new and better definitions
of what it is to be a man.

lueprints

Viagra in the Media

> Thanks to Viagra I've come to understand
> Zeus's amorous transformations.
> That's what they should have called Viagra.
> They should have called it Zeus.
> —PHILIP ROTH, *THE HUMAN STAIN* (2000)

Before, during, and after David Letterman and Jay Leno found nightly monologue material in a seemingly endless parade of Viagra jokes, the popular press found that Viagra (and Pfizer) had many dimensions. Pfizer became a Wall Street darling: never before had the addition of a single drug to a pharmaceutical company's product line resulted in such a significant increase in a stock's value. Viagra added another layer of complexity to ongoing health insurance disputes: if Viagra use was covered by an insurance company, then why wasn't birth control also covered? Moreover, debates waged over what should constitute a monthly supply of Viagra. Viagra was also a source for fashionable human relationship stories. And Viagra raised important questions about gender and sexuality. Viagra is drama. As late-night television tapped into and enlivened the general giddiness of water cooler humor across the country, the popular press didn't seem to be able to write stories fast enough to satisfy the public's interest in the topic. Thousands of stories were written in the popular press about Viagra between September 1996 and the product's eventual debut in late March 1998. In this chapter I examine fifty-two news stories appearing in the *New York Times, U.S. News & World Report,* and *Newsweek*.[1]

The media coverage of Viagra can be roughly divided into four phases. First, the prerelease Viagra articles (September 1996–March 1998) outline the nature of erectile dysfunction with existing or proposed solutions driving the drama. Second, articles reporting on Viagra's availability appeared (March 1998–June 1998). These focus on the success of the clinical trials and the scientific clamor that accompanied the release. The third phase of articles emerged in the months following the unprecedented success of Viagra (June 1998–February 1999). These news stories focus on three things: (1) the personal relationship aspects of Viagra; (2) the insurance controversies surrounding Viagra; and (3) the risks of Viagra. The final stage of Viagra news takes us from a year after Viagra's debut to the recent past (February 1999–October 2002). These articles tend to focus on the cultural implications of Viagra, particularly the scientific management of male and female sexuality and its concomitant political economy.

Several components are emblematic of nearly every Viagra article. First, there are portraits of American males. These portraits reveal ages, occupations, values, and disappointments and successes. Second, there is personal (or lay) testimony—both by users and would-be users of Viagra—and expert testimony by a variety of sexual-health professionals, including urologists, primary care physicians, obstetricians and gynecologists, sex therapists, and government officials. And third, there are statistics—statistics attesting to the preponderance of erectile dysfunction, the success rate of Viagra, and the cost of Viagra to insurance companies, and statistics establishing normative levels of a range of bodily systems.

Frequently in these news articles, Viagra is introduced through the use of emphatic epithets. Eighteen months before its debut, Viagra was characterized as "the ultimate erection aid" in a *Newsweek* article by Geoffrey Cowley titled "Attention, Aging Men."[2] Other cognomina for Pfizer's capillary chemistry followed in quick succession. The *New York Times* called Viagra "a wonder of the modern age,"[3] "the new miracle drug,"[4] and "the new national drug of choice."[5] *Newsweek* followed with "the potency wonder drug,"[6] while *U.S. News & World Report* countered with "the sexual potency drug."[7] Dorothy Nelkin, author of *Selling Science,* points out how descriptions like these both exaggerate the promise of new drugs and oversimplify the intricacies of chemistry to the body.[8] Implied by the prevalence of these monikers is the idea that this technology is something we've all been waiting for.[9]

This chapter explores media messages as they reveal the constructed nature of bodies, both personal and political. Media critic Peter Parisi writes, "Examining news stories as examples of discourse, narrative, or framing implies that a news report is formulated and narrated out of a virtually infinite number of events and facts."[10] As narratives, news stories reveal assumptions and values, ideologies and politics.[11] These ideologies, of course, have a tremendous influence on how we construct ourselves as individuals. Magazines and newspapers not only supply the public with particulars about health and medicine; this knowledge also shapes attitudes, actions, and decisions about the risks and benefits of health-related behaviors.[12]

Communication scholar Julia Wood points out how media influence both cultural images of gender and individual identities, controlling what we see and know, reproducing expectations, values, and ideals, and "pathologizing" the human body. She stresses how "one of the most damaging consequences of media's images of women and men is that these images encourage us to perceive normal bodies and normal physical functions as problems."[13] With regard to health issues in the media, health communication scholar Athena du Pré is suspicious of the tendency toward sensationalism, while encouraged by the ways in which media can increase the public's awareness of health-related issues.[14] News agencies are quick to respond to stories that examine the medicalization of sexuality because, according to Leonore Tiefer, a scientific perspective *legitimizes* stories about sex.[15] Medical news about sex in the popular press satisfies the public's craving for such news and simultaneously remains "clean" rather than pornographic.

As a group, the fifty-two news stories in my sample tell us a great deal about erectile dysfunction generally and Viagra's impact on how men communicate about their bodies and sexuality specifically. Some are written with a great deal of social reflexivity—exposing assumptions made by physicians and therapists, questioning the ease with which Viagra passed through the Food and Drug Administration (FDA), and zeroing in on the relational fallout in a "take a pill" society. And yet, other aspects of Viagra's impact remain unexamined. By examining these news stories—as a group—I locate a *genealogy* of factors that produce, maintain, and (for some) transform assumptions of the sexualized male body. I then interpret these assumptions, exposing the dominant discourse of biomedicine. Feminist political scientist Kathy Ferguson suggests that it is through the lenses of interpretation and genealogy that the social critic can trace the "threads" of discourse. Genealogies not only imply multiple beginnings but also draw "attention to that which has been omitted."[16]

The content of these articles touch upon five primary subject areas. Specifically, the media messages reveal assumptions and values about (1) pre-Viagra erectile dysfunction technology; (2) the impact of Viagra on romantic relationships; (3) testimonials of masculinity; (4) Viagra and death; and (5) the political economy of healthcare. The ordering of these themes is not indicative of "most important" or "least important." Rather, they are thoroughly interconnected and overlapping. I order them in this way in the interest of telling the story about Viagra as reported in our nation's recognized news outlets and to suggest a genealogy of factors that maintain masculinity's sexual socialization. A discourse analysis of the Viagra story as reported in these news sources reveals the creation of a significant cultural narrative, thereby illuminating assumptions, ideals, and beliefs about sexuality and masculinity.

Sensationalizing the New/Debunking the Old

Among the three sources considered here, *Newsweek* was the first to mention Viagra. In his September 1996 article "Attention: Aging Men," Geoffrey Cowley explores the burgeoning market of structures, elixirs, injections, and concoctions available (or being developed) in order to perpetuate signifiers of masculine youth. His article reveals the extent to which hormone treatments and cosmetic surgery for aging male baby boomers have become big business.[17]

Viagra, of course, is not the only technological solution for erectile dysfunction, but it is widely available, cheap, and subtle. Many of the early articles surveyed cast a blight on the alternatives, all but dismissing them as cumbersome, costly, and, perhaps most damnable, unromantic. Before Viagra came along, a number of devices—developed by what would be considered legitimate medical industries—treated erectile dysfunction. Testosterone therapies, vacuum treatments, penile implants, prostheses, pumps, and pharmaceutical injections and suppositories have all claimed to successfully treat ED. "Success" here is relative. Viagra's success rate (depending on who does the reporting) has ranged from 45 to 90 percent. The alternatives claim a similar rate of success. Nonetheless, the language in these news stories all but dismisses the value of these devices and/or their legitimacy.

In a November 1997 *Newsweek* article titled "A Pill for Impotence," John Leland writes, "Until recently, the only options would have involved body-shop mechanics, either a surgical implant or a pump of the sort advertised in the back of men's magazines."[18] In this example, the mention of body shops and men's magazines gives an underworld if not "underclass" quality to a particularly sophisticated surgical procedure and a noninvasive, comparatively inexpensive, and successful mechanism. Each produces and sustains erections. By comparison, "Viagra is something very different," writes Douglas Martin in a May 1998 article for the *New York Times,* "much easier to use than previous generations of suppositories, injections, and vacuum pumps."[19] The appeal of Viagra is in its purported simplicity: just take a single pill and wait thirty minutes for an erection. No surgeons, no devices. Masculinity is maintained best by reducing the austere architecture to its bare necessities. Look Ma, no hands.

In this example, from *U.S. News & World Report,* it is the patient (rather than the author of the story, the physician, or the pharmaceutical company) who rebuffs the use of surgical procedures or machinelike devices to restore his erectile function.

> The doctor said [the patient] could try mechanical contrivances like a vacuum cuff or pump. Or he could have bendable rods surgically implanted. Or, using a small, fine needle, he could inject alprostadil, a drug that mimics a natural substance produced during sexual arousal, into the penis, to encourage blood flow. [The patient] did not care for any of these options.[20]

Is it any wonder men don't enjoy going to the doctor? These other therapies "act" upon the would-be user. Moreover, in order to be effective, these remedies must exert force on the male body, as Jane Brody writes in the *New York Times*,

> There are half a dozen other effective remedies. But unlike the others, Viagra is a pill, making it a far simpler and more discreet remedy than its rivals, which include drugs *injected* or *inserted* into the penis and devices *implanted* and *inflated* [my emphasis].[21]

From a masculinist scientific perspective, these actions align with *female bodies* as they imply an invasion of bodily space and better suit the complexities of *reproduction* (rather than the production for which men are rewarded in the public sphere). Female bodies are acted upon: penises are inserted, sperm is injected, eggs are implanted, and wombs are inflated. Meanwhile, Viagra is represented as requiring no accompanying "props" and appears—through ease and discretion—to take effect almost by divine right when compared with other options. Swallowing a pill, it seems, has become so much a part of our society that it is considered noninvasive when, of course, it is invasive. It is important to point out, however, that the active chemical in Viagra—sildenafil citrate—does not work instantly (as does the injected or inserted alprostadil); desire is required and stimulation is recommended. I suggest that this delay in Viagra's efficacy—coupled with the sexual scripts of passion and foreplay—can be construed by its users as a "natural" response.[22]

The variety of methods summarized here represents both invasive and noninvasive options. And although Viagra is certainly invasive, it is rendered almost neutral in these stories. One gets the impression that these alternatives were *never* desirable and yet, as they were once the only other medically sanctioned remedies, they had no shortage of users and benefits.[23]

Literary critic and philosopher Kenneth Burke suggests it is through "strategic ambiguity" that the "debunker" combats opposing arguments (or, in this case, alternatives to Viagra) by discarding them overtly, only to advance the new argument covertly. His analogy, I think, is worth reproducing here:

> Matches may be used either to light our pipes or burn down our houses. And
> one can well understand why, if they were being used entirely for the purpose of
> burning down our houses, a thinker should arise to say: "Let us have no more
> matches." By preventing the use, he [*sic*] could prevent the misuse. And then, if
> he still had occasion to light his pipe, he might make an altered recommendation
> of this sort: "What we really need is *lighters*." He might go on to show that
> matches are largely derived from tradition, whereas lighters are modern. And in
> our eagerness for the solution, we might be willing to meet the thinker halfway,
> failing thereby to note that lighters could be misused in quite the same way as
> matches were [emphasis original].[24]

So when we "light our pipes" with Viagra, as it were, rather than, for
instance, a vacuum pump, we are thinking of Viagra as noninvasive (of both
romance and the body). This is an ambiguous distinction at best insofar as
taking a pill is an act that has been rendered routine in this culture. The consequence of the myriad medicines we ingest unthinkingly is cause for concern. But Burke is suspicious of debunking generally. As he describes the
process, the typical debunker constructs "a mode of argument that would, if
carried out consistently, also knock the underpinnings from beneath his own
argument."[25]

Given the speed with which technology changes, it is no surprise that
even Viagra (as Burke predicted) was being debunked by rival technologies.
John Leland of *Newsweek* points out:

> Others, though, are less sold on Viagra. Some doctors insist the future belongs
> to local medications, not a pill that circulates through the entire body. And for all
> Viagra's publicity, Pfizer's research has not yet been through peer review.
> "They've presented the data in the most positive light," says one top researcher,
> *who is working on an alternative treatment* [my emphasis].[26]

An impartial argument, then, questions the need to "correct" erectile dysfunction (however defined) at all.

The first theme in these news accounts is to sensationalize Viagra and to
debunk the other, traditional therapies. This double strategy fails to take into
account the vast differences among these therapies regarding ease of acquisition, cost effectiveness, and most importantly, side effects. But the popularity
of Viagra has also produced side effects of a different kind. *Relational* side
effects often stem from the resurgence of (or potential for) sexual interest
long since retired.

Viagra and Communicating Couples

The second major theme I identify is that erectile dysfunction—both in professional journals and the popular press—is often described as a couple's disease. This implies that although impotence may afflict only one member of

the relationship, both members of the relationship (or all three for that matter!) are affected. The stories in the popular press devote a great deal of ink to the issue of communication between couples. In fact, the longest stories of those in the sample are concerned with the derivative relational consequences of Viagra's effectiveness. This subsection addresses a number of motifs with regard to communication and relationships reported in these news stories including (1) the silence between partners about ED; (2) the meaning of a biomedical (rather than a communicative) solution; and (3) the need for relational repair that "no pill will cure."

An important motif has to do with the communication about erectile dysfunction that takes place and, perhaps more frequently, does *not* take place between couples. "I felt as if we were colleagues," confides a man in an article in *U.S. News & World Report*. "We'd go places, we'd get done what needed to get done around the house, but there was this huge, dark subject we wouldn't discuss."[27]

Along with fueling the stand-up routines for dozens of comedians, Douglas Martin's *New York Times* article, "Thanks a Bunch Viagra; The Pill That Revived Sex, Or at Least Talking About It," suggested that Viagra's availability got people talking about sex generally *and* got men to visit their doctors.[28] But once prescribed, couples were confronted with more than the capability of (hetero)sexual expression. Jennifer Steinhauer of the *New York Times* reports:

> When the possibility of sex resurfaces, a couple is often at a loss. They never talked much about their problems before, and now they have no idea how to approach the change. In the meantime, all the issues that contributed to the impotence or resulted from it have been long swept under the rug.[29]

As Steinhauer implies, impotence has both organic and psychological etiologies and Viagra impacts both happy couples and unhappy couples. These issues are, of course, related. Jane Brody, also of the *New York Times*, uncovers similar sentiments when she writes:

> [Viagra] does nothing per se to reawaken sexual desire and foster communication and loving feelings between loving partners who may have long ago put these aside. Men who are impotent often refrain from any physical or verbal expressions of tenderness and desire for fear of raising false hopes in their partners, who may do likewise to avoid inducing guilt in a man unable to *perform* sexually [my emphasis].[30]

The frequency with which "performance" is used to describe sexual health has been established as an ongoing theme in this book. Its use here points out the functional—or efficacious—definition of performance and provides an opening for the ways in which performance is a presentation of self, a self sometimes compromised by a stigmatized condition.

Regarding the performance of social stigma, Erving Goffman distinguishes *passing* from *covering*. "Passing" conceals a stigma from unknowing persons while "covering" assuages concerns for those in the know, or those he calls "the wise." It would be difficult for a man to conceal his impotence from a partner with whom he has previously enjoyed sexual relations—that is, to pass. "Covering," on the other hand, is a tactic requiring the participation—whether active or passive—of both partners. Covering intimates complicity of some kind.[31]

By representing erectile dysfunction as organic and developing a pill as the cure, biological sexologists are aligned with passing. Goffman writes, "[A] strategy of those who pass is to present the signs of their stigmatized failing as signs of another attribute, one that is less significantly a stigma."[32] When erectile dysfunction can be attributed to an organic—or physiological—cause rather than a psychological or relational cause, three things happen simultaneously: (1) the ED sufferer situates the source of the problem outside of his ego and places it resolutely in his body; (2) the dreaded visit to the physician lasts only as long as it takes to get a prescription for Viagra;[33] and (3) discussions with his partner concerning their romantic desires, differences, and difficulties can be avoided. At the risk of reinforcing stereotypes, I'd guess that these consequences would be pretty attractive to the typical American baby boomer male. "[That] impotence is a problem of mechanics can be appealing," writes John Leland in *Newsweek*. "It takes all the blame and guilt out of the equation."[34]

These media stories are clear in this conclusion: although Viagra may have people talking about sex, it doesn't necessarily get *couples* talking about it. As long as impotence is attached to an organic etiology, couples are likely to avoid an interrogation of relational obstacles and obstructions. I turn now to the second motif in this theme of communication between couples—the mind/body split in biomedicine.

The purported cause of impotence—and this relates significantly to why the condition is now referred to as erectile dysfunction—has undergone a radical shift. Perhaps due in large part to the influence of Sigmund Freud's ideas in our culture, the inability to sustain an erection was, for most of the twentieth century, thought to stem from psychological problems. Over the past twenty years, however, physiologists have reversed this tenet. Concomitantly, erectile dysfunction has all but replaced impotence in the scientific arena. "Impotence" has a rhetorical quality that erectile dysfunction does not. The condition of impotence implies the sufferer *himself* is impotent—that is, a powerless man. We don't make this same implication with erectile dysfunction. Those suffering from ED are not considered "the erectily defunct."

That men with erectile dysfunction are most often cast as sufferers—rather than patients, victims, or "cases"—merits further scrutiny. The verb "to suffer" has its etymological root in the Latin *ferre*, meaning "to bear" (as in "bear in mind" or "he couldn't bear to think about her"). This particular verb has always evoked for me the image of one who willingly endures substantial psychic weight without relief. It would seem, then, that while the condition has undergone a name change, the characterization of its embodiment remains one that—simultaneously—maintains both a psychological etiology and the ever-elusive cure. By manufacturing a treatment, rather than a cure, Pfizer guarantees a constant customer base for its product.

The separation of mind and body fortified by the change from "impotence" to "erectile dysfunction" raises important questions for the couples portrayed in these news stories. Wray Herbert's *U.S. News & World Report* article "Not Tonight, Dear" encapsulates some of the research in the area of psychological and physiological interconnectedness. For example, Herbert's article reveals how financial stress has been linked to sexual dysfunction in both men *and* women. Because depression is a characteristic response of many kinds of stress and because stress is a major contributor to heart disease, it is no wonder that discovering a single cause of sexual dysfunction is complicated. Also in Herbert's article, Harvard psychiatrist John Ratey argues for combination therapy under the assumption that prescribing a drug is insufficient if depression is the culprit.[35] Similarly, sex therapist (and author of *The New Male Sexuality*) Dr. Bernie Zilbergeld suggests, in an interview with *Newsweek's* John Leland, that erectile dysfunction remedies *can* be useful, but not if they are being used "to get around other problems."[36]

The news stories that forefront the relational aspects of Viagra show exactly how and where mind and body are divided and applied. In another article, Leland describes how trends in dysfunction therapy "reflect the different natures" of approaches for men and women.

> For many women, fixing the problem means fixing the relationship, "establishing proper conditions for good sexuality," says Dr. Richard Kogan, a New York psychiatrist and sex therapist. "Male dysfunction is better studied from a physiological standpoint."[37]

I find this quotation especially interesting because, according to feminist critiques of binary thinking, women are typically associated with the body (and nature) and men are associated with the mind (and culture). The male body—as a body—is celebrated in sport and sex, but only until something goes wrong. Whenever things "go wrong" on the ballfield or in bed, the male body is othered, abject, and accused of betraying the command of the "real" rational self. Men are "alienated" from their bodies, then, because to be aligned *with* the body would mean being aligned with femininity.

Yet another *Newsweek* article by John Leland, "The Science of Women Sex," includes the perspectives of sisters Jennifer and Laura Berman. Jennifer is a urologist and Laura is a sex therapist. Together they are "the telegenic faces of female sexual dysfunction, a two-headed Oprah for the erotically aggrieved."[38] Despite the seemingly multiple-disciplinary approach—a "tag-team" of mind and body therapy—the Bermans reinforce cultural expectations of gendered attitudes toward health, sexual and otherwise, in their report:

> For women, more so than for men, simply "medicalizing" the problem is too reductive. While many Viagra-enhanced men are happy just to get erections, fixing women's blood flow will cure little if libido-killing stresses still assail the relationship, the home life and the woman's self-esteem. Women presenting identical complaints might require a drug, a weekend retreat or a sex toy, or some combination of the three.[39]

Because men are aligned with the mind (and rational thinking) it seems that any aberration to the otherwise invisible body must be masked quickly. The male body must never become a site of investigation—a subject of the medical gaze. For the imperfect male body to become a subject of the gaze—through prolonged examination (whether physiological or psychological)—would render the male body feminine.

What makes Kogan's and the Bermans' attitude about gendered treatments for sexual dysfunction predictable, however, is that our society's expectations and stereotypes make it a woman's responsibility for maintaining relational health.[40] And despite cultural assumptions that men want sex for fun and women want sex for love, survey research concludes that most men do prefer relational sex to recreational sex.[41] The combination of relational silence due to a stigmatized condition and the biomedically endorsed mind/body split regarding the etiology of impotence can lead then to a kind of matrimony acrimony. But the major revelation here is that gendered social behavior is often perpetuated by "hard" science that claims to objectively describe reality without acknowledging how its own solutions propel stereotypes.

The third motif in this theme of relational communication has to do with the puzzle that Viagra *can't* solve. Studies have demonstrated that mediated depictions of relationships promote fanciful versions of what a "normal" relationship is.[42] Despite the overwhelming public perception that Viagra is revolutionary in its ability to quickly repair the relational costs of erectile dysfunction, I was surprised (and encouraged) by some of the news stories that questioned Viagra's value to relational harmony. An article by Stacey Schultz in *U.S. News & World Report,* "When Sex Pales, Women May Need More Than Viagra," unveils the complexity of relational desire:

> Stress, anger, or a cooling relationship can kill desire as surely as a disturbance in hormones or blood flow, and "no pill is going to fix that," says Aline Zoldbrod, a sex therapist in Peabody, Massachusetts.[43]

In a *New York Times* article, Douglas Martin interviews sex therapist Karen Martin, who worries about the perception of Viagra as a cure-all.

> "This is not going to make years of emotional damage disappear." . . . Viagra could have the effect of focusing sexual experience too narrowly, something she says already limits many couples. "In this culture we see being sexual as having intercourse," she said. "We're a very meat-and-potatoes culture. In other cultures, they toss in a few mushrooms."[44]

Similarly, a Jon Nordheimer article in the *New York Times,* "Some Couples May Find Viagra a Home Wrecker," reveals other complications. Although this article demonstrates (refreshingly) that medical doctors, too, are capable of recognizing the entanglements of emotion, desire, identity, and the dynamics fundamental to sexual relationships, other assumptions and stereotypes emblematic of larger societal expectations are promulgated. In this lengthy article,[45] Nordheimer reports that

> [w]omen who suffer medical afflictions associated with age or a severely reduced sex drive may be disturbed by a husband's restored potency and cool to his advances, experts said. Moreover, when other problems have derailed a relationship, they said, no little blue pill is going to make them magically disappear. . . . For some men . . . restored sexual function can create issues of fidelity that previously had been moot. A man suddenly empowered sexually after years of inactivity may go flying out the door looking for someone else if his partner doesn't share his enthusiasm or flatly rejects him. . . . Many impotent men compensated in the past by becoming very attentive lovers. If they now turn sex into prolonged athletic contests their partners may quickly rebel.[46]

In these articles that do important work in questioning the perceived value of Viagra for relationships, several assumptions should be examined:

First, we should question the expectation that all couples need to maintain the sexual vigor of their youth—a vigor that is unabashedly masculine in its emphasis (both in therapeutic and practical arenas) on models of conquest and performance.

Second, we should critique the assumption that it is only the man in these relationships (who *suffers* from a lack of sexual ability) who must come to terms with what medical sociologist Kathy Charmaz calls "contingent personal identity."[47] In the example above, note that the female partner is not assumed to have gone "flying out the door" in search of a capable lover when her husband was impotent. Overwhelmingly, the cost of erectile dysfunction to women in the relationship goes unexamined, unless it is coded within the frame of Viagra: a boon to a long passionless drought.[48] And while cuddling is implied as the default substitute for impossible intercourse, no other forms of sexual play are considered in these articles. As Russell Watson's *Newsweek* story "The Globe Is Gaga for Viagra" reminds us, "A poor lover plus Viagra does not make a good lover, but merely a poor lover with an erection."[49]

Finally, despite the frequent use of the term "partner"—a descriptor that is used in the long-term committed relationships of both gay and straight couples—the articles quoted in this subsection refer exclusively to heterosexual behavior, a tendency that will be examined more thoroughly in the subsection to follow.[50]

Returning to the perpetuation of the mind/body split in the treatment of erectile dysfunction, the question must be asked—What is at stake when integrating the two (especially in a heterosexual model of relational dynamics)? By acquiescing to an emergency room ideology of "treat 'em and street 'em," and accepting the biomedical solution to the putative sexual dysfunction within a relationship, the female partner enables the male partner to "save face," but often at the expense of her own sexual needs and desires (or lack thereof). Within a relationship marked by traditional performances of masculine authority and feminine servility, it is the woman who feels the pressure to equalize the anxiety resulting from the compromised male ego. Writing about the experience of "first heterosex" (or perhaps, more colloquially, "losing virginity"), Janet Holland, Caroline Ramzanoglu, and Rachel Thomson suggest that it is

> through *her participation* in *his performance* [that] she is inducted to the world of heterosexual sexuality, where she must learn to play by the masculine rules of the game, or take the consequences of resistance. . . . Within this game, her sexual identity, subjectivity and desire are silent. To succeed as a woman, and to be rewarded, she must become proficient in supporting and satisfying masculine values and needs [my emphasis].[51]

The woman's complicity in the man's performance is achieved through silence. Her proficiency in supporting and satisfying his values (and thereby demonstrating her success as a woman) is guaranteed by the biomedical endorsement and attributions of gender in the mind/body dualism. Something that "no pill will cure" is also subject to this gender dichotomy: none of the articles suggested that a man taking Viagra might be concerned with intimacy dynamics.

The areas of relational communication I've addressed here illustrate the ways in which Viagra's benefits have been challenged by the popular press. The subtlety of taking a pill is an appealing antidote to the silence and secrecy surrounding sexuality and its (presumed) impediments. Biomedicine's embrace of pharmaceutical solutions reveals its advocacy of the mind/body split. The mind/body split not only fixes erectile dysfunction in organic causes and normalizes the chemical solution, but also divides solutions along gendered lines, suggesting that men don't require the communicative therapy that women do. This divide has a profound affect on both individual partnerships and attitudes about gendered performances. These attitudes are discernible when men are quoted in these stories. Men in these articles—who speak anecdotally and metaphorically—reveal values and needs. Here I look at how masculine values and needs are portrayed in these news stories and how the masculine virtues of risk taking and sexual prowess are upheld.

Testimonials of Masculinity

"Testimony" has a relevant etymology in the discussion of male sexuality. The word derives from the Latin *testis,* meaning "witness." Testimony is evidence—an authentication, a sign, an acknowledgment. By virtue of the sperm from a man's testicles, the birth of a child is "proof," so to speak, of a couple's sexual congress. More to the point, offspring serve as evidence of a man's ownership of wife and family.[52] The testimony from sufferers of erectile dysfunction and/or users of Viagra serve, for Pfizer Pharmaceutical's purposes, as evidence of both need and success. Men quoted in these Viagra news stories communicate three distinct attitudes about how erectile function intersects with their beliefs about masculinity.[53] These beliefs are organized around (1) status; (2) utilitarian and architectural metaphors for male sexual organs; and (3) an imagined return to youthful virility.

The gendered nature of communication styles has been a frequent site of academic investigation.[54] Although early studies chose to address the ways in which *men* and *women* differ in how they participate in a communicative event, more recent investigations into the nature of communication have come to recognize the importance of describing gendered styles as *masculine* and *feminine.* Nevertheless, masculine styles and feminine styles typically correspond with men and women, respectively. Those who employ a feminine style of communication do *rapport* talk, while the masculine style is orchestrated around the strategy of *report* talk. Deborah Tannen explains:

> For most women, the language of conversation is primarily a language of rapport: a way of establishing connections and negotiating relationships. . . . For most men, talk is primarily a means to preserve independence and negotiate and maintain status in a hierarchical social order.[55]

Even though we're not talking here about conversation per se, an analysis of masculine testimony about sexuality can take into account the same stakes. For many women, talk about sexual practices is about relationship validation. A mutual acknowledgment of barricades to the bedroom *authenticates* the partnership. While often an occasion for braggadocio, sex talk for many men draws attention to inadequacies—a direct affront to male status—not only in relationships, but also in the real and imagined arena of men. Indeed, a patient's lack of erectile function prompts the writer of this passage to steep him in a feminized countenance:

> The patient . . . was accidentally kicked in the groin years ago. The damage was severe. A beefy, *rounded* man, he sits on the examination table *sidesaddle,* his ankles crossed *coyly.* Both he and his Rubenesque wife curl their shoulders inward and keep their heads bowed, as if in shame [my emphasis].[56]

This man clearly lacks the markers of masculine status and, instead, is portrayed as the embodiment of feminine deportment. An example of elevated status, on the other hand, can be found in Geoffrey Cowley's *Newsweek* article in which a man banters with his physician about the success of his hormone therapy: "My wife would like a word with you . . . and that word is stop."[57] In this instance, the man's recovered virility is an occasion to elevate his status among men.

If erectile dysfunction is regarded as a couple's disease, then Viagra is depicted as the couple's cure. The testimonials offered in twenty-four separate news accounts reinforce the importance of communication about sexual activity and happiness (through sexual fulfillment) in relationships. Communication between partners about sexual preferences, turnoffs, and frequency is essential to the successful relationship according to physicians, sex therapists, counselors, and the partners themselves. But although references to marriage, partners, and sexual relationships were regularly featured *aspects* of these news stories, specific *examples* of dialogic communication were rare: Viagra users, their physicians, sex therapists, and counselors constantly refer to sexual fulfillment but always from a hypothetical and/or generic sense. The few examples that are included construct an overwhelming assumption of marriage (or, at least, monogamous heterosexuality) among Viagra users *and* reinforce status as a traditional aspect of masculine communication style.

It is worth noting that not one of the fifty-two news stories includes a report of a gay man or gay couple being treated for erectile dysfunction. The "wife" is the default partner when the relational dynamics of erectile dysfunction are described. And while she might be frustrated by her husband's erectile difficulties, she is patient and "stands by her man." These characterizations come through in discourse both by ED sufferers and by the physicians and therapists who treat them. In addition, "she" is also portrayed as more likely to initiate talk about bedroom frustrations and is the obligatory driving force in the decision to seek professional help about sexual difficulties.[58]

A required component of the male sex role is independence.[59] Men are supposed to be self-reliant and confident, never admitting to a lack. In a *New York Times* article a man recalls, "[My wife] wanted me to see a doctor because I no longer had erections."[60] Meanwhile, he is less than concerned, busying himself with his golf game and ignoring the relational fallout. "To tell the truth," he confesses, "I was more concerned about my putting than playing around."[61] Another article in the *Times* illustrates another kind of aloofness. A man who has had erectile dysfunction (the result of testicular cancer) since the beginning of his marriage confides, "One thing that amazed me when we finally opened the lines of communication was that my sexual performance was not satisfactory for her."[62] In the same article, another man suggests that ED "isn't an easy topic to deal with" because "it goes to the heart of masculinity."[63]

Independence, heterosexuality, and penetrative sexual activity are dominant themes in these testimonials. Altogether, they signal the motif of status as an important consideration for the men portrayed in these news stories. What is more, men maintain both status and the mind/body dichotomy by utilizing metaphors to describe their bodies.

Because virility is viewed as an integral part of what it means to be masculine, a loss in virility is often considered a loss in masculinity: "I feel less than a man," comments the subject of a *Newsweek* article.[64] Uncertainty and real or imagined deficiency of one's virility generates an "othering" of the fallen phallus. It is not the man who is lacking but his member. This transfer is carried out through the use of mechanistic metaphors, for example, the title of a 1997 *Newsweek* article by Geoffrey Cowley: "Rebuilding the Male Machine." In its perceived failure, the penis goes from erect and performing phallus to an object as useless as "a flat tire"[65] or stopped-up "plumbing,"[66] or as revealing as "a chink in their armor."[67] Likewise, the solution or recovery is viewed "as insurance,"[68] "a full tank,"[69] or a "revolution."[70]

The men using these metaphors take their cues from medicine. Dr. Irwin Goldstein is one urologist and researcher who sees the process of erections as a mechanical one. Profiled in Jack Hitt's February 2000 *New York Times Magazine* feature story about the medicalization of sexuality, Goldstein works with Drs. Jennifer and Laura Berman at Boston University's Sexual Health Clinic. This is the team that treated Bob Dole. Goldstein remarks:

> Not to discount psychological aspects . . . but at a certain point all sex is mechanical. The man needs a sufficient axial rigidity so his penis can penetrate through labia, and he has to sustain that in order to have sex. This is a mechanical structure, and mechanical structures follow scientific principles. . . . I am an engineer . . . and I can apply the principles of hydraulics to these problems. I can utilize medical strategies to assess, diagnose and manipulate things that are not so straightforward in psychiatry.[71]

The use of architectural and mechanistic metaphors here does more than simply provide useful models for grasping the specifics of ED; they are also utilized rhetorically to create distance between the physiological and psychological approaches. In more than one article, Goldstein emphatically declares, "It's all hydraulics!"

"The penis as a 'tool,'" writes Peter F. Murphy, "makes explicit the association between male heterosexuality and the machine." Murphy's book *Studs, Tools, and the Family Jewels* examines the metaphors men live by as well as the shrewdness of discourse common among heterosexual males.

> The penis as a device for performing a chore or doing a job is one metaphor that dominates the lexicon of male bonding. The idea of the penis as an instrument to accomplish something (usually penetration of a woman to allow a man to have a quick and easy orgasm), or as an implement to get a particular job done, pervades the way men think about their sexuality.[72]

This points to another important meaning of the word "tool"—it is also used to describe those who blindly follow artificial standards. A tool here is an "implement" of oppression—a dupe, a stooge. A tool is somebody who, unthinkingly, does what he is told to do. If the penis is supposed to function when called upon to do so, then there is a clear hierarchy between a man and his penis. In these news stories, this hierarchy is maintained—both by patients and physicians—through the use of mechanistic metaphors. But it is in adolescence that this hierarchy is established.

In the discourse of erectile dysfunction, the benchmark for healthy sexual response is based on recollections of youth and/or early relationship activity. From the "I wish I knew then what I do now" department comes the idealization of youthful sexuality, as evidenced by comments made by those for whom Viagra has worked successfully. "I'm 60 years old but I think I'm 16"[73] and "It's time for me to be a stud again"[74] are two examples of how the recovery of erectile function is equated with reminiscences of a glorious sexual past.

It is has been argued that women experience distinct, biological moments that punctuate the course of their lives whereas men do not. Whether or not these moments are absent for men, women's biological experiences are imbued with cultural significance; menarche, menstruation, pregnancy, and menopause not only mark time in a woman's adulthood but are also indicative of sexual readiness, availability, and outcome.[75] That is, in a culture of male dominance, women's bodies are marked. With regard to men's bodies, no matching reproductive indicator is available, nor is there an expectation of changing function. Once boys reach puberty and begin to experience erections and produce sperm, science tells us there is little variation on sexual physiology until death—at least nothing as dramatic as pregnancy, nor as culturally loaded.

The popular press stories depicted here do seem to want to find some significance in the statistics on erectile function. One subtext to the story of Viagra's success is the recognition of "manopause" accompanied by the apparent ability to circumvent it. "Manopause"—an unimaginative euphemism for a life change in masculine middle age—is set up as the condition of which erectile dysfunction is a symptom.[76] Eluding the inevitability of aging is what much of the testimony here suggests as the motivation for perpetual virility. If the *before* Viagra remark sounds like this—"My eye doesn't wander anymore, because I can't do anything about it"[77] then the *after* comment sounds like this—"It's just like when we were first married."[78]

"It" is twofold: the ability to have penetrative sex, and the perception that having sex is a sign of youthful vigor. An article by Susan Brink in *U.S. News & World Report* establishes the connections among masculinity, sex, communication, and youth. "The Do or Die Decade" is a look at how poor health among men in their fifties is both a result of a lifetime of masculine socialization *and* an opportunity for change. Brink writes, "Viagra has given men an entrée into the healthcare world to talk about a nearly universal underlying fear."[79] This doctor's visit should create an opportunity for a physician to uncover other potential health problems, many of which may be directly related to impotence. But admitting physical vulnerabilities, particularly impotence, is not in alignment with the masculine directives "Be self-reliant" and "Be sexual."[80] Revealing weaknesses (particularly after a lifetime of masculine independence) is a reminder of the inevitability of aging and its distance from youth. Brink quotes one man as saying,

> Being able to do it. I worry about that. I think every man does. No one will tell you . . ., "You know son, you'll be able to do it when you're 100." When you're a teenager, sex is all guys talk about. Then all of a sudden, you don't talk about it.[81]

Health communication researcher Michael Arrington's research of prostate cancer patients in a support group reveals how a culture of marginalization and silence is likely perpetuated by social structures rather than a lack of interest in the topic of sexuality. When a psychologist replaced a physician as the facilitator of this support group, the group's members were provided with a space to talk about emotional issues, physical pain, and sexual intimacy. Arrington found that these men were able to "negotiate sexuality with their partners in a wide variety of ways, ranging from abstinence to redefining sexual intimacy to seeking other forms of intimacy altogether." The definition of "real" sex—defined as spontaneous penile-vaginal penetration—is one that begins in adolescence. Changing that definition might require a shift in consciousness, something that a serious illness and/or a talented facilitator might enable.

Testimonies of masculinity contained in these news stories suggest a puerile and stagnant relationship between men and sexuality—one that Viagra preserves with its emphasis on subtlety, organic causes, and universal remedies. These testimonials—which feature status, mechanistic metaphors, and youthful virility as their primary themes—reinforce how the male sex role is steeped in tradition and slow to change. But here I must ask as others have—Are these roles actually what men perform, or what they are expected to perform? And if these roles are expectations, who is the audience? Because definitions of American masculinity are so carefully regulated through models of hegemony and the practices of complicity, it is not surprising that these testimonials replicate traditional norms. But the perpetuation of norms (whether or not they are performed) does have a price. This price is evidenced both by the lengths to which men will pursue the sexual expectations of heterosexual masculinity and by the costs absorbed by the state in that pursuit. As Lynne Segal observes,

> Many feminists simply equate "masculinity" and "male dominance." On this view the psychology of men inevitably perpetuates the social structures of male dominance, as a result of either their biological *or* their social construction [emphasis original].[82]

As I'm sure Segal would agree, the perpetuity of male-dominated social structures is not a question of *either* biological *or* social interplay but of both/and. The three motifs of status, architectural metaphors, and youth comprising the theme of testimonials of masculinity demonstrate the degree to which the fantasy of hegemonic masculinity holds sway over the reality and inevitability of aging. The fourth theme wrenches that reality to the forefront.

Viagra and Death: Guinea Pigs and Scapegoats

Shortly after Viagra's debut, dozens of news stories surfaced that addressed the possible risks of taking the drug.[83] Although the willingness to endure side effects lies somewhere on the continuum of risk-taking behavior, risking *death* must surely occupy the extreme.[84] Within a couple of months of Viagra's release, news stories addressed the allegations that some Viagra users had underestimated the risks involved when combining sexual exertion and a weak heart. More problematically, a significant number of Viagra users died within hours of taking the popular new pill. This news—aggressively downplayed by Pfizer—prompted headlines like "Dying for Sex" in *U.S. News & World Report,* "Just How Safe Is Sex?" in *Newsweek,* and, most emphatically, "Six Taking Viagra Die" in the *New York Times.* But even as the drug's safety record raises questions, there is a rhetoric in these news stories that distinguishes between legitimate and illegitimate risk among Viagra users. This rhetoric, I will argue, divides risk into either (a) legitimate or anticipated risk—risk that is approved as characteristic of hegemonic male norms and expectations; or (b) illegitimate or unanticipated risk—risk that is contrary to hegemonic male norms and is, in fact, suggestive of subordinate masculinities.

By July 1998—barely three months after Viagra's release—the FDA had received reports of seventy-seven deaths.[85] Major side effects occurred by the hundreds, according to the FDA, including nonfatal heart attacks, strokes, and impaired vision. Even as the public was made aware of these side effects, Pfizer's consumers revealed their biases. In *Newsweek* a sixty-four-year-old Maryland man remarks with characteristic masculine bravado, "I think about [the risk]. But the tradeoff is worth it."[86] In the *New York Times* a man opines, "Some of these old guys will drop dead from it."[87]

In a May 1998 *New York Times* article, Jane Brody reports how "in the wave of enthusiasm surrounding this drug over the last two months, many physicians and their patients have ignored its limitations and side effects" and that "millions of sufferers are likely to forsake caution."[88] Published some nine months after Viagra came sailing into the harbor of the public's awareness as the "potency pill," Shannon Brownlee's *U.S. News & World Report* article, "Dying for Sex,"[89] encapsulates the casualties attributed to Viagra and intimates the causalities. In particular, Brownlee is suspicious of the methods by which Pfizer managed the drug's clinical trials and the FDA's approval process. And by the time her report hit the newsstands, the FDA had confirmed that at least 130 Americans had died after taking Viagra.[90] Brownlee's article is not the first among those surveyed to report on Viagra's impediments, but it is the first to provide critical analysis that points out the possible obliquities practiced by Pfizer Pharmaceuticals and the FDA. Brownlee's thesis is twofold. She first argues that Pfizer's clinical trials failed to include patients with heart problems:

> The company went to full-scale clinical trials, using sildenafil to treat impotence in more than 3,000 men. The researchers were careful to exclude men with serious heart conditions or high blood pressure, or those who had had a stroke or heart attack in the past six months.[91]

The second part of her thesis is that the FDA moved too quickly in approving Viagra, without its usual and necessary precautions: "The drug's approval came just as Congress was concluding four years of congressional pressure on the FDA to approve drugs—even lifestyle-enhancing drugs—more quickly."[92] Brownlee's article is supported by illuminative expert testimony. The rebuttals provided by Pfizer, however, are the most revealing; Pfizer is shameless in its refusal of accountability.

Included among Brownlee's experts are representatives from the Public Citizen's Health Research Group that charge Pfizer with purposely excluding men with heart conditions from their clinical trials *specifically* because of "safety worries." To this accusation, Brownlee quotes Pfizer's director of clinical trials, Ian Osterloh: "We thought [heart and high blood pressure patients] wouldn't be thinking about sex."[93] Meanwhile, death as a side effect is something Pfizer can somehow both deny and soft-pedal. Brownlee writes,

> Pfizer maintains that Viagra is safe when used as directed. "I don't think there is any evidence this drug is dangerous," says Ian Osterloh, who directs Pfizer's clinical trials, the tests on people that determine a drug's safety and efficacy. The number of deaths, says Osterloh, is not unexpected considering that many of the men using Viagra are old and have failing hearts. In fact, he says, Pfizer expected more deaths. It is precisely because Viagra is being used by older, often ailing men, and because it is a sexual aid and not a lifesaving drug, that critics are questioning the speeded-up process that led to its approval.[94]

Perhaps what is surprising is the extent to which this phenomenon of risk taking at the expense of health is understood, condoned, and reported by the popular press.

By June 1998, when the first sixteen deaths had been reported, *Newsweek* journalist Rana Dogar discloses in her article "Just How Safe Is Sex?" that

> The details of each death aren't yet clear. . . . But there appear to be some common denominators. At least 13 of the men were reportedly over 50, the key age for both heart attacks and Viagra use. Many suffered from ailments like heart disease or high blood pressure; some were taking medications for them.[95]

In the *New York Times,* Gina Kolata defends Pfizer's position when she writes, "Of course, patients taking nitroglycerin have serious heart disease so even if such patients died while taking Viagra, that in itself would not mean that they had died because they had taken Viagra."[96] *Newsweek's* John Leland also effects a remarkably benign position when he concludes, "The risks, though, are easily inflated. . . . Most of the men who died were elderly, and 51 had other risk factors like high cholesterol, high blood pressure or diabetes."[97] The ways in which these news stories characterize the deaths that followed the ingestion of Viagra legitimizes both the response of Pfizer Pharmaceuticals and the larger societal structure that grants the process of developing drugs to organizations with a primary focus on profit.

But the risks of Viagra could not be completely ignored. Death notwithstanding, these news stories had other ways to talk about the perils of the potency pill. Along with legitimizing risk, many of these news stories located illegitimate risk. In order to appease the public's interest in safety and to demonstrate responsibility, these news stories concoct numerous scapegoats upon whose backs the burden of evil is loaded.

In his introduction to Kenneth Burke's *Permanence and Change,* Hugh Duncan explains how the use of the scapegoat is "only a rationalization of other motives" including sexual, political, and economic motives.[98] In *The Rhetoric of Religion,* Burke differentiates between the ritualistic scapegoat and the pseudoscientific scapegoat. In ritual, the scapegoat is "delegated" insofar as the attributes in need of purgation are contrived. But for the pseudoscientific scapegoat, negative attributes have been retroactively assigned.[99]

These negative attributes disproportionately fall on "queer" users of Viagra. By "queer" I refer to those who, according to certain writers, ingest Viagra illegitimately—that is, those outside of the boundaries sanctioned by Pfizer, by technoscientific discourse, and even by society at large. Performance studies scholar Elizabeth Bell points out how "each culture maintains elaborate cultural constraints against and rewards for coupling in/appropriately."[100] In these news stories, those men who couple inappropriately—or, illegitimately—and are made scapegoats as a result include homosexuals, rave party drug users, and nonimpotent heterosexuals (both male and female).

Pfizer has always considered Viagra contraindicated by the use of a class of drugs called nitrates—medication often employed to manage angina, cardiovascular disease, and high blood pressure. The combination of Viagra and nitrates can result in a life-threatening drop in blood pressure.[101] From the beginning, Pfizer included on its patient summary of information a warning against the use of Viagra for those taking nitrates. The class of nitrates includes amyl nitrate or "poppers," a recreational drug popular in the gay community and used to intensify sexual response and heighten excitement. In early May 1998, *New York Times* writer David Kirby reported how members of New York City's gay community began circulating the danger of the Viagra/poppers combination through social circles after AIDS activists began receiving calls from Pfizer representatives.

> [Pfizer spokeswoman Maryann Caprino] said the warning about nitrates appears in Viagra's federally approved package insert. But, she said, "You can't use words like 'poppers' in your insert." And sales representatives making the rounds to New York doctors in the last two weeks "could only talk off the package insert," she said, which meant they couldn't use the word poppers, either.[102]

After receiving a warning from a representative of an advocacy group, a physician with a large gay clientele "began warning patients about not mixing poppers and Viagra." He thought a call from Pfizer to activists (and not physicians) was "a funny way to tell people."[103] By early 1999, however, Pfizer explicitly included a warning on its patient summary information about "poppers." When asked about a public education campaign for gay men, Pfizer responded that such a campaign was only "a possibility."[104]

Over four years later Pfizer still hadn't produced any educational literature for gay men. An October 2001 *New York Times* story, "Experts Fear a Risky Recipe," reports how

> [Pfizer spokesman Geoff Cook] said he did not know whether the company would pursue a gay-oriented educational campaign. He stressed, however, that

Pfizer had long warned against the use of Viagra for *nonapproved* purposes. . . . "Our position to not use Viagra for *recreational* purposes is well-known, but any pharmaceutical product can be abused," Mr. Cook said. He added that Pfizer also advised caution when the drug was used with protease inhibitors, an important class of HIV medications [my emphasis].[105]

By this account, it would seem that Pfizer equates gay sex with the adjectives "recreational" and "nonapproved." Writer David Tuller opens the story by acknowledging the similarities between gay men and straight men: "Many gay men, like straight men, are using Viagra solely for its approved purpose—as a remedy for persistent erectile dysfunction." He then chastises gay men for "treating [Viagra] as a recreational drug and taking it along with Ecstacy [*sic*] and other illegal substances." The article includes examples of medical misfortunes befalling gay men who've combined Viagra with other drugs (including poppers). Distressingly, the article singles out gay men using Viagra as contributing to the spread of HIV through a roundabout argument that would have readers thinking that all gay Viagra users have multiple partners, are recreational drug users, and frequent bathhouses. Fortunately, this news story does attempt a reflexive stance when Tuller reports that it is unclear "whether Viagra use itself can lead to an increase in risky behavior or whether those who tend to engage in risky behavior are simply more likely to take Viagra."[106] He adds,

Some Viagra advocates say the drug may actually reduce HIV transmission by making it easier for men to maintain erections while using condoms. And others say that focusing on recreational Viagra use among gay men smacks of prejudice.[107]

Given the prevalence of straight men using Viagra even under the threat of death, heart attacks, and the panoply of other side effects, I would suggest there is prejudice at work here. And if Pfizer is marketing its product to straight men for whom *procreation* is no longer a goal (and, in some cases, impossible) then it seems clear that cultural constraints against sex as *recreation* is something reserved only for gay men. The double use of the adjective "recreational" for gay drug use *and* gay sex maligns both.[108]

Pfizer's target market is heterosexual baby boomers and aging Xers. But when Jack Hitt explains in the *New York Times Magazine* how "the practice of poly-pharmacy, taking a couple of different rave drugs . . . kills the sex drive," it is no surprise that the "club kids in the big cities use it as a party drug."[109] It is also no surprise that Pfizer damns these uses but, once again, is unwilling to make any edifying improvements, either to its package insert or through marketing strategies. In her article "The 'Sextasy' Craze," Karen Breslau of *Newsweek* writes,

At Pfizer, . . . officials take a dim view of the surging recreational popularity of their product. . . . The company . . . rejected a request from officials in San Francisco to put a warning on Viagra about high-risk sexual behavior. "This is a public-health issue that needs to be addressed by public health campaigns on safe-sex practices, not by focusing on one drug," says spokesman Geoff Cook.[110]

Finally, nonimpotent heterosexual males are portrayed as illegitimate users and scapegoats, but in a different way. From the "be careful what you ask for" department appear the cautionary tales of men who "just want some fun."[111]

These stories stress the fact that Viagra is not an aphrodisiac and only intended for "the clinically impotent patients for whom it was intended."[112] These men, too, are subject to side effects—in particular, priapism, a prolonged, painful erection that, if untreated, can cause permanent impotence. But there is a wink-wink, nudge-nudge quality to these warnings, as well.[113] Indeed, many of these articles fully acknowledge Viagra's nefarious uses. One such user proclaimed that Viagra "helped him last twice as long as usual."[114] Another discloses, "My girlfriend always knows when I use it. . . . Instead of this carefully choreographed single episode, suddenly I'm a nuclear reactor of love."[115] Such exposure is, without question, good for Viagra's reputation among men. Indeed, my own unsolicited informants have revealed a similar response. None of the people who've told me they've used Viagra has ever had it prescribed to them personally—such a revelation would be tantamount to admitting that they had erectile dysfunction—rather, it is always acquired through a friend or relative, giving the "street" distribution of Viagra an urban legend quality. Susan Brink writes,

> [Tested] and approved for erectile dysfunction, [Viagra] is almost certainly being used to enhance sexual performance, a purpose for which it has never been tested. . . . It's practically impossible to curtail such "off-label" drug use, since physicians can prescribe drugs for any purpose they choose and drug companies are always looking to expand their markets.[116]

Pfizer can (and does) play both ends against the middle here. By condemning these off-label uses, Pfizer demonstrates its corporate responsibility even as it enjoys the financial benefits of such underground talk—true or false. The illegitimate users are already society's scapegoats: drug users, homosexuals, and, to a lesser extent, lascivious heterosexual single men and some married men (who use Viagra only with mistresses). Meanwhile, the popular press legitimates the rightful users, even those whose penchant for risk taking earned them the final reward.

As these news sources allay the possible detrimental effects of Viagra, they create the likelihood of risk-taking behavior. For legitimate users, the possibility of regaining lost erectile function trumps the threat to general health and well-being. Because the loss of erectile function so threatens a loss in masculinity, many men turn uncritically to the promise of technoscientific marvels like Viagra. Likewise, the news stories legitimate its use among men at risk, equating the FDA's approval with objectivity and ignoring the subjectivity of individuals.

Kenneth Burke explains how authorities impress us with their wisdom. In the case of Viagra these authorities are sanctioned by virtue of their technoscientific expertise. As their wisdom becomes social stock knowledge through the efficiency of the mainstream press, we become susceptible to guilty feelings when we defy its advantages. Many men continuously assert their sense of masculine identity through overt and covert displays of sexuality. So when erectile dysfunction threatens this marker of masculinity and there is a ready antidote that fulfills all the requirements of a quick-fix, high-tech society, it is no wonder that men feel compelled to try it. Furthermore, the risk of death does nothing to assuage this compulsion. Men may be sacrificing their mortality, but not their status in the hierarchy.[117] After all, there is probably no physical demise more hegemonically masculine than a heart attack.

Pfizer markets Viagra as a treatment for erectile dysfunction. By what ever means *physicians* arrive at the definition of erectile dysfunction,[118] there is no doubt that the target market for its treatment (and the financial success of that treatment) rests in the fifty-plus age group of American males—the demographic cohort most at risk for heart ailments stemming from cardiovascular disease and high blood pressure. What is more, in its roll call of the organic causes of erectile dysfunction, Pfizer specifically names the drugs that are prescribed to treat high blood pressure and heart disease as contributing "to a man's inability to get and keep an erection"[119] and recommends Viagra as a treatment. So Ian Osterloh's claim that "we thought [heart and high blood pressure patients] wouldn't be thinking about sex" rings hollow; Pfizer both anticipated an interest in sex among men with high blood pressure and heart disease *and* systematically kept such men from its clinical trials.[120]

Here, I'd like to turn to a discussion of risk and redemption. Pfizer Pharmaceuticals claims that it expected more deaths. But why? What is it about sex that drives thousands (if not millions) of American men to compromise their health, whether by ingesting a pill or through physical exertion? The answer, again, may be found among James Doyle's five themes of American masculinity. Socialization emphasizes both virility and achievement as imperatives for the performance of masculinity. "Be sexual," "Be aggressive," and "Be successful" all come into play here. In childhood, boys are rarely reprimanded for risky behavior; in fact, risk-taking behavior among young males is rewarded by peers, if not by parents. Organized sports—particularly football[121]—often intensify the performance of risk taking and aggression, as physical training emphasizes strength, the endurance of pain, and, above all, winning. This adolescent socialization, of course, becomes part and parcel of adult masculine socialization, albeit more subtly. Viagra "works" on several levels because it provides men with an assertive (or active) role in their treatment and, as it is advertised in the popular press, this treatment promises success. Most importantly, it does so without compromising a man's status in his social hierarchy. The way in which these news stories address the issue of death calls attention to the fact that death is always big news. This is not surprising. No matter what the context or circumstances—whether the issue is an airplane crash, disease, or catastrophe—the drama of death is exhaustively narrated and examined in the media. And after scenes have been created and recreated, shock has been expressed and acknowledged, and the aggrieved have been listened to and consoled, the question of blame surfaces and demands a response.

Some articles blame Pfizer and others blame people. Pfizer is drawn as a company that is irresponsible: in testing Viagra, in ignoring the myriad health problems of the drug's target market, and in pressuring the FDA in the interest of profit and stock prices. People are blamed for not taking the drug as directed, for being out of the hegemonic masculine loop, for wanting better sex and sensory experiences, and for performing sex irresponsibly/illegitimately. Most apparent in these reports that attempt to make sense of fault is that Pfizer, as much as the media doing the reporting, exculpates itself and directs blame toward the users of its drug.

With regard to these *legitimized* risks of Viagra, there is more to be revealed. Data in the *Journal of the American Medical Association* indicated that 564 Viagra-related deaths had been reported through July 8, 1999—a mere fourteen months after Viagra was approved by the FDA.[122] And in January 2003, researchers at the University of Chicago discovered how some of those deaths were *not* the simple result of combining Viagra with contraindicated nitrates, but rather, from unexpected platelet clumping.[123] Inexplicably, none of the news sources considered here reported these findings.

Clearly, as evidenced by the comments from spokespersons dismissing the risks of its product, Pfizer has demonstrated its commitment to profits, rather than any of the altruistic motives some of its literature boasts. For Pfizer, these deaths signify an embarrassment more than a legitimate hazard for which it might be responsible. Dead men tell no tales. *Newsweek's* John Leland writes, "To atone, let us now honor the Viagra 130, those brave men who died before they could fulfill the drug's true promise: to spew intimate details from the boudoir, preferably in public, even in front of the kids."[124]

In the final section of this chapter, I look at how the rhetoric of the social "costs" of Viagra continues in a larger institutional structure. The fifth major theme of the news stories I examine is the economic impact of Viagra on a societal scale.

Viagra and the Political Economy of Healthcare

An important focus of the media coverage of Viagra has been the drug's macroeconomic impact. Viagra caused major ripples in the ongoing national debate over health insurance. Almost immediately, controversy raged over the status of erectile dysfunction as a health problem. Comparisons were made between Viagra and the birth control pill in the effort to point out glaring inconsistencies in policy making.[125] In this section I look at two of the areas in which news stories reported Viagra's impact on healthcare's political economy: the debate over insurance coverage (including the inevitable comparison with the birth control pill) and Internet sales. Pharmaceutical sales on the Internet raise important questions about healthcare: specifically, the role of the physician–patient relationship.

As a nation, we do like our pills. A pill satisfies both our love of techno-science and our culture's quick-fix mentality. Indeed, taking a pill is—in miniature—a useful metaphor for instant gratification.[126] As a culture, Americans have grown to rely on prescription drugs for both their efficacy and reliability.[127] In her *New York Times* report, Jennifer Steinhauer quotes Eileen Palace, director of the Center for Sexual Health at Tulane University who notes:

> We are in a very high-tech society, and people are used to having things done very quickly. . . . We saw in the 1960s how the pill could control biology. Later we saw how to control fertility. People want a simple, easy, fast, solution. And many physicians assume that just because there is a physical problem means there is no psychological cause.[128]

In a 2002 *U.S. News & World Report* article that gives a historical account of impotence "cures," the president of the National Council Against Health Fraud agrees, "People want simple quick answers to complex problems."[129] The etiology of erectile dysfunction, the status of ED as a quality-of-life condition, and restrictions on prescription allotments are all controversial issues with tremendous financial stakes. Along with reports trumpeting Viagra's remarkable success as a treatment for erectile dysfunction came the specifics regarding Viagra's popularity and economic impact. So it wasn't long before government–sponsored Medicaid and a number of private insurance companies entered into the discussion. This subsection addresses how these three motifs—etiology, coverage, and prescription allotment—were reported in the news.

The stories published in the early months of Viagra's release (spring 1998) were fascinated with statistics, reporting, for example, that some doctors wrote as many as 100 prescriptions for Viagra a day[130] and that over 75,000 prescriptions were written in the first two weeks after its release.[131] A high of 120,000 new prescriptions were written for Viagra during the third week in April according to *Newsweek*.[132] By mid-June 1998 doctors had "scribbled out 1.7 million prescriptions."[133] By the end of calendar year 1998 "nearly 6 million prescriptions worth more than $441 million" had been filled.[134] Less than two years after its release, with both new users and repeat customers contributing to the total, almost 200,000 prescriptions were being filled each week.[135] By comparison, the sum *total* of all other prescription erection aids *before* Viagra—including urethral suppositories, penile injections, and hormone therapies—amounted to approximately one-tenth of that total, or 20,000 prescriptions a week.[136] Two years after its release (April 2000), "physicians [had] written more than 17 million prescriptions" for Viagra.[137] The average prescription of ten to fifteen pills (at approximately $10 per pill) helped make Viagra a $1-billion-a-year product almost instantly.[138]

On May 28, 1998, Robert Pear of the *New York Times* reported that the "Clinton Administration has told state officials that it intends to require their Medicaid programs to pay for medically approved uses of the impotence drug Viagra."[139] As states maintained that they should make their own decisions, lawmakers argued that "a nationwide mandate for coverage of Viagra through Medicaid would cost the states and the Federal Government more than $100 million a year."[140] Because more than 40 percent of Medicaid costs are absorbed by each state, some states argued that the cost would hinder the delivery of care to patients with more serious medical conditions. Amazingly, the federal directive requiring states to pay for Viagra was promulgated even as an increasing number of Viagra-related deaths were being reported. A spokeswoman for New York State Governor George Pataki said, "The Federal Government should not be requiring New York or any other state to pay for Viagra until there is a better understanding of the impact this drug has on patients."[141]

Insurance company Kaiser Permanente similarly challenged the idea that a pill for erectile dysfunction would be something they would be required to cover. "Kaiser decided that it would not raise the premiums for all its members to pay for treatment of a nonlethal, noncrippling condition that almost all of its members could afford to treat on their own," wrote Michael Weinstein in the *New York Times*.[142]

The introduction of the subject of cost to both the state and private enterprise reopened the debate over both the severity of erectile dysfunction and Viagra's intended use. What made Kaiser's decision so interesting, according to Weinstein, is that insurance companies "often restrict or exclude treatments because of cost"[143] but don't usually admit that cost is the reason. Weinstein reports how decision makers for insurance companies "invoke code words—experimental, cosmetic, risky—to mask their motives, which they can't say publicly."[144] Kaiser estimated that adding Viagra to its coverage would cost the company (and eventually its members) $100 million a year, "far more than it spends on all antiviral drugs, including the expensive drugs used to treat H.I.V."[145]

Insurance companies were not the only institutions that had to adjust their accounting estimates as result of Viagra. An October 1998 *New York Times* story revealed that the Defense Department had to adjust their 1999 budget to include Viagra:

> The Pentagon estimated that it would spend about $50 million in the coming year to provide the impotence drug Viagra to American troops and military retirees. . . . Based on the number of soldiers, sailors, pilots, Marines and retirees who have asked for Viagra so far at military clinics and hospitals, Defense Department health officials estimated that if the drug were given to everyone who wanted it, the cost could top $100 million.[146]

One of the issues at stake with regard to cost had to do with the number of pills contained in a prescription. Unlike most pharmaceutical drugs that have to be taken in specific doses a certain number of times a days, Viagra is a use-as-needed medication. So both Medicaid and private insurance companies that would cover Viagra had to decide on what constitutes an appropriate supply. The military allows no more than six pills a month.[147] In the *New York Times,* Robert Pear writes that Pfizer "suggests covering 10 pills a month if states insist on a limit. But some states have set lower limits. Florida, for example, pays for 4 pills a month."[148] In *Newsweek,* Daniel McGinn reports that, according to Pfizer's market research director, the subject of how many pills could send messages about what "a 'normal' sex life" is.[149] As result, Pfizer made no recommendations initially, but felt compelled to do so once insurance became an issue. Cigna Healthcare decided to limit the prescription to six pills a month "based on estimates of an average couple's needs."[150]

At the center of this debate is the question of the severity of erectile dysfunction. Since ED is " nonlethal [and] noncrippling,"[151] states and insurance companies are loath to cover the costs of Viagra when other services would have to be limited, cut back, and/or eliminated altogether as a result of funding it. Meanwhile, Pfizer responded by saying that impotence "is a bona fide medical condition that has a tremendous impact on patients and their partners."[152] Like New York and other states such as Wisconsin, insurance companies such as Kaiser, Prudential, and Humana expressed their reluctance to cover Viagra by pointing out how the cost for a drug that is medically unnecessary would infringe on treatment for more serious conditions. Other states and insurers required a documented diagnosis of organic impotence in order to qualify[153] or "more stringent criteria for evaluating a patient's medical need for the drug."[154] The military eventually "limited Viagra to men in whom erectile dysfunction has been diagnosed by a doctor."[155] Indeed, it was reported that even Secretary of Health and Human

Services Donna Shalala considered Viagra's potential for both clinical and financial abuse.[156]

Another important consideration regarding Viagra's impact on health-care's political economy was revealed when mandatory insurance coverage for Viagra catalyzed the discussion over birth control pills and their infrequent coverage. Carey Goldberg of the *New York Times* writes that, "For decades, women's advocates had little success in pushing insurance coverage of contraceptives."[157] When Viagra was included in many insurance plans, "[these groups] have been able to add to their arsenal of arguments the tough-to-beat issue of basic fairness."[158] Opponents to contraception coverage ranged from the Catholic Church to antiabortion groups to business leaders to the U.S. Chamber of Commerce.[159] While one-half to two-thirds of insurance companies do cover oral contraceptives, the significant difference in overall out-of-pocket health costs between men and women—women spend 68 percent more—can be traced to those insurance companies that don't.[160] In June 2001, a federal judge ruled that not covering birth control "violated the Pregnancy Discrimination Act," bringing the issue of coverage to a decisive moment.

The roles of birth control pills and Viagra in women and men, though not parallel, each in different ways impact and significantly influence sexual agency for both sexes. The debates concerning these medications have pointed out the gendered inconsistencies inherent in the U.S. healthcare's political economy[161] and revealed the ways in which insurance companies and nonmedical U.S. government agencies influence health decisions. While this is not, in itself, *news,* unpredictable and seemingly arbitrary decision making reveals how our health system is negatively impacted by the combined power of pharmaceutical companies defining illness, insurance companies regulating payment, and masculinist perspectives driving research. Of course, the way all of this is reported by the media provides most of the public's information and framework for debate.

Another debate over access to Viagra concerns its ease of acquisition on the Internet. Shortly after Viagra became available, news stories appeared that trumpeted the little blue pill's other contribution to the health of the American man: more men were making appointments to see their doctor.[162] "Men are so consistently no-shows at doctors' offices that insurers have come to count on it," writes Susan Brink in *U.S. News & World Report.*[163] Viagra's availability resulted in men keeping their appointments, enabling doctors to diagnose problems aside from (but related to) erectile dysfunction. In the *New York Times,* Fred Brock writes that "for every million [men] who asked for Viagra, it was also discovered than an estimated 30,000 had untreated diabetes, 140,000 had untreated high blood pressure and 50,000 had untreated heart disease."[164] *Newsweek's* Dan McGinn confirms these estimates, adding that a heart disease diagnosis "warms the heart of Pfizer VP

Marie-Caroline Sainpy, whose cardiac-drug team sells treatments for those ailments."[165] Why am I not surprised?

"Need Viagra? No prescription? No problem!" is the way online pharmacy advertisers pitch Viagra.[166] Despite the manufacturer's claims that erectile dysfunction is a serious medical condition that requires a physician diagnosis, Pfizer is not averse to Internet sales. Patient–physician communication in such a context is not capable of either diagnosing or treating the plethora of conditions of which erectile dysfunction is an unwanted result.

The procedure for ordering prescription drugs online was revealed in these news stories. At least two writers of the articles surveyed purchased Viagra over the Internet in order to demonstrate how easy this was to accomplish. In an article titled "Electric Kool-Aid Viagra," Frank Rich of the *New York Times* reports that, after being charged a "consultation" fee and filling out an online medical history, a bottle of pills arrives by UPS from San Antonio, Texas. Of interest to Rich was the fact that he didn't really have to communicate with a physician. He learns the name of his physician/consultant only by reading the pill bottle:

> [This doctor] not only didn't talk to me, but he didn't consult with my primary-care physician to verify my purported medical history or see if I was telling the truth when I said I was not taking medications known to interact dangerously with Viagra.[167]

Similarly, Jack Hitt, writing for the *New York Times Magazine*, fills out an online medical interview and answers a couple of questions. The next day, "barely 12 hours after I had clicked the send button, the FedEx guy appeared with an envelope that rattled when he handed it to me."[168] Similarly, an article in *U.S. News & World Report* gives the details of a staffer who attempts to purchase Viagra online, including in the health questionnaire the fact "that he had had two open-heart surgeries."[169] Like Frank Rich and Jack Hitt, he too is "approved" and receives his supply of Viagra.

The ease of purchasing Viagra on the Internet raises a number of questions when side effects are considered. Frank Rich's point is that for patients whose physicians have refused to prescribe them Viagra due to, for example, a weak heart, the Internet is the logical source. In *Newsweek,* journalist Jerry Adler observes, "You need a license to open a pharmacy, but anyone can put up a Web site and start mailing pills all over the world."[170] Adler's article includes a quotation from Jeff Stier of the American Council on Science and Health, who suggests that the Internet "is the new medium for the snake-oil salesman."[171]

Buying Viagra on the Internet inhibits meaningful doctor–patient communication. The FDA Modernization Act of 1997 relaxed the restrictions of direct-to-consumer advertising: television advertising copy, for example, is no longer required to mention side effects. Rather, advertisers are required only to direct the consumer to other sources for information. The physician, then, "becomes the informational intermediary between the patient and the drug."[172] The availability of prescription drugs on the Internet is cause for further concern as the services of physician/consultants are paid for by pharmaceutical companies, specifically to approve the prescriptions of online applicants.[173]

The status of quality-of-life conditions is, of course, a huge "money" issue. Erectile dysfunction—as a quality-of-life condition—and Viagra—its cure—define expectations for "normal" masculine performances of sexual health. The fact that pharmaceutical companies drive these expectations for the primary purpose of increasing stock market share prices is extremely problematic. The introduction of quality-of-life condition reimbursement and treatment, in and of themselves, creates expectations for health coverage that will, no doubt, tax an already financially vulnerable and inequitable U.S. healthcare system. The body's absorption of a pill—simple and discreet—has become, in microcosm, a symbol of the quick-fix mentality of a society not interested in repairing underlying and multiple causes. Expectations for the body, driven by financial goals, demonstrate the precarious relationships among political economy and identity, capitalism and sexuality, and gendered performances and normalcy.

This chapter has provided a retrospective of how Viagra has been reported in the news. The analysis uncovers hidden assumptions about the male body, male sexuality, and masculinity and health. These assumptions are not revised or transformed by Viagra; rather, they are upheld. Male bodies are expected to perform on demand—if not "naturally," then with a naturally performing pill. Male sexuality is defined in one way; performing sexuality requires a mechanistic erection and vaginal penetration, even at the risk of one's health. Ideally, sex mirrors the youthful experiences of early adulthood with frequent and explosive orgasms defining the norm for all men at all ages. Above all, heterosexual performances of sexuality are valued with deviant, or "queer," performances scapegoated. These traditional expectations for sexual health are maintained by the current political economy.

Regarding the media in general and these stories in particular, it is significant that today's Viagra news stories are no longer concerned with how the little blue pill impacts relationships or how taking it is potentially life-threatening. Instead, stories revolve around competing pharmaceutical equivalents of Viagra (i.e., Cialis, Levitra). Today, stories in the media—by, for instance, CNN's medical correspondent Dr. Sanjay Gupta—matter-of-factly report that 30 million American men have erectile dysfunction without any of the critical feedback that a few stories in my sample provided. Here we see the difference between reporters (who merely parrot press releases) and journalists (who dig deeper). The next chapter, "Shims and Shills: Viagra and the Marketing of Transcendence," explains how Pfizer's own promotional materials have contributed to the absence of those important critical perspectives in today's news stories about men, health, and erectile dysfunction.

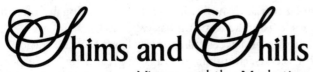hims and hills

Viagra and the Marketing of Transcendence

We are consumers. We are by-products of a lifestyle obsession.
Murder, poverty—these things don't concern me.
What concerns me is celebrity magazines, television with 500 channels,
Rogaine, Viagra, Olestra, Martha Stewart—
we're all just polishing brass on the Titanic.
It's all goin' down, man! So fuck off with your sofa units and your spring
green stripe patterns—I say never be complete.
I say stop being perfect. I say let's evolve.

—*Fight Club* (1999)

When you hear the name "Bob Dole," do you think of the senator from Kansas or the 1996 Republican presidential candidate? Or maybe you think of the husband of former Red Cross president and current Republican Senator Elizabeth Dole? Or do you think of the spokesperson for Viagra? If you're reading this book, you're probably thinking about the Bob Dole of Viagra fame. Then again, you just might think about Bob Dole in that context no matter what you are doing.

It seems that I can't watch more than fifteen minutes of television before I am subjected to one of the dozens of direct-to-consumer (DTC) pharmaceutical ads that have only recently become an acceptable part of television broadcasting. Before 1997, the Food and Drug Administration (FDA) had all but banned direct-to-consumer prescription drug advertising of the kind we now witness regularly.[1] The FDA has two responsibilities: The first is to determine whether or not products are safe and effective. The second is to make sure those products are marketed responsibly.[2] Prior to 1997, the FDA required television advertising copy to include "patient summary information." This information details, among other data, side effects, cautions, and consumer warnings. Furthermore, television pharmaceutical ads—prior to 1997—could name the illness *or* the drug, but not both. Since then the FDA has relaxed these regulations and, not coincidentally, spending by pharmaceutical companies on television advertising has exploded.[3]

In May 1998, discussing his successful recovery from prostate surgery on *Larry King Live*, Bob Dole asserted that Viagra is "a great drug" in response to King's questions about prostate cancer and impotence. As a result, Pfizer contacted Dole about heading an awareness campaign for erectile dysfunction and promoting Viagra. Like the news stories surveyed in the previous chapter, testimony is a prominent feature of Pfizer's marketing of Viagra. Of these testimonials, none has matched Bob Dole's for either name recognition or sales results. Seven years later, he is still strongly linked with the brand. But testimony—and celebrity testimony, specifically—is just one feature among many that Pfizer utilizes in its marketing approach.

In this chapter, I continue an exploration of Viagra's cultural significance by identifying the ways in which Pfizer Pharmaceuticals has produced and maintained its economic currency in an era in which pharmaceutical companies have moved from manufacturing products to manufacturing medical conditions that their products treat. Laura Mamo and Jennifer Fishman use the term "biomedicalization" to refer to the ways in which technoscience and the biomedical industrial complex "have increasingly infiltrated into people's conceptions of health, illness, the body and what it means to be 'human.'"[4] In this chapter, I argue that the kind of marketing practiced by Pfizer Pharmaceuticals normalizes biomedicalization in the pharmaceutical industry; it also negatively influences the relationship among the public, their physicians, and the larger healthcare industry.

In one of the few scholarly treatments of Viagra from a critical humanities perspective, Mamo and Fishman deconstruct several of Pfizer's promotional materials, including the Bob Dole television commercial.[5] This chapter endeavors to expand on the observations of Mamo and Fishman, offering examples from a wider range of materials and responding to their call for more critical and alternative readings. As a result of both the range of promotional texts and their high production values, I interpret the images that accompany these messages as much as the messages themselves. In particular, I look at four types of direct-to-consumer advertising utilized by Pfizer: (1) television commercials; (2) product brochures and pamphlets; (3) the Viagra magazine *LifeDrive;* and (4) informational videos. Additionally, I closely examine the book *Viagra: The Remarkable Story of the Discovery and Launch* and Pfizer's print ads in the *Journal of the American Medical Association,* a prestigious medical journal (a complete list of these promotional materials can be found in Appendix B).

Viagra's ongoing marketing efforts raise important questions through the way masculinity and sexuality are defined, created, and performed in their promotional materials. I identify five themes in these promotional materials that contribute to the unparalleled commercial success of Viagra. I begin the analysis in this chapter by considering the way in which Pfizer through its promotional materials defines erectile dysfunction (ED). The second theme examines the etiology of ED. How is the etiology of ED characterized by Pfizer and how does Viagra as treatment overcome these causes? The prevalence of ED is the third theme—How does Viagra arrive at its estimates of ED sufferers? The fourth theme is traditional performances of the male sex role. Pfizer perpetuates traditional male sex roles in its marketing and promotional materials. How are assumptions about men and masculine behavior, beliefs, and values incorporated in these promotional materials? The fifth theme is intimacy. Pfizer defines intimacy one way and markets Viagra as the remedy that helps men achieve intimacy by helping them overcome ED. But how is intimacy defined, depicted, and delineated? Before moving to these themes and my analysis, I provide a descriptive overview of my sample of promotional texts and locate them within the history of American advertising.

Advertising as Cultural Artifact

In "The Hard Sell: Advertising in America," author Bill Bryson provides a historical overview of how advertising has undergone various changes as a fundamental component of American culture.[6] In so doing, he examines the three strategies developed in the late nineteenth century by George Eastman in the marketing of the Kodak camera. Eastman set the standard for consumer goods advertising by (1) targeting the mass market; (2) embracing the concept of planned obsolescence; and (3) spending lavishly on advertising.

Advertising was new in Eastman's era and immediately influential.[7] In his essay, Bryson explores advertising's discovery of the "slogan," the "free sample," and, most importantly, "the identification and exploitation" of American anxieties. These anxieties focused predominantly on the human body. The Gillette safety razor is identified by Bryson as the first product that, *if not used,* would result in the acquisition of diseases "you never knew existed."[8] Along with creating our awareness of heretofore nonexistent maladies, advertising also tells us how we the public should feel about them, what our response should be, and, most importantly, how to prevent, get rid of, or, at least, "live with" various afflictions. This management of the body—as something to be regulated—is in many important respects a modern phenomenon.

In a 2003 *New York Times Magazine* article Shannon Brownlee addresses the cost to Americans of biomedicine's embrace of prevention rhetoric. The idea of identifying symptoms early in the hopes of warding off a more serious malady is, perhaps, *the* dominant ideology in twenty-first-century medicine. She writes, "belief in this sort of interventionist preventive medicine has ascended in lock step with the proliferation of diagnostic tests, which allow doctors to detect signs of disease in people who have few or no symptoms."[9] The implicit belief—and one Brownlee attempts to enervate in her article— is that early detection and aggressive treatment will result in longer and bet- ter life. In the meantime, prevention rhetoric is one embraced by pharma- ceutical companies, for they have become quite adept at formulating simplistic questionnaires that help to define social norms.

Lisa Belkin reports in *Mother Jones* that "pharmaceutical companies spent an estimated $1.7 billion on TV advertising in 2000, 50 percent more than what they spent in 1999, more than double the 1998 amount."[10] Belkin fur- ther explores how DTC ads have created a shift in how patients are informed of their treatment options; control of treatment options is no longer wielded by doctors. The article's title, "Prime Time Pushers," reveals the author's bias against the current trend in television advertising, but this doesn't stop her from pointing out some of the benefits of this recent shift:

> In the years since ads for Viagra first began to air, millions of men have visited their doctors specifically to get that drug—and thousands of them were diag- nosed with serious underlying conditions. The Pharmaceutical Research and Manufacturers of America estimates that for every million men who asked for the medicine, it was discovered that 30,000 had untreated diabetes, 140,000 had untreated high blood pressure, and 50,000 had untreated heart disease.[11]

As important as these discoveries are, they are not what drive the decision to advertise, or even to develop new drugs. "Let's face it," cautions Belkin, "even the drug companies would agree they are not spending all this money just to be helpful."[12] Belkin's main question is whether the same "telegenic tinsel" that results in the purchase of a Mercedes-Benz or a McDonald's hamburger also results in Americans pushing for prescriptions they might not need.

Because Viagra is such a heavily marketed product and because Pfizer uses so many different types of marketing vehicles to promote it, I character- ize the different features of the media before moving to an analysis of the dominant codes, constructions, cultural assumptions, connotations, values, and beliefs of this advertising. I order my presentation of these advertising vehicles by the likelihood of public exposure: television commercials, product brochures and pamphlets, *LifeDrive* magazine, promotional videos, print advertisements, and an advertising premium—a book titled *Viagra: The Remarkable Story of the Discovery and Launch.*

Television Commercials

Following the success of the Bob Dole commercial, Pfizer has continued to utilize television as a way to promote its product. The company's commercials have frequently featured celebrity endorsements. In addition to Bob Dole, NASCAR driver Mark Martin and Major League Baseball star Rafael Palmeiro have urged men to visit their doctors to "see if a free sample of Viagra is right for you." Other commercials construct a scenario of an average "Joe" who has recently returned from a doctor's visit. His exterior demeanor has remarkably changed, prompting friends and coworkers to venture guesses as to the source of the transformation. The celebrity endorsement, then, instructs the viewer to visit the doctor, whereas the average "Joe" commercial shows the viewer what happens when he does. These commercials, between thirty seconds and one minute in length, are often seen on all-sports networks (e.g., ESPN, Fox Sports Net) as well as on more family-oriented networks like A&E and American Movie Classics. I have also seen these commercials on the TV Guide Channel. On sports channels, they are frequently aired along with other products that appeal to a man's desire for a more youthful appearance such as hair dyes and exercise equipment.

Product Brochures and Pamphlets

A number of product brochures and pamphlets promote Viagra. Designed for distribution by healthcare personnel (i.e., urologists, primary care physicians), these full-color promotional materials are emblematic of high-end advertising and range between twelve and thirty pages in length. Like the television commercials, some of the product brochures feature sports celebrities Mark Martin and Rafael Palmeiro; others utilize an "everyman" subject who has questions and concerns about his erectile dysfunction or, alternatively, assures the reader that Viagra "does what it says it does." Included in every example of these product brochures is personal testimony, patient summary information, and the Sexual Heath Inventory for Men (SHIM), a "simple self test for ED." These brochures and pamphlets also include toll-free phone numbers and web addresses; a postage-paid mail-in reply card is also a common feature. With titles such as "Start Something Over Again," "Prime Time," and "Viagra Stories: Recover Your Love Life," these brochures introduce the reader to men and women who once had "intimacy," lost it, and have now found it again thanks to Viagra.

LifeDrive Magazine

Besides marijuana and *High Times*, can any other drug claim its own magazine? Originally titled *Voices*, *LifeDrive*, a dedicated magazine for Viagra users, epitomizes the extent to which Pfizer is committed to marketing its product. Along with the SHIM test and ample lay and professional testimony, *LifeDrive* features brief articles about travel, sports, music, food, and relationship advice in a thirty-two- to forty-page format. The language used in the titles of these articles is delightfully ambiguous: "10 tips to put some spring in your step," "In a fix? How to finish that refinishing project," "Home-grown romance," and "Quietly making a comeback." Interestingly, the common denominator among the articles in *LifeDrive* is the valorization of persistence. This is especially true of the cover stories that feature athletes and musicians who are "outnumbering their peers," "still making an impact," and "still burning up the stage." Another interesting aspect of this quarterly is a pullout card "that you can hand to your doctor to get the conversation started" about ED and Viagra. By all accounts, the arrival of Viagra has made a meaningful contribution to alleviating the taboo on discussing sexual problems. Nonetheless, *LifeDrive* seems committed to perpetuating the norms of male silence by uniformly alluding to this stereotype in its promotional materials. What is, perhaps, most interesting about this magazine is the way in which advertisements are embedded among feature stories. Ads and features are set in a similar font size and style, breaking conventions for graphic design and layout.

Promotional Videos

Although it remains rare for the users of a single drug to have their own magazine, more and more pharmaceutical companies *are* offering educational videos to help explain the benefits and dispel the "myths" of a particular pharmaceutical product. Pfizer's expensively packaged thirteen- to sixteen-minute videos for Viagra contain both lay and expert testimony, as well as graphics and charts that model the causes of erectile dysfunction and show how Viagra works to combat it. Each video is also accompanied by a helpful booklet that contains facts, figures, patient summary information, and, of course, the ubiquitous SHIM test. Their titles promote correctable life changes: "The New Facts of Life," "What Every Man (and Woman) Should Know about Erectile Dysfunction," and "Real People: Real Stories." Unlike any of the other promotional materials, these videos give prominence to nameless narrators, men in their late forties to mid-fifties, who act as intermediaries between the viewer's concerns and first-person accounts.

Print Advertisements

While Viagra is marketed to "ordinary Americans" through a variety of popular media and promotional materials, physicians are confronted with variations of Pfizer's pitch for Viagra in one of the most prestigious journals in medicine: the *Journal of the American Medical Association (JAMA)*. I surveyed one hundred issues of *JAMA* between July 1998 and December 2002 and discovered that Pfizer had placed advertisements for Viagra in seventy of them.[13]

Viagra: The Remarkable Story of the Discovery and Launch

Published by Medical Information Press (a division of Pfizer), this ninety-page hardbound book is, quite literally, a glorified bible of Viagra's development. The book is divided into seven "chapters" that (1) chronicle the history of erectile dysfunction; (2) recount the discovery of sildenafil; (3) clarify how Viagra works; (4) describe the clinical trials; (5) relate the marketing "launch" of Viagra; (6) theorize its impact on diagnosis and treatment; and (7) prophesy the future of sexual health. Containing full-color illustrations, photographs, historical archives, and pages of graphs, charts, and questionnaires, this book is an advertising premium—a product that is frequently given to physicians by sales representatives as a promotional "thank you." Written by medical writer Larry Katzenstein, it is beautifully designed and includes a foreword by Nobel Laureate Louis Ignarro.

As a group, these promotional materials are extremely rich for analysis—they encompass a range of media, supply a historical look at how Pfizer's rhetoric has changed and adjusted, and attest to the impact of this new trend in DTC advertising in the pharmaceutical industry. Furthermore, the range and perpetuity of Pfizer's advertising and promotional materials imply what Michel Foucault might call "an uninterrupted, constant coercion, supervising the processes of activity rather than its result."[14]

Because successful advertising strategies typically rely on consumer "hot buttons," I look at the way Pfizer's videos, magazines, brochures, and television commercials "speak" to consumers. Gender is frequently used in advertisments as an ideological device that works to define men and women by utilizing idealized themes of masculinity and femininity.[15] Communication scholar Valerie Hartouni has suggested that advertising, marketing, and promotional materials—as cultural artifacts—circulate within distinctive discursive arenas. Such artifacts presume, produce, and compel certain ways of seeing. As a result, specific knowledge is organized by a culture's "shared fantasies and anxieties."[16] By looking at Viagra as a cultural artifact, I explore how Pfizer Pharmaceuticals markets Viagra both to the public and to physicians. It is important to mention that these "texts" have become available at various points in Pfizer's marketing scheme and seem to assume that the audience of these texts has kept up with both "Viagra" as a trade name and the drama of Viagra as it has unfolded across the cultural landscape. Defining erectile dysfunction is the first of five major themes I investigate in these promotional materials.

Defining Erectile Dysfunction: What's in a Name?

In 1970, Masters and Johnson concluded in *Human Sexual Inadequacy* that most cases of impotence stemmed from psychological causes. Through the 1970s, the elimination of "anxiety-producing elements" was touted by sex therapists as a necessary aspect of treating erectile difficulty.[17] Indeed, *treating* impotence was formerly the uncontested domain of psychology even as psychological therapies were divided into scientific and humanistic camps.

Pharmacology's successful venture into the domain of sexual dysfunction can be traced to four significant developments. The first was the 1975 declaration by a World Health Organization (WHO) panel of experts that "problems in human sexuality are more pervasive and more important to the well-being and health of individuals in many cultures than has been previously recognized."[18] Guy Brindley's "demonstration" recounted in the introduction of this book might be considered the second. The third major development came in a 1993 report from the National Institutes of Health (NIH) Consensus Development Panel on Impotence that proposed that the term "impotence" be replaced with "erectile dysfunction."[19] The fourth was the publication in 1994 of what has come to be known as the Massachusetts Male Aging Study.[20] Based on questionnaires distributed to fewer than 1,300 men in the greater Boston area, it was determined that at the age of forty, 40 percent of men had *some degree* of erectile dysfunction.[21] By the age of fifty, 48 percent had *some degree* of ED, and by the age of seventy, almost 70 percent of the men surveyed claimed *some degree* of erectile dysfunction. The use of degrees, it seems, suggests that definitions of *impotence* are significantly affected by expressions of *potential*.

Etymologically, "potent" has the distinction of arising from the Latin verb *potere* (to be powerful), from the Greek noun *posis* (husband), and from the Sanskrit noun *pati* (master). Indeed, each of these roots is at work in the variety of definitions *Webster's New Collegiate Dictionary* offers for "potent":

> 1) having or wielding force, authority or influence: powerful; 2) achieving or bringing about a particular result: effective; 3) chemically or medicinally effective or rich in a characteristic constituent; and 4) able to copulate—usually used of the male.

It doesn't take too much effort to notice the similarities among the definitions of potent, traditional masculine roles, and the benefits promised in the variety of promotional materials for Viagra. "Impotent" is the logical opposite of potent and according to *Webster's* means "lacking in power, strength, and vigor." Susan Bordo notes, "The word [impotence] rings with disgrace and humiliation. . . . Unlike other disorders, impotence implicates the whole man, not merely the body part."[22] Erectile dysfunction, on the other hand, implicates only a body part—the penis—so it is only the penis that science endeavors to repair and only that body part that men locate as the root of their erection difficulties. The patient summary of information about Viagra describes "how sex affects the body":

> When a man is sexually excited, the penis fills with more blood than usual. The penis then expands and hardens. This is called an erection. After the man is done having sex, this extra blood flows out of the penis *back into the body*. The erection goes away [my emphasis].

This description doesn't really describe what happens during sex. Instead, it describes what happens to the penis upon arousal and after ejaculation.[23] But what is of particular interest to me is the way in which the penis is described as something *other than* part of the body. What is also worth noting is the way "sex" stands in for orgasm and the way sex is male-ordered: automatic, routinized, and predictable. In other words, when working properly, the penis works the same way, every time, for every body. Absent from the description, however, is any mention of *desire*. Indeed, Katzenstein's Viagra story calls the erection process "a triumphant mixture of nerves, arteries, muscle fibers, blood, hormones, and other chemicals, and a dash of erotic stimuli."[24] Both of these descriptions foreground a biomedical perspective— "after the man is done having sex"—and are dismissive of how much desire impacts the process.

Along with the WHO's support for new scientific research in the area of sexual health, it seems likely that the name change—to erectile dysfunction— dramatically changes perceptions for both medical professionals and patients alike. With erectile dysfunction and its organic etiology upheld by "hard science," the pharmacology industry saw fit to pursue legitimate research and development. And here is where Pfizer had a head start.

While developing an angina medication in 1992, Pfizer researchers noticed three things: (1) the active ingredient—sildenafil citrate—didn't really work very well to combat angina; (2) patients "reported an increased tendency to get erections" as the result of the medication;[25] and (3) patients didn't want to return their unused samples.[26]

Whether we're talking about impotence or erectile dysfunction, Pfizer's promotional materials establish "facts" and debunk "myths" concerning definitions, prevalence, and causes. Just as "ED" replaced "impotence" as the signifier of choice, so did a new story emerge regarding its etiology—one that exploited spurious divisions between mind and body and between psychology and physiology.

Etiology

With a photograph of the ancient architectural structure known as Stonehenge supplying the backdrop, Pfizer's Spring 2001 issue of its Viagra magazine, then known as *Voices*,[27] includes an article titled "Myths and Facts." One of the myths reads as follows: "Erectile dysfunction, also known as erectile difficulty, is a problem that is in your head." The following fact clarifies this fiction when it states:

> Studies have shown that most ED is caused by health problems. These problems can be high blood pressure, high cholesterol, and diabetes. ED can also be linked to smoking, drinking too much, or stress. Viagra can help with ED caused by these problems.[28]

And in a pamphlet titled "Prime Time," a section addressing "the real causes of ED" suggests that "It was once mistakenly believed that ED was largely 'all in your mind.' . . . We now know that the majority of ED cases are associated with common physical conditions."[29] Some of the physical conditions listed in this pamphlet that are distinguished from those "all in your mind" include: "psychological conditions, such as anxiety and stress," "medical conditions such as depression," and "lifestyle factors, such as cigarette smoking, excessive alcohol consumption, and/or illicit drug use." Another brochure intones, "ED—it's not in your head. Erectile difficulty says as little about your masculinity as high cholesterol or diabetes does. It's a common medical condition that can affect men of all ages to some degree."[30] And in one of Pfizer's promotional videos, titled "What Every Man (and Woman) Should Know about Erectile Dysfunction," a pair of good-natured narrators tell the viewer:

> One of the most common misconceptions is that erectile problems start with psychological problems. In some men, psychological issues can be a factor. But we now know that the majority of ED cases are associated with a physical—not a psychological—situation. . . . One reason erectile dysfunction is common is because it's often associated with other common conditions that can affect the blood vessels, such as heart disease, diabetes, high cholesterol, high blood pressure. Depression is *another medical condition* that can be a factor [my emphasis].

By suggesting that the majority of ED cases are not caused by psychological "situations" and then including depression as a medical condition, I find myself wanting to know just what—according to Pfizer—a psychological situation might involve. On the one hand, categorizing depression as a medical condition does give credit to the efforts made by both patients and physicians to better educate the public about both the prevalence and gravity of depression.[31] On the other hand, Pfizer both reinscribes a mind/body dichotomy and creates a hierarchy among psychological causes, with depression, anxiety, and stress at the top of the hierarchy and cryptic and unsung causes at the bottom. Nevertheless, by focusing on the body as the chief culprit in the etiology of erectile dysfunction, Pfizer endeavors to alleviate from the potential Viagra user any possibility of personal responsibility. This is not to say, however, that Pfizer is beyond suggesting other agentic factors.

"Start Something All Over Again" is a brochure expressly written for partners of impotent men.[32] The use of the term "partner," however, ultimately does little to include a range of sexual practitioners. Rather, the use of "partner" is most likely intended to bridge divides in how heterosexual males might refer to girlfriends, lovers, wives, or spouses. The twenty-three photographs in this brochure attest to only five different couples—racially diverse, yes, but all heterosexual. What is most curious about this brochure is the extent to which Pfizer attempts to pacify the concerns of the partner that his erectile dysfunction has anything to do with her. But while men are assured emphatically over and over again in these promotional materials that the problem is physically based (and therefore not a character flaw) the same emphasis is not granted his partner: "Even though ED is a physiologic condition that *may have nothing to do with you as a partner*, it can still have an unfavorable affect on your relationship" (my emphasis).[33]

Rhetorical qualifiers modify and limit claims. By introducing claims with qualifiers, the brochure signals to the partner that there are exceptions to the claim. And Pfizer provides the partner with several opportunities to help her consider herself exempt. If she wonders what it is that may (or may not) have to do with her, she may (or may not) want to consider her physical appeal: "If your partner's inability to respond *to you* sexually has become a recurring problem, he may be suffering from ED, a treatable medical condition" (my emphasis).[34] In this example, it is not *his* inability to get it up, but his inability to respond *to her* that reveals the possibility of a psychological cause. Never questioned in any of Pfizer's promotional materials analyzed in this chapter is *his* interest in sex or even *her ability to respond* to him. Attractiveness, readiness, and desire are always her concerns. Physical etiologies absolve him from thinking about his ED in terms of a relationship but her part in the relationship is always at issue: "You *might* have started to believe that *your partner no longer finds you* attractive" (my emphasis).[35]

Whether or not—via these qualifiers and exceptions—the consumer of this brochure considers herself partly (or wholly) responsible as the source of his ED, she will be called upon to help solve it. For example, "His ED *may not be a reflection of you*—but you can help him do something about it" (my emphasis).[36] It is her responsibility—as caregiver—to procure the doctor's visit:

> You should know from the start that ED *probably has nothing to do with you*. But getting treatment does. Because without the encouragement, support, openness,

interest, and love of a partner, many men will simply not seek treatment [my emphasis].[37]

Here is where Pfizer strategically reclaims psychology. If she doesn't share his concern and help him get to the doctor, then his self-esteem will suffer and she *will* be to blame. In a bizarre switch from the singular "your partner" to the plural "they," the female caregiver is implicated in the wholesale resurrection of American masculinity when the brochure implores,

> They need someone to tell them that ED is a medical condition, not a lack of manliness. They need to hear that you still love them and that their sexual ability is as important to you as it is to them. They need to feel that you want to help find a solution, together. And they need to know that there's hope.[38]

As this passage calls attention to her interest in his (or peculiarly, *their*) ability, her desire (or lack of) as well as her expectations are also implicated. Pfizer is there to educate her regarding these expectations:

> [You may have started to believe] that losing interest in sex is a normal part of life. You might have also assumed that ED is a natural part of aging, an inevitable by-product of time. However, millions of Americans are enjoying sex into their sixties and beyond.[39]

As this last quotation exemplifies, another myth that Pfizer debunks is that ED is a natural consequence of aging. In Pfizer's promotional video "The New Facts of Life," one of the narrators avows,

> It's true that ED is more common in older men. But that's because they are more likely to have one or more . . . risk factors. Older men should expect some changes in how their bodies function sexually. But ED should not be expected as an inevitable part of aging. Sexuality does not have an expiration date.[40]

In another video, a sixty-three-year-old man declares, "You can accept baldness, gray hair, glasses, an aching back, [and] hearing aids. But I definitely don't accept the fact that [my] love life has gone away with the grays."[41] It is interesting to note that Pfizer's focus on debunking this myth has lessened in more recent materials. This is especially interesting because many of these more recent promotional materials display much younger men as candidates for ED than the earlier pieces did.

Promotional brochures from 1998 and 1999 feature gray-haired or balding men with similarly mature female partners. Brochures from 2000 through 2002 display much younger couples. Indeed, many of these younger couples do double duty for Pfizer as they appear in promotional videos as well as print materials. It is in these videos that they reveal their ages. One man is thirty-six years old.[42] While it is, perhaps, dangerous for me to speculate about how old someone looks or acts, one need only look at the television commercials for proof of Viagra's shifting target market in Pfizer's choice of celebrity spokesmen: seventy-seven-year-old retired U.S. Senator Bob Dole in 1999; thirty-nine-year-old active professional baseball star Rafael Palmeiro in 2002.

Pfizer's marketing choices notwithstanding, Barbara Marshall and Stephen Katz suggest that Pfizer's rhetoric of "age as risk factor" (rather than as cause) results in a sweeping estrangement: "Age, then, is a 'risk factor' among many. While there is an acknowledged link between age and the prevalence of erectile dysfunction, a simple causal link is now severed."[43] When Pfizer debunks the "myths" about ED, the company hopes to both increase the potential customer base for Viagra and endeavor to alleviate the stigma of ED by tapping into the public's general anxieties over perceptions of normalcy and, specifically, the anxiety of aging and mortality. Debunking myths as lies and advancing facts as truth is a common rhetorical move both in advertising and public speaking. It is also a move that—while economical and effective—is also polarizing and far too simplistic to be useful to consumers. Pfizer's claims about the pervasiveness of erectile dysfunction give emphasis to capricious divisions of organic versus psychological causes; the dubious categories, questionnaires, and statistics accentuated and created only further manipulate this division.

ED Is Everywhere

With animated graphics, PowerPoint-type banners and titles, and—most importantly—spokesmen and testimonials, Pfizer spares no expense in the production of its promotional videos. Featured in these videos are unnamed narrators, men ranging in age from the late forties to late fifties, who conduct themselves as good "pill" ambassadors. They negotiate between the viewer's concerns and the "real" men (and their partners) whose personal testimony attests to the importance of Viagra in men's lives and relationships. The "real" in these promotional videos help buttress the claim that ED is everywhere. And cleverly presented statistics reinforce the points that "every man" needs to know.

Stamped against a computer-generated wall of marble, the graphic reads "MYTH: Erectile Dysfunction is rare." Meanwhile, one of three hosts in the video "What Every Man (and Woman) Needs to Know about Erectile Dysfunction" advises the viewer that

> The National Institute of Health estimates that as many as 30 million American men have *some degree* of erection problems. So if you have ED, you're not alone. Chances are you know someone—your boss, your uncle, your next door neighbor—who's dealing with the same problem [my emphasis].[44]

The first myth that Pfizer endeavors to uproot is the infrequency of erectile dysfunction. A brochure titled "Start Something All Over Again" urges, "You and your partner should take comfort in the fact that when it comes to ED, you're certainly not alone."[45] In *Viagra: The Remarkable Story of the Discovery and Launch,* Larry Katzenstein declares that erectile dysfunction is "a problem that to *some degree* affects more than half of all men aged 40 to 70" (my emphasis).[46] A brochure titled "Take the Pfizer Health Challenge" includes this claim: "An estimated 30 million men in the United States—about 1 in 3—suffer from *some form* of ED" (my emphasis).[47] What Pfizer means when it defines ED in *forms* and *degrees* is articulated in the following exchange of myths and facts that appeared in an early issue of the Viagra magazine:

> MYTH: I don't have erectile dysfunction because the problem doesn't happen often. This means Viagra is not for me.

> FACT: Even if it happens once in while, it is still ED. Most men with ED have it just some of the time. Viagra is the #1 prescribed medicine for ED that happens once in a while.[48]

An interview with New York City urologist Jed Kaminetsky appearing in another issue of the Viagra magazine and titled "Good Medicine" shows exactly how the criteria for the condition of erectile dysfunction has been expanded and how Viagra has become the number-one prescribed medicine for ED when he remarks,

> People think they have to have severe ED to take Viagra. But that's not true. It works well for men who can get erections, but the erections aren't as rigid as they once were. Or they don't last as long as they used to. Or there may be a longer interval between erections. Now, I prescribe Viagra to men of all ages. But I think just about every sexually active man over 50 with ED could benefit from Viagra.[49]

With these kinds of parameters it is no wonder that the estimates for ED are so high in the United States, and it is no surprise that Dr. Kaminetsky can boast, "It's gotten to the point where I have the biggest ED practice in New York City. I've prescribed Viagra for ED to over 2,500 men."[50] It is obvious that Dr. Kaminetsky is satisfied with Viagra. The statistics and numbers that measure satisfaction among his patients and their partners, however, are absent.

Viagra's reputation in the medical community, it seems, is based at least as much on its commercial success as on its ability to treat ED. This commercial success is due in larger part to expanding the uses of Viagra to include more and more prospective "patients." Perhaps most alarming along these lines is a recent report in the *British Medical Journal* that suggests that taking

Viagra *daily* could *prevent* erectile dysfunction.[51] This position is endorsed by none other than Dr. Irwin ("It's all hydraulics!") Goldstein of Boston University Medical Center. The rhetorical appeal of "ED for everyone" rests not only in the numbers and estimates but also in how ED has been characterized.

The 1993 NIH study that Pfizer cites in its materials is explicit in its declaration that "estimates of prevalence (the number of men with the condition) will vary depending on the definition of erectile dysfunction used."[52] Furthermore, the NIH study contends that "anecdotal evidence points to the existence of racial, ethnic, and other cultural diversity in the perceptions and expectation levels for satisfactory sexual functioning."[53] For the record, the NIH study states

> Data on erectile dysfunction available from the 1940s applied to the current US male population produce an estimate of erectile dysfunction prevalence of 7 million. More recent estimates suggest that the number of US men with erectile dysfunction may more likely be near 10 to 20 million. Inclusion of individuals with partial erectile dysfunction increases the estimate to about 30 million.[54]

It is worth noting here that "[d]ata on erectile dysfunction available from the 1940s" represents an example of Ian Hacking's *semantic contagion*. Semantic contagion occurs when we retrospectively apply contemporary conceptual terms and endow past events with a connotation those phenomena did not have at the time. Statistics attesting to the prevalence of erectile dysfunction in the 1940s sidestep the fact that the condition now known as erectile dysfunction existed then only under the psychologically loaded label of "impotence." Admittedly, a social scientist might argue that the 1940s estimates are, indeed, low given this psychological component. What I argue here, however, is that this kind of semantic contagion is representative of the lack of reflexivity in the scientific construction of health conditions generally and male sexuality specifically.

The indiscriminant use of the term "erectile dysfunction" implies that the condition has always been conceived as predominantly a physical disorder rather than the psychological disorder it was thought to be through the 1970s. Furthermore, the oft-repeated figure of thirty million erectile dysfunction sufferers is extrapolated from the Massachusetts Male Aging Study conducted from 1987 to 1989. Amazingly, erectile dysfunction's supposed frequency is derived from the results of a study of 1,300 Boston area men between forty and seventy years old. This study was admittedly limited in racial sampling but "consistent with the composition of the Massachusetts population."[55] Given this data, it seems plausible that erectile dysfunction may have as much to do with rooting for the Red Sox—and having to wait eighty-six years for a World Series title!—as with any physical condition. By citing these two studies, Pfizer utilizes apparently objective, verifiable, and external studies to support its claims for the seriousness and prevalence of erectile dysfunction. But the company also constructs its own versions of objectivity in its promotional materials.

Propping Up Erectile Dysfunction with a SHIM

In architectural parlance, a "shim" is a thin piece of material used to fill in or prop up an otherwise stable structure. When Pfizer claims that there are thirty million ED sufferers in America, there is little doubt in my mind that a five-question health inventory found in nearly every one of its Viagra brochures helps validate these estimates: the SHIM (Sexual Health Inventory for Men). The SHIM contains five questions that concern the respondent's impotence or erectile function over the previous six months:

1. How do you rate your *confidence* that you could get and keep an erection?
   [1] Very low
   [2] Low
   [3] Moderate
   [4] High
   [5] Very high
2. When you had erections with sexual stimulation, *how often* were your erections hard enough for penetration (entering your partner)?
   [0] No sexual activity
   [1] Almost never or never
   [2] A few times (much less than half the time)
   [3] Sometimes (about half the time)
   [4] Most times (much more than half the time)
   [5] Almost always or always
3. During sexual intercourse, *how often* were you able to maintain your erection after you had penetrated (entered) your partner?
   [0] Did not attempt intercourse
   [1] Almost never or never
   [2] A few times (much less than half the time)
   [3] Sometimes (about half the time)
   [4] Most times (much more than half the time)
   [5] Almost always or always
4. During sexual intercourse, *how difficult* was it to maintain your erection to completion of intercourse?
   [0] Did not attempt intercourse
   [1] Extremely difficult
   [2] Very difficult
   [3] Difficult

[4] Slightly difficult

[5] Not difficult

5. When you attempted sexual intercourse, *how often* was it satisfactory for you?

[0] Did not attempt intercourse

[1] Almost never or never

[2] A few times (much less than half the time)

[3] Sometimes (about half the time)

[4] Most times (much more than half the time)

[5] Almost always or always

The respondent is asked to "pick just one answer for each question" and then add up the numbers. Although the maximum score is 25 points, a score of 21 or less (i.e., 84 percent of maximum or less) signifies a visit to the doctor. What makes this noteworthy is the way in which Pfizer constructs these questions, oversimplifying the dynamics of sexual pleasure.

Laura Mamo and Jennifer Fishman point out how Viagra's efficacy hinges on the sexual script of vaginal penetration with the penis, reflecting and reinforcing "dominant cultural narratives about appropriate and legitimate male sexuality" and denying other forms of sexual expression, thereby enforcing compulsory heterosexuality.[56] For Mamo and Fishman, an alternate reading of question 3 would ask, "Hard enough to enter my partner where?"[57] To this alternate reading I add more. Of question 2, I can ask, "What about my morning erections that occur without sexual stimulation—what do I do with those?" To question 4, I can respond, "It wasn't difficult at all, I completed intercourse in 40 seconds." Of question 5, I can wonder, "How satisfactory was intercourse for her (or him)?"

The answers provided are as revealing as the questions. Besides its obvious heterosexist design, this sexual health inventory is also at fault for its disregard of relational dynamics, its emphasis on quantity, and its ignorance of other psychosocial dynamics at play. A question asking for a one-sided account of satisfaction ignores the relational complexities of the couple involved. A question that assumes penetration ignores the possibility of Viagra as an enhancement for masturbation and/or oral sex. "How often" (rather than "how enjoyable") forefronts the emphasis on quantity rather than quality. And all the questions ignore the ways in which alcohol and drugs (both legal and illegal, prescription, and over-the-counter) not only wreak havoc with the vascular system but also affect psychic factors. Both alcohol and drugs may interfere with *and* enhance sexual enjoyment.

Pfizer uses a definition of erectile dysfunction attributed to the 1993 NIH Consensus Development Panel: "the inability to attain and/or maintain penile erection sufficient for satisfactory sexual performance."[58] And yet even this definition—carefully worded to avoid the implications of "impotence"—

is loaded with ambiguities: "sufficient," "satisfactory," "sexual," and "performance" are all terms open to multiple interpretations. In the pharmaceutical industry—where quantitative data rules—it is peculiar that the numbers used to establish the market for impotence rely on a self-evaluation of subjective interpretation.

Two other inventory scales for erectile function preceded the SHIM. The Massachusetts Male Aging Study utilized a sexual activity questionnaire that includes nine items "related to potency."[59] Most importantly, this questionnaire includes a question about partner satisfaction: "How satisfied do you think your partner(s) is (are) with your sexual relationship?"[60] Two aspects of this question are worthy of elaboration. First, I sincerely doubt any questionnaire that explores women's sexual health would ever assert the possibility of concurrent multiple partners. Second, the results of this particular question reveal that in each of the self-rated categories—not impotent, minimally impotent, moderately impotent, and completely impotent—"partner satisfaction" was reported *higher* than the respondent's "satisfaction with partner." In other words, men almost always report that their partner is more satisfied with sex than they themselves are, independent of the degree of impotence.

The SHIM is directly adapted from the 1997 Pfizer-funded International Index of Erectile Function (IIEF)—a fifteen-item questionnaire that asks its respondents to reply based on "the past four weeks" rather than the last six months as the SHIM does.[61] While demonstrating the same propensity for penetration as the SHIM, this version does ask questions about desire such as "How often have you felt sexual desire?" and "How would you rate your level of sexual desire?"[62] What the SHIM test does is reduce the dynamics of sexual response to its simplest correlates and lengthens the response frame, thereby expanding the market for Viagra. In this way, Pfizer exploits what Gail Sheehy calls the "pervasive fear of sexual decline."[63] When Pfizer speaks in terms of erectile dysfunction in *some form* or *some degree* it creates steps and stairs. These steps and stairs lead the climber to a single outcome that concludes with something like this: "My erections, like those of most men my age, aren't what they used to be—but they *could* be with Viagra."

Just how serious is erectile dysfunction? According to Pfizer it is very serious. Pfizer's Katzenstein describes erectile dysfunction as "a devastating problem."[64] The Massachusetts Male Aging Study researchers conclude that "impotence is a major health concern in light of the high prevalence."[65] And a study "supported by a grant from Pfizer" and using Viagra as a "treatment" determines that the International Index of Erectile Function "would be suitable for use by clinicians and researchers."[66] The NIH Consensus Conference Report suggests that erectile dysfunction is "poorly understood by the general population and by most health care professionals."[67] The emergence of self-diagnostic tests, the name change from "impotence" to "erectile dysfunction," and the development of Viagra have, no doubt, increased the understanding of erectile dysfunction's causes and treatments as defined by Pfizer. And yet the term "impotence" appears strategically in many of the promotional materials. "In keeping the term 'impotence,'" Susan Bordo reasons, "drug companies would get to have it both ways: reduce a complex human condition to a matter of chemistry, while keeping the old shame mechanism working, helping to assure the flow of men to their doors."[68] Pfizer manipulates the definition of erectile dysfunction in a way that exploits men's anxieties, generates a rationale for more sponsored research, and creates categories that balloon prevalence. These promotional materials also define what erectile dysfunction *means* to men and their partners.

The previous three sections have examined a variety of Pfizer's promotional materials for the themes related to the definition, etiology, and prevalence of ED. Judith Lorber and Lisa Jean Moore contend that a major concern of *social* epidemiologists is determining how data are collected and analyzed:

> Hefty profit margins and expandable markets determine research and development priorities; thus, Viagra for erectile dysfunction gets produced, as well as antidepressants and allergy medications. In such a system, the essence of illness—its diversified social context—is suppressed.[69]

The social context of masculinity, like the healthcare system, is diverse. This next section draws attention to the ways in which Pfizer's promotional materials both perform diversity and preserve traditional stereotypes of male behavior.

Traditional Masculinity

In this section, I begin by looking at two television commercials. As the principal subjects, the first commercial employs a Latino man and the second an African American man. By including men of color in its advertisements, Pfizer appears sensitive to the challenge of addressing diversity among masculinities. A closer examination, however, reveals established bastions of the male sex role: the sportsman and the stud. The strong silent type—another traditional male role—is examined further along in this section when I look at how doctor–patient interaction is portrayed and imagined by Pfizer.

Sportsman

With a sports-themed chant accompanying the sights and sounds of a major league baseball stadium, we are introduced to a ballplayer involved in the ritual behavior of practice. Rafael Palmeiro, a veteran of seventeen-plus seasons in the major leagues, is one of baseball's most consistent players, an excellent hitter as evidenced by his batting average, runs batted in, and home run statistics. A member of the Baltimore Orioles during the 2004 season, he played for the Texas Rangers when the Viagra commercial featuring him first aired in the spring of 2002. At the start of this commercial, Palmeiro is moving quickly, deftly, and accurately—handling ground balls, making throws, covering his position. In voice-over he tells us, "I take fielding practice." A graphic informs us that he has won several Gold Glove awards—the annual honor bestowed on the premier fielder at each position. Next, Palmeiro appears in the batter's box, stroking practice pitch after practice pitch deep, out over the spacious outfield and beyond the fence. The voice-over returns: "I take batting practice." The graphic that accompanies these images tells us that he has hit over 475 lifetime home runs. All the while we take note of his quiet confidence as the commercial segues seamlessly from batting practice pitches into a pitch for Viagra. Here, Rafael Palmeiro looks directly into the camera and says, "I take Viagra." Thankfully, there are no "practice" field video clips to accompany this piece of news; instead, we are left to our own statistical imagination. Lest we get too invested in the details, Rafael Palmeiro appeases our curiosity when he adds, "Let's just say it works for me." As the commercial transitions to its conclusion, the graphics supply us not with statistics but the required legal subtext. And we watch him emerge from the dugout, bat in hand, presumably to hit yet another home run. The camera pans back and we are treated to the image of a dozen baseball bats, mushroom-capped handles pointing skyward. "Step up to the plate," urges the Texas slugger, "and ask your doctor if Viagra is right for you."

When it comes to marketing products, the male sports hero has no equal.[70] What makes the Palmeiro commercial especially interesting is the way professional baseball is used to sell sexual identity to men who are at an age when they have to admit that their childhood ambition of playing baseball in the majors can now only be fantasy.[71] And yet they still want to hit home runs.[72]

As teenagers, the language of baseball is employed by boys to describe and measure sexual conquest.[73] Kissing is getting to first base. Fondling a girl's breasts is getting to second base. Third base is reached by penetrating a girl's vagina with a finger or receiving oral sex. Sexual intercourse—going all the way—is a home run.[74] Interestingly, for most boys, the end of organized baseball coincides with the beginning of sexual experimentation. So as the promise of a career in sports dwindles, boys in a culture without societal rites of passage seek out other ways of assessing their prospects as adult men. Sexual experience is one way. But let us not depart the significance of organized baseball too quickly. Michael Kimmel suggests that "organized participatory sports were offered as a corrective to a perceived erosion of traditional masculinity in the late 19th century."[75] Additionally, Kimmel points out how spectator sports—particularly baseball—signified the shift in the United States from a culture of production to one of consumption.

The late nineteenth century coincided with significant social changes that, according to Kimmel, resulted in

> a crisis of middle-class white masculinity, a crisis in the dominant paradigm of masculinity that was perceived as threatened by the simultaneous erosion of traditional structural foundations (e.g. economic autonomy and the frontier), new gains for women, and the tremendous infusion of nonwhite immigrants into major industrial cities. It was a crisis of economic control, a struggle against larger units of capital that eroded work-place autonomy and new workers (immigrants and women), who were seen as displacing traditional American men.[76]

When Kimmel lays out these structural changes, I can't help but notice how late-twentieth-century advancements by women and gay men (e.g., financial autonomy and expanding sexual frontiers) have similarly threatened traditional American men. Using baseball as a vehicle, Viagra both reinscribes the phallic power of heterosexual penetrative sex *and* connects traditional American males with each other through the promise of youthful virility, creating what Robert Connell has described as *collective practices.*[77]

Poet Donald Hall writes, "Baseball connects American males with each other, not only through bleacher friendships and neighbor loyalties, not only through barroom fights, but most importantly, through generations."[78] Baseball—among other sports—promotes stick-to-itiveness, dogged perseverance, and tenacity, themes that Pfizer incorporates into other aspects of its advertising as well. According to Varda Burstyn, the use of statistics in sports—including the pursuit of world records and the bestowing of awards based primarily on statistics—signals the "systematic breaching of the natural limits of the human body."[79] Pfizer's use of Palmeiro's lifetime statistical accomplishments is significant. The pursuit of statistical milestones—whether hitting real or symbolic home runs—is indicative of an American ideology of capitalism and expansion. Enhancing the "body"—becoming stronger, bigger, faster, and harder—is encouraged.

LifeDrive magazine regularly features cover stories that celebrate James Doyle's masculine commandments of "Be independent" and "Be aggressive." Music group Earth, Wind, and Fire are "still burning up the stage" on the cover of the spring 2001 issue. On the fall 2001 cover, we see NFL Hall of Famer Ronnie Lott "still making an impact." Tony Gwynn, former major league star and current baseball coach at San Diego State University, graces the cover of the summer 2002 issue along with text that promises an explanation of "why college baseball may be tougher than the pros."[80] Rafael Palmeiro (confidently cradling a baseball bat that seems to extend from his crotch) is the subject of a story that examines "how one man has most of his peers outnumbered."

These cover stories and many other aspects of Pfizer's marketing call attention to the ways in which real men "do something" in the face of life's changes and contingencies. To do nothing is passive and feminine; to do something is active and masculine.[81] In keeping with this tendency to extol traditional masculine virtues, Pfizer recognizes that *doing something* is good enough—it is not necessary to also talk about it. Consequently, many of Pfizer's promotional materials feature the strong, silent type. This type of man doesn't talk about what he does, he just does it. No single character in any of Pfizer's promotional materials does this as thoroughly as "Joe."

Stud

A tall, handsome black man is seen emerging from the office of the "Medical Group." He wears a smile—the wry smile of a man who has learned a valuable secret. "Joe" is a white-collar professional and appears to be in his late thirties to early forties.[82] Dressed in an expensive suit, we see him enter and cross the vast lobby of a high-rise office building and go into an elevator. In the elevator he encounters a coworker who takes notice of Joe and, presumably, Joe's quiet confidence. This coworker—a white man, wearing spectacles, and much shorter than Joe—asks, "Hey Joe, did you get a haircut?"[83] Joe replies simply, "No." Even though there is no request for elaboration and none offered, Joe's coworker appears to be pondering a mystery.[84] Once the elevator arrives on the floor of their workplace and they disembark, Joe encounters more questions—"Did you just get back from vacation?"—not only from the bewildered white man but also from certain female colleagues: "Did you shave your mustache?" "Is that a new suit?" "Are those new shoes?" To all of these questions Joe answers, "No." He does not engage any of his inquisitive colleagues any further. But even sequestered in his office, Joe fields more questions: "Did you get a promotion?" his male sidekick asks. "No," Joe replies. "Did I?" the coworker inquires. "No," responds Joe yet again. Still answering questions, Joe leaves the office and walks confidently through the parking lot, presumably on his way to his car. His cellular telephone rings, whereupon, after a laugh, Joe remarks to the mystery caller, "Yes."

Joe is the boss. We know this because he is not beholden to any of his colleagues, he occupies a large office, and he comes and goes as he pleases. Several dynamics add complexity to this scene. One is the fact that while Joe has questions asked of him by two women of color, he is not addressed by any white women. Furthermore, the women ask Joe questions about his appearance while the white man mostly asks questions about status.

The lack of interaction between Joe and any white women is conspicuous in its absence. In their article "Potency in All the Right Places: Viagra as a Technology of the Gendered Body," Laura Mamo and Jennifer Fishman observe that Viagra print advertisements depict either white couples *or* black couples and, in so doing, maintain the black/white binary even as Pfizer strives toward racial diversity.[85] Following Mamo and Fishman, I also utilize the words of Anne Balsamo who suggests that "when seemingly stable boundaries are displaced by technological innovation . . . other boundaries are more vigilantly guarded."[86] Although "Joe" must satisfy the diversity goals of Pfizer's marketing division (called Team Viagra), his race is carefully considered in terms of how and with whom this studliness is performed. Lynne Segal reminds us how "Black is the color of the dirty secrets of sex—relentlessly represented in the image of Black 'boy' as stud, and Black woman as whore."[87] So in order for the (white) audience (and target market) for this commercial to accept Joe as spokesman, Joe is silent. His performance as stud is presented by way of his quiet confidence and coolness, which are cryptic and concealed.

Pfizer once again gets to have it both ways: Joe exemplifies black male potency, power, and (implied) size while also being quiet, confident, and cool. Here is where Pfizer plays both with and against the image of the powerfully sexual black man. Robert Staples suggests that black men must always "confront the contradiction between the normative expectations attached to being male in this society and the proscriptions on his behavior and achievement of goals."[88] In its efforts to construct the potent male, Pfizer creates in Joe its own balance in this contradiction. In this appropriation, Pfizer reveals its expectations: black men can be sexual and successful as long as they are modeling hypersexuality for white men and only if this sexuality and success is not practiced with white women.[89] Pfizer provides Joe with a penis, but not a phallus. Kaja Silverman claims that an individual penis can never achieve the status of the phallus as privileged signifier within the symbolic order. And while the penis provides a partial phallus, the racial "other" lacks the phallus completely.[90] In American society, the black man is denied the phallus. He can be, instead, only a model of hypersexuality.

In the "Joe" commercial—as in many of the Viagra marketing and promotional materials that debuted in 2002—the protagonist's partner is not only unnamed, she/he is irrelevant. Indeed, by virtue of his position in the workplace and the flagrant freedom it affords, Joe represents the masculine passage Gail Sheehy calls "the flourishing 40s."[91] By the time the "Joe" commercial aired in the spring of 2002, *everybody* knew what Viagra is and does; all that had to be demonstrated were its ancillary affects: on confidence, on masculinity, and on power. What Viagra does (or *is*, for that matter) is not mentioned. The assumption is that the audience knows what Viagra is. This commercial demonstrates the effects of Viagra—a taller, studlier, more confident man. All this as the result of simply "asking your physician for a sample to see if Viagra is right for you."

While Viagra has now been peddled by sports stars such as Palmeiro and Mark Martin, it is, for me, the "Joe" commercial that most clearly signals the shift in Pfizer's marketing interests. By expanding Viagra's targeted customer base from men over fifty to men in their early forties (and younger), Pfizer appears intent on selling a particular sexual persona—that of a "stud"—as much as a treatment for ED.

Newspaper stories claimed that Viagra catalyzed talk about sex. But what I've observed is that people aren't talking about their own sexual behavior—only other people's. Pfizer estimates that erectile dysfunction affects thirty million American men. The company also claims that most of this ED goes unreported. Even as Rafael Palmeiro asks men to "step up to the plate" and Joe demonstrates what happens when you do "ask your doctor," Pfizer seems overly sensitive to the possibility that men don't or won't ask. Several aspects of its marketing perpetuate the traditional stereotype that men "don't ask for directions."

The Strong Silent Type

The masculine directive "don't ask for directions" has moved from an observation made by sociolinguists to a routinized plot gimmick in situation comedies and popular culture. It is also an inexhaustible trope in Pfizer's promotional materials. A Viagra advertisement in *JAMA* features a sample six-pack of pills resting on top of a road map of Missouri (the "show-me" state). The ad copy reads, "Finally, directions your patients are willing to ask for." Another *JAMA* ad depicts a couple at a scenic overlook, awkwardly embracing as they lean against a motorcycle. In the background are rolling hills and rocky outcrops, reminiscent of a cowboy movie. The copy reads, "Your patients are looking for your help. Ask your patients if they'd like to talk about Viagra." Another brochure describes it this way: "It is not uncommon for men to feel embarrassed by ED. They may avoid talking about the condition."[92]

Another brochure, showing Rafael Palmeiro in a classic batter's stance, includes a number of "coaching tips" styled after the kind of advice sometimes found on the backs of baseball cards:

> Coaching Tip: Relax. There's nothing to worry about. Millions of men have already asked about Viagra.
> Coaching Tip: Keep your eye on the doctor. Good eye contact is the key to any conversation.
> Coaching Tip: Don't slouch. Asking for Viagra is a sign of courage. So keep your chin up and feel confident.[93]

Included in every issue of *LifeDrive* magazine are detachable cards, intended to be handed over to a physician in lieu of vocal exchange. On one side the card reads "Straight Talk," furthering the implication that Viagra is intended only for legitimate heterosexual sex.[94] The other side of the card offers different types of messages customized for the individual concerns and medical provisions of the potential patient. The directions read as follows:

> We know how difficult it can be to talk to your doctor about ED and Viagra. It's normal to feel a bit uncomfortable at first. To make it easier for you, we have attached pullout cards that you can hand to your doctor to get the conversation started.[95]

Another double-page advertisement in *LifeDrive* depicts a couple in their late thirties smiling out at the reader. They are obviously satisfied, their smiles signaling that they have already "stepped up to the plate," that they were "up to the challenge." As determined by the advertising copy, however, she does the talking:

> I'm proud of him because he asked about Viagra. I love him because he did it for us. When my husband first started experiencing erection difficulties, such as erectile dysfunction (ED), he didn't want to admit there was anything wrong. But when it started to put a real strain on our relationship, he talked to his doctor about Viagra.[96]

The reluctance of men to talk about problems, visit their physicians, and ask for directions is a well-studied phenomenon in a number of academic fields. This research fuels the stereotype that men avoid any communication that reveals personal weakness or vulnerability. The extent to which Pfizer capitalizes on this phenomenon, however, is overdone. By providing the cue cards that facilitate doctor–patient conversations about ED, Pfizer perpetuates the attitude that having ED is shameful. Viagra, claims Pfizer, "has prompted some 10 million men in the United States and around the world to seek treatment and get results for a problem that many have lived with in silence and shame." Pfizer, like most pharmaceutical companies, is not interested in explaining the interpersonal dynamics that result when men feel compromised in the doctor–patient communicative exchange any more than they are interested in investigating the multiple factors that contribute to hypertension, depression, and alcoholism among their prospective client/customers.

Everyman

Another way Pfizer stereotypes traditional performances of masculinity is through a number of subtle signs. Samples of Viagra come in a six-pack—a two-week supply or a packaging strategy men will recognize? More recently, Viagra offers a promotion of "buy six prescriptions, get the seventh free."[97] On the back cover of one issue of *LifeDrive*, for example, we see the diamond-shaped pill simulating a football being kicked toward the goalposts, presumably to win the game.[98] On the back cover of another *LifeDrive* edition, Pfizer's little blue pill is a button on a black tuxedo; the accompanying copy reads, "Blue never goes out of style."[99] Obviously, the blue that was chosen as Viagra's color is, for masculinity, symbolism par excellence.

Judith Williamson writes that advertising in its myriad forms "creates a structure of meaning."[100] Advertising does this by inviting the consumer "to make a transaction" between a product and already-established systems of meaning.[101] Pfizer does this by connecting Viagra to a variety of male signifiers. Most (if not all) of these signifiers are drawn from very traditional symbols for maleness. Dominant are images of upright structures accompanied in some way by the powder blue color of Viagra. Bottles, tools, buildings, flag poles, masts, columns, picket fences, and baseball bats always and everywhere accompanied by the color blue, represented in and through images of water, sculpture, professional sports uniforms and helmets, and, most ubiquitously, through graphics and representations of the diamond-shaped pill itself.[102] The message here is that the objects have the same qualities as what Viagra will provide. More than connecting the color blue with masculinity, the blue in these advertisements connects masculinity to hardness, vitality, and endurance.

The promotional materials also re-create traditional expectations for women. An article in the spring 2001 issue of *LifeDrive* explains how to go "from couch potato to Casanova in just 5 easy steps."[103] Step 3 suggests giving the "gift of time." Accompanied by a photograph of a pair of soapy rubber gloves washing a Viagra-blue plate, the copy reads: "This is a gift she will truly love. Do some of *her* chores" (my emphasis). Step 5 involves creating "the perfect night," and the article suggests visiting a local hotel for the weekend because "two days without chores can be like a vacation."

This section has described the ways in which Pfizer's promotional materials utilize stereotypical images of masculinity to sell Viagra. Participation in sports, studliness, and silence closely match James Doyle's themes of American masculinity, especially "Be aggressive," "Be sexual," and "Don't be feminine." The Viagra man can demonstrate his worthiness of and his right to Viagra by exemplifying these masculine virtues. Equally important is the tendency to construct performances of masculinity and sexuality in standardized and traditional ways. The next section of this chapter analyzes Pfizer's use of the term "intimacy," another example of how standardized treatments rely on standardized (and traditional) definitions.

Intimacy

"Intimacy" has its etymological foundation in the Latin *intimus,* meaning innermost. Indeed, the "oceanic feeling of oneness" that M. Scott Peck describes as physical intimacy in *The Road Less Traveled* has its origin in the womb. Pfizer's promotional materials take this "innermost" root far too literally. "Intimacy" is Pfizer's shorthand for penile-vaginal intercourse. What is more, Pfizer's use of the word "intimacy" in these promotional materials carries with it an expectation of some kind of masculine exertion, operationalized by the use of "performance" metaphors and giving an added dimension to the phrase "working stiff."

In a spring 2001 issue of *LifeDrive*, "John" demonstrates how "intimacy" is something that has a performance quality that is assessable (in the same way an automobile or employee is assessable) when he observes,

> Well, ED makes you feel less masculine because you're *unable to perform* . . . I was hopeful and excited when I heard about Viagra coming out. I thought it was a real opportunity to *bring intimacy back* into our relationship (my emphasis).[104]

In a brochure titled "Prime Time," the testimony of "SG" (a retired mechanic) establishes the correlative between sex, work, and performance when he confides, "when you are not performing . . . you wonder if you are doing your job."[105] In the promotional video "What Every Man (and Woman) Should Know about Erectile Dysfunction," a man recounts how ED affected his marriage:

> It was not a happy scene—it became quite dysfunctional between us. It was a real struggle. Every time we approached *an intimate moment* it was a very major thought in my mind and concern that this, it, I, was not going to *function* normally (my emphasis).[106]

The way intimacy is described as performance based is also endorsed by medical authorities in Pfizer's promotional materials. An interview with psychiatrist Sandra Leiblum in the fall 2001 issue of *LifeDrive* reveals a functional definition of performance when she advises that

> [c]ouples need to be prepared that this is not a magic pill that the man swallows and suddenly they're having the best sex of their lives. It's going to be nice *to be physically intimate again*, but it may not be *a 5 star event*. . . . Couples need to be prepared to *fine-tune* their sex life once they reinitiate sexual intimacy (my emphasis).[107]

Similarly, partners employ Pfizer's use of "intimacy" as a rhetorical substitute for penetrative penile-vaginal intercourse. In the following example, "Diane" describes the emotional consequences of her husband's ED as she experiences it:

> But on the nights *we tried to get intimate and failed*, I felt frustrated. And afterward, he would face one way, I'd face the other, and I would cry, tears soaking

my pillow, wondering, what do I do now? And at 6 months into the marriage, pretty much *all intimacy had come to a dead stop* (my emphasis).[108]

Pfizer's use of "intimacy" as a replacement term for "penile-vaginal penetration"—which is itself a replacement for the more colloquial "fucking"—is an example of Kenneth Burke's logologic distinction between "dramatism" and "scientism."[109] "Intimacy" here becomes a god-term. Sanctioned by their privileged place in American society as heterosexual married couples, those offering testimony in the examples above demonstrate their rightful claim to something hierarchically superior to "fucking," and more action-oriented than the scientific and object-oriented "penile-vaginal penetration" emphasized by the SHIM test.

Interpersonal communication scholars Ronald Adler, Lawrence Rosenfield, and Neil Towne suggest, however, that "intimacy" has several dimensions, including intellectual, emotional, and shared activities. The *physical* intimacy Pfizer describes is just one of the forms of intimacy a relationship can exhibit. Furthermore, according to Adler et al.,

> Some physical intimacy is sexual, but this category can also include affectionate hugs, kisses, and even struggles. Companions who have endured physical challenges together . . . form a bond that can last a lifetime.[110]

Intimacy, then, is something much more multifaceted than sex. Interestingly, "intimacy" as a euphemism for sexual intercourse dates from 1676, when it specifically referred to "illicit sexual intercourse."[111]

Amazingly, Pfizer's early clinical trials using sildenafil citrate as a treatment for ED did not utilize these stories of "failed intimacy" to help assess the seriousness of the complaint. Nor were couples employed to test the efficacy of Viagra. Instead, men were hooked up to a piece of laboratory equipment called the RigiScan—a monitor developed to measure "penile rigidity"—and asked to "view erotic material for 2 hours."[112] In Larry Katzenstein's Viagra bible, Dr. Mitra Boolell of Pfizer's British facility, located in Sandwich, describes these early clinical trials this way:

> Since sildenafil citrate works only when there is sexual stimulation, we needed a standardized technique for providing more or less the same degree of stimulation—and that basically meant getting patients to watch blue movies. In the UK, the laws that govern sexually explicit materials are very strict, and it was difficult for us to get permission to import this material from Europe. . . . Then we had to find a relaxed setting, the optimal environment for patients to respond. We couldn't run that kind of study in the average hospital environment. So we negotiated to use a private hospital room and run the study in the evenings and on weekends to ensure privacy for the patients.[113]

I find it fascinating that the "optimal environment for patients to respond" was not with their regular partner in the privacy of their bedrooms, but in—

what I imagine to be—a stark clinical setting, wired to a medically endorsed cock ring, and treated to the British equivalent of *Debbie Does Dallas*.[114]

Journalist Jon Cohen points out, however, that the "twelve RigiScan-outfitted men" watching "porn movies" played only a small part in the FDA's approval of Viagra.[115] The significant data came from the study involving the fifteen-question International Index of Erectile Function mentioned earlier in this chapter.[116] But according to *New England Journal of Medicine* editor Robert Utiger, quoted in Cohen's *New Yorker* article, this study was the first erectile dysfunction study ever published "that contained no laboratory or clinic component."[117]

Also quoted in Cohen's article is University of Virginia chief of urology William Steers, who suggests that the most reliable ED questionnaire-based studies are the ones in which *spouses* rate the success of the treatment. Cohen explains:

> When you ask women about sex with their Viagra-enhanced husbands, [Steers] said, their response "is always lower than the men's." Depending on how strictly questionnaires defined "successful intercourse," men in ten different studies reported rates of success ranging from forty-eight to seventy-three percent. In a study Steers conducted with wives, though, the definition of success had little impact on the responses, which consistently hovered around forty-eight percent. [118]

The question of "successful intercourse," as Pfizer defines it, is worthy of further consideration. According to Pfizer's promotional video "The *New* Facts of Life," three out of four men "reported improved erections." But of this 75 percent, only two out of three "reported successful intercourse."[119] Remarkably, only 50 percent of those who use Viagra are able to achieve the kind of intimacy Pfizer has narrowly defined on its SHIM test. Based on the sales figures then, it seems that attaining a "better" erection (whether adequate for penetration or not) is the primary goal, not only for Pfizer, but for many American men as well.

It is here that I'd like to return to an alternative definition of intimacy, namely, what Adler, Rosenfield, and Towne refer to as *emotional* intimacy: the exchange of important feelings.[120] To *intimate*, after all, also means to make known, to suggest, or to imply.

Pfizer's singular usage of intimacy as a substitute for sexual intercourse is a glaring example of how science defines reality. Throughout this section, I have demonstrated how, through its promotional materials, Pfizer encourages couples who may or may not have "suffered" sexual limitations to improve their lot through the undertaking of a single act—the ingestion of a pill. The transcendent force that will enable the audience to overcome the limitations of their relationships is simply to take Viagra. This eliminates the possibility for expanded definitions of intimacy and, instead, puts inappropriate power in the hands of a profit-driven company whose decisions can markedly influence how both bodies and relationships perform.

Pfizer's promotional materials—in their abundance—define erectile dysfunction, factor its etiology, and marvel at its prevalence. With regard to these aspects of its subject matter, the promotional materials do so explicitly. With no less verve, but with rhetorically strategic subtlety, these materials define masculinity and intimacy in problematically unimaginative ways. Masculinity is represented in a very traditional manner—through athleticism and sexual prowess. Similarly, intimacy is seen as something that can only be achieved via penetrative sex, which is itself characterized as something that requires, at least from the male partner, a singularity of focus, of function, of performance, of workmanship. This chapter reveals the ways in which marketing and those that drive its standards have a profound impact on the health and welfare of a society.

Through the Viagra (ad)venture, Pfizer demonstrates how to successfully market a product for a condition that—historically—most men would not admit to. They accomplish this by creating a relationship between the condition and the "cure" and creating a name that medically legitimizes this previously embarrassing condition. The term "erectile dysfunction" refocuses the condition from being associated with a male's lack of potency to the more enlightened concept of a physical loss of function that can simply be (e)rectified. The acronym "ED," used by Pfizer—particularly in direct-to-consumer promotion—to embody this condition, is offered as a password with which to initiate a difficult conversation between physician and patient.[121] Furthermore, ED has a *brand-name* personality—simple, discreet, and empowering—and, as such, aligns beautifully with Viagra, a seemingly graceful and effective solution to this redefined condition. Contributing to this alignment, unfortunately, is a medical industry that seems uninterested in critiquing blatant examples of conflict of interest in its research. In June 2002, the *New England Journal of Medicine* announced it would be "relaxing" its stringent conflict-of-interest policy because of the difficulty it reported in finding consultants who didn't have financial connections to pharmaceutical manufacturers.[122]

The fifth and final chapter of this book, "Bare Necessities: Masculinity, Architecture, and Sexuality," examines the combined effects of Pfizer's advertising and the news stories surveyed in chapter 3 through a lens of contemporary architectural theory, and offers a corrective.

$\mathscr{B}$are $\mathscr{N}$ecessities

Masculinity, Sexuality, and Architecture

A building's architectural integrity derives from the masculinization of its materials, made to bear the weight of all the cultural values masculinity purportedly connotes, above all austerity, authenticity, and permanence.
—JOEL SANDERS, *STUD: ARCHITECTURES OF MASCULINITY* (1996)

Deconstruction resembles the demolition of an old, unstable, and outdated building (that of patriarchal heterosexualism) ravaged by the passage of time (historical time) and the ever-present eroding elements of the surrounding physical environment (the sociocultural environment). Continuing the analogy, the old building will be replaced by reconstructing new buildings that enhance sexual agency.
—ANDREAS PHILARETOU AND KATHERINE ALLEN,
"RECONSTRUCTING MASCULINITY AND SEXUALITY" (2001)

We perform many roles, any or all of which could influence the bodily workings. Meanwhile, our internal organs and tissues also perform. Physiological language is deeply mechanistic—it speaks of control systems, and feedback loops serving to stabilize them. Yet implicit in these systems is active response to change and contingency, bodily interiors that constantly react to change inside and out, and act upon the world.
—LYNDA BIRKE, "BODIES AND BIOLOGY" (1999)

After the frustrated rescue efforts had subsided, a primary objective following the catastrophe of September 11, 2001 was the restoration of normalcy. Returning to normal—this urgency to be made whole again—seemed a necessary step in our ability to recover as a nation. From atop a pile of rubble at

Ground Zero in New York City and with a flag at half staff behind him, President George W. Bush forecast the inevitable military strikes in Afghanistan, even while hailing the heroism of New York City's rescue workers.

Following a two-week bereavement period, our nation's leaders urged us to get back to business; the official end of mourning signaled by restoring the stars and stripes to full staff at Camp David. Florida governor Jeb Bush advised his constituents that "the best way to defeat terrorism is to get back to work."[1] The stock market, the National Football League, and Major League Baseball resumed their schedules, kicked off by renditions of "God Bless America."

For many Americans, these institutional recoveries were not enough. A material recovery was sought as well. The Twin Towers of the World Trade Center needed to be restored: a collective of architects and artists in New York City even proposed a "virtual re-creation" of the towers in the form of projected light—a ghost—generated by laser beams or searchlights to demonstrate that "New York is unbroken, and that we're here, and vibrant, and alive."[2] And indeed, on the six-month anniversary of what has come to be known as 9/11, the urban spectacle titled "Tribute in Light" was unveiled. This "architectonic illusion"—each of the two towers was re-created by forty-four high-powered searchlights—"gives the impression of an image revealed, rather than designed" and "proposes that, together, we look *for* something," rather than at something.[3] This project, designed as a temporary installation, became an instant landmark.[4] Mayor Michael Bloomberg is receptive to "reerecting the lights" but doesn't know how to pay for it.[5]

These architectural repairs were, perhaps, instigated by talk about architectural motives. Terrorist experts debated two positions in the weeks following 9/11: did Usama bin Laden and Al Qaeda choose the World Trade Center and the Pentagon as targets for their metaphorical significance (as representative sites of American money and military strength) or for their potential as sites for the devastating loss of human life? While no one won this debate, all agreed that the damage to the different targets, both in human life and structural ruin, was immense. Symbolizing expanding business interests and domestic defense, the World Trade Center and the Pentagon are decidedly masculine; the shapes in which their masculinity is incorporated, however, are significantly different. While the 110-story Twin Towers were leveled, the injury done to the similarly peopled weblike configuration of the insular Pentagon was minor by comparison. It is also worth noting that the "scar" of land in southwestern Pennsylvania created by the crash of the fourth plane hijacked in the September 11th attacks was, no doubt, recovering beneath an insular blanket of winter snow even as the wreckage in New York City and Washington, D.C. was being steadily cleared away.

In a discussion of American architecture since World War II, architecture theorist Joan Ockman describes the ideology represented by the modern skyscraper as "the strong silent type."[6] Modernist architects, Ockman explains, eliminated embellishments and flourishes from their designs in favor of function, leaving only the bare necessities. This style embodied rationalism and symbolized the virility of American technoscientific progress. Social anthropologist Henrietta Moore suggests that buildings in space reproduce not only "the dominant male ideology," but also other characteristics on which we base our constructions of gender.[7] Architect Diana Agrest has argued that architecture is an illustration of the male pattern of "appropriating an exclusively female privilege: maternity."[8] Architecture is aligned with production rather than consumption, exteriority rather than interiority, and with taking up space as opposed to yielding space.[9] As metaphor, architecture has frequently been summoned to define the body's functions. Medical anthropologist Emily Martin has shown how, following dominant ideologies of business, the medicalized body has moved from "machine" to "fortress" to "factory."[10] The skeleton is the body's scaffolding and the gastrointestinal system is the plumbing. The circulatory system, maintaining an oxygen supply in the blood, is the electricity. Invisibly flowing through all those bodily systems, says British sociologist Ken Plummer, is power, "a flow of negotiations and shifting outcomes."[11] Mechanistic metaphors are utilized by biomedicine to impose order on the body.[12] A masculine concept of power (power *over*, rather than power *with*) undergirds both the prevalence of architecture as an archetypal metaphor and architectural practice. Architectural metaphors are typically aligned with the biomedical (or functional) view of the body while modernist architecture (the skyscraper in particular) reflects traditional masculinity.

Architectural metaphors inform my study of the themes within the discourse surrounding Viagra's introduction to the American marketplace. But of course there is a difference between architectural theory and architectural practice. As a profeminist male, I am interested in troubling the unquestioned, inquiring of the unasked, and continuing my vocation as "gender traitor."[13] Architectural metaphors help me do that. Examining the discourse of hegemonic masculinity is, in Jeff Hearn's words, to "deconstruct the dominant" and "make the one(s) the other(s)."[14] Cultural studies scholar Lawrence Grossberg writes,

> At the heart of contemporary critical theory is the recognition that experience itself is a product of power and that, therefore, that which is the most obvious, the most unquestionable, is often the most saturated by relations of power.[15]

As epitomized by the World Trade Center catastrophe, even modern skyscrapers have a limited staying power. Whether due to decay, design, or deliberate destruction, skyscrapers do fall and, at times, the strong silent types have trouble getting it up. If the modern skyscraper is symbolic of both corporate identity and the nation's corporeal masculinity, then the development of the drug Viagra helps secure a material masculinity. A Robert Mankoff cartoon in *The New Yorker* cleverly synthesizes both of these sentiments. Two Madison Avenue advertising executives are looking out an office window at the side of the Empire State Building, which displays the word Viagra vertically, each letter two stories high: "Now, that's product placement!" one says to the other admiringly. Just as skyscrapers are erected to provide "horizons of significance"[16] representative of this nation's financial strength, so does Viagra re-create the significance of the male erection as constituting American masculinity.[17]

Both the news stories and Pfizer's promotional materials construct the erection as essential in performances of male sexuality. Rather than question the position of the erection as the sine qua non of manliness and male pleasure, however, the news stories debunk the rival technologies that produce erections (i.e., pumps, implants, prostheses, pharmaceutical injections) in favor of Viagra's "naturalness." Furthermore, the erection (and its absence) is frequently represented using architectural or mechanistic metaphors. Pfizer's materials *isolate* the erection as the culmination of "erotic stimuli," routinizing and standardizing male sexuality. To be sure, the erection (as Pfizer would have it) is the medium for orgasm and men have a right to it. The erection—as the male experience par excellence—is a saturated and unquestionable symbol of power.

Viagra discourse perpetuates the towering illusion that is the male sex role and reinscribes James Doyle's "themes" of American masculinity. Men depicted in both news stories and promotional materials perpetuate the "Be sexual" command by maintaining an ageless interest in (hetero)sex, desiring the imagined virility of their youth both in frequency and intensity. Men are no less concerned with status according to these texts. Viagra is portrayed as the avenue whereby independence and success can be achieved through the correct performance of sexual health maintenance. The surreptitious means by which Viagra is acquired (via the Internet) and consumed (in the form of a tiny pill taken an hour before sex) contributes to the masculine directive "Be independent." And achieving the "Be successful" maxim is all but promised by the promotional materials wherein Pfizer measures success by erectile *improvement*. In addition, Pfizer's materials are relentless in the demand that men *do something* about their erectile dysfunction (whether real or imagined). As a result, the "Be aggressive" requirement demanded of American men is fulfilled. In television commercials, Pfizer appeals to traditional aspects of masculinity through the use of sportsman and stud stereotypes. Finally, both Pfizer Pharmaceuticals and news stories advocate the physiological solution to erectile dysfunction. Psychological causes and their solutions—communication, therapy, lifestyle changes—are thereby rendered feminine. As a result, to consider the psychological etiology of erectile dysfunction would be to violate the masculine edict "Don't be feminine." Each of Doyle's five requirements of American masculinity is undergirded by a sixth: "Be healthy." As a *treatment* (rather than a cure), what Viagra does best is cover up the range of possible physical and mental causes for erectile dysfunction. As a treatment, Viagra is a *masked utility* for masculinity.

Pharmaceutical companies have moved from manufacturing products to manufacturing medical conditions that their products treat. Advertising now instructs the viewer to visit the doctor and ask for a drug, then shows the viewer *what happens when he does.* The emergence of self-diagnostic tests, the name change from "impotence" to "erectile dysfunction" (ED), and the development of Viagra have, without question, increased Pfizer's stakes in the understanding of ED's causes and treatments. Pfizer manipulates men's anxieties, sponsors research, and creates categories that balloon prevalence.

My examination of Viagra, however, has not only been an endeavor to reveal how masculine performances of sexual health are dangerous to men: hegemonic performances of masculine health inhibit the delivery of health to all social groups. The cost of Viagra impacts private health insurance premiums, public access to healthcare via Medicaid, and even the U.S. military budget. As social mechanisms, power and privilege impact our social experiences. Power and privilege are exerted and maintained through symbolic constructions. Mary Douglas writes, "The human body is common to us all. Only our social condition varies. The symbols based on the human body are used to express different social experiences."[18] Viagra, as it socially constructs sexuality, impacts men, women, and relationships. Viagra, as a symbol of masculine virility, expresses a specific and privileged social experience—that of hegemonic masculinity—bringing with it a significant social cost to men and women alike.

As the couple's solution to the couple's disease, Viagra obstructs the possibilities for sexual improvisation. Pfizer Pharmaceuticals defines erectile dysfunction and makes claims about its prevalence—which are, in turn, parroted more or less uncritically in news accounts—*and* develops a treatment that reinforces the status quo of penetrative heterosexual intercourse as the epitome of intimacy. As a gender scholar, a critical thinker, and a man, I must question the ways in which biomedicine might stall sexual experimentation and elaboration insofar as it ruthlessly excludes the possibilities of sexual variation. These exclusions produce and maintain social disparities among sexualities and between men and women.

Male Sexuality as Vertical Architecture

By looking specifically at two sets of texts—news stories and promotional materials—this book reveals how Viagra has impacted our understanding of sexual health in the seven years since its well-promoted debut. Dominating these texts are the twin discourses of masculinity and science. These discourses frame, reflect, deflect, and insinuate expectations for sexual health and not only for men. Male sexuality, in particular, has been shown to be a social performance, reinforced by appeals to what I will call here "vertical architecture." In this section, I describe how the discourse of Viagra accomplishes vertical architecture in three ways. Viagra accomplishes vertical architecture by (1) representing a corrective to a hierarchical malfunction; (2) reinforcing both the mind/body split in scientific discourse and the metaphor of body as machine; and (3) perpetuating the stereotype of heterosexuality as the correct performance of sexual identity. Hierarchy, the mind/body split, and heterosexism are vertical impulses. Hierarchy is the impulse toward power over others, characterized by performances of hegemonic masculinity. The Cartesian mind/body split has its foundation in the vertical impulse toward immortality when confronted with the mortal body. Heteronormativity is a vertical impulse that reinscribes traditional roles, with men having power over women and heterosexual men having power over homosexual men.

Viagra as Hierarchy

Kenneth Burke argues that we must be critics of the human drama; by failing to be critical of the human drama, we remain ignorant of how we are motivated toward action in the world.[19] In our human drama, Burke claims we are "goaded by the spirit of hierarchy," always seeking to climb the ladder toward the highest place in the hierarchical model of perfection. Furthermore, Burke claims we are attracted to hierarchy because we are moved by a sense of order, the structure by which we believe we can attain perfection.[20] In describing the key assumptions of Burke's critical system, Burke scholar David Payne states that "hierarchy is fundamental to human symbolism."[21] Hierarchy is the principal means by which things are placed in relation to each other—either valued above or below other things. This valuation can concern the material (e.g., money, television sets, homes) as well as the conceptual (e.g., education, religion, happiness).

Burke contends that audiences are motivated by discourse and its appeals to perfection. But while discourse tells us what we want through a language of hierarchy, the rhetoric of transcendence tells us why we should want perfection and how we can attain perfection. According to Payne, "rhetoric has transcendent themes because people want to believe they are doing something important in their lives, that they are rising above the ordinary."[22] Our drive for transcendence, however, creates conflicts over values that require choices about which authoritative symbols we accept or reject.

As a health condition, Pfizer Pharmaceuticals has succeeded in elevating erectile dysfunction from its former position as the trivial, yet socially embarrassing condition known as impotence to the treatable, yet seemingly inevitable circumstance of mature masculinity. Pfizer has succeeded in this redefinition primarily by building a link between erectile dysfunction and its product, Viagra.

Pfizer reinforces the hierarchy between youth and age in its promotional materials; a hegemonic fantasy of constant masculine virility trumps the reality and inevitability of aging. The audience for these promotional materials must choose to accept or reject these symbolic constructions. Unfortunately, both Pfizer and the popular press have proved relentless in their efforts to sway an audience upward, an audience driven by the promise of transcendence.

Pfizer creates a hierarchy among the supposed causes of erectile dysfunction while news stories create a hierarchy between legitimate and illegitimate risk. In the rhetoric of Pfizer, physiological causes are preferred over psychological causes and, among psychological causes, legitimate (or medically diagnosable) causes are preferred over cryptic, relational causes. News stories valorize the heroic, legitimate risks of heart patients who—in their efforts to rise above the ordinary—combine nitrates with Viagra. Meanwhile, Viagra's illegitimate users—gay men, drug users, and indiscriminant, lascivious heterosexuals—"queer" the rightful intent of what we are led to believe is a conscientious pharmaceutical company.

A hierarchy is maintained between physicians and patients by constructing the male patient as someone unable (or afraid) even to articulate his own health concerns. Meanwhile, there is a hierarchy portrayed among doctors with Viagra prescription writing as the final arbiter. Witness the doctor interviewed in the Viagra magazine who declares, "I have the biggest ED practice in New York" (the biggest city!). And with patients acquiescing to physicians and physicians creating hierarchies among themselves, is it any wonder that the patient (or sufferer) must then create a hierarchy between his subjective "self" and his penis? As a "tool," the penis is supposed to function when called upon.

The rhetoric of Viagra—found in both news stories and promotional materials—overwhelmingly supports the notion that men who maintain the ability to achieve erections perform their role as men better than those who can't (or won't). The rhetoric of Viagra is a rhetoric of hierarchy. Men without erections experience guilt for not being real men. But because Viagra is not a cure for ED but only a treatment, those men who take it continue to have erectile dysfunction—they just don't *suffer* from it. Furthermore, the implication is that men who choose *not* to take Viagra are agents who consciously choose to forfeit their agency. Consequently, the man who chooses not to take Viagra—not to act—chooses to have erectile dysfunction and must accept his lower position in the hierarchy, forgoing his chance for transcendence. Hierarchy is a vertical architecture.

Viagra as an Illustration of the Mind/Body Split

Because the body has been reduced to parts, men are concerned only with how they have made a move toward perfection. As a physiologically based impairment, Viagra doesn't create for the man a recognition of himself as a subject. Rather, it reaffirms the otherness of his body. The mind/body split is another example of vertical architecture.

A psychosis, according to Kenneth Burke, is "a particular recipe of over-stressings and understressings peculiar to the given institutional structure."[23] As a necessary component of what Burke would call a technological psychosis, the mind/body split serves to enhance the prestige of the institution of scientific discourse within healthcare. As my analysis shows, how and when medical etiologies are labeled physiological versus psychological is a matter of overstressing and understressing.

First and foremost, Pfizer reinscribes the mind/body dichotomy in its description of ED's causes. Physicians often assume because there is a physical problem there is no psychological cause. Meanwhile, news stories reinforce cultural expectations and gendered attitudes toward health by sponsoring the myth that men's sexual problems can be solved physiologically while women's sexual problems require a consideration of relational dynamics. I contend that wholesale solutions based solely on biological sex create distinctions that perpetuate damaging and detrimental relationships between men and women.

Pfizer's adoption, embrace, and wholesale endorsement of the rhetorical switch from "impotence" to "erectile dysfunction" in its promotional materials is another example of how Viagra perpetuates the mind/body split in biomedicine. Unlike impotence, which implicates the whole man, ED implicates only a body part—the penis—so it is only the penis that Viagra repairs and only that body part that men locate as the root of their erection difficulties. This transfer of responsibility is accomplished through the use of mechanistic, utilitarian, and architectural metaphors as described through testimonials of masculinity in the Viagra news stories. It is worth reflecting on why this separation of mind/body was so successful as a strategy in the rhetoric of Viagra.

As a concept of Marxist theory that examines the process of separating human beings from their work, their minds from their bodies, and nature from human experience, *alienation* is, according to Allison Jagger, a "gender-mediated experience."[24] Just as Jagger claims women are alienated from their bodies in the process of reproductive labor, I suggest that, by taking a pill, men are alienated from their bodies in the process of securing this corrective therapy for erectile dysfunction. Put differently, a drug like Viagra is successful (and rhetorically acceptable) precisely because of its alienating effect. Furthermore, Susan Bordo has suggested that maintaining traditional ideals of masculinity through chemical enhancement (e.g., Rogaine, DHEA testosterone, Viagra) and/or elective surgery (e.g., liposuction, phalloplasty) reflects a pursuit for the approval of other men (that is, the male gaze) as well as for the approval of women.[25] This is similar to Jagger's observation that, in the process of slimming, shaving, and implanting, women construct their bodies in ways that create competition among women for the attention of men. Perhaps in a youth culture, men seek calf and pectoral implants, undergo liposuction and even phalloplasty in an effort to appear viable in the corporate locker room, where, evidently, success is measured by more than sales quotas.

In the last twenty-five years, health communication specialists and medical anthropologists have paid a great deal of attention to the distinctions between biomedical and psychosocial models in healthcare.[26] The biomedical "disease" model, for example, emphasizes objective diagnosis, treatment, and cure by physicians conducting relevant tests, recognizing abnormalities, and prescribing successfully tested therapy. In contrast, the psychosocial "illness" model forefronts the individual's subjective experience and refers to how the patient shapes meaning in a spatially and temporally bound personal, cultural, and societal environment. As Carole Vance writes, "Biomedical models tend to be the most unreflective about the influence of science and medical practice in constructing categories like 'the body' and 'health.'"[27] That men in particular may favor the biomedical model in response to sexual health concerns is best explained by a genealogy of factors that include social, cultural, political, and biological conditioning. For many men, for example, in circumstances where "normal" performance is closely aligned with masculine identity (e.g., sports and sex), an objective cause that blames the body—deviant and external to the "self"—reduces personal responsibility for "failure."[28]

Viagra has taken a firm hold in the American imaginary as *the* answer to the problem of erectile dysfunction. Biomedicine's embrace of pharmaceutical solutions reveals its advocacy of the mind/body split. My aim, however, is not to return to humanist sexologists and psychologists the control of the sexual dysfunction market. Nor do I express a preference for "psychological" over "organic" etiologies. Rather, I believe it is necessary to question the degree to which consumers have been amenable to biomedicine's interpretations and to its inherently conservative definitions of sexual expression. As an integral feature of Viagra's rhetoric, the mind/body split is a vertical architecture.

Viagra as an Accomplishment of Heteronormativity

For most American men, the loss of virginity through the act of penile-vaginal penetration is a significant step toward adult masculinity, manhood, and heterosexuality. And while many men will experience other aspects of sexual behavior that are pleasurable, none will reify their masculinity more than "straight" sex (or what Carole Vance calls "meat and potatoes" and Pat Califia calls "vanilla" sex). In the texts examined here, men who fail to accomplish this act—whatever the cause—have demonstrated significant doubts about their own subjective experiences of masculinity. That most heterosexual men appear to consider the erect penis as the only means toward sexual fulfillment indicates a narrowness of thought that doesn't take into account what has been learned about the practices of alternative sexualities.

I define heteronormativity as the cultural inclination to position heterosexuality as the default socio/sexual experience—perhaps the grandest of "grand narratives."[29] What I mean by this is that heterosexuality is viewed as the expected path of sexual development. A rhetoric of heteronormativity not only upholds this expectation, but grants the experience of heterosexuality unearned power and privilege through the repetitive endorsement of its social, political, and cultural values, both real and imagined. And it does all of this by pretending that other ways of being a socio/sexual human being don't exist. Stevi Jackson writes:

> An effective critique of heterosexuality—at the levels of social structure, meaning, social practice and subjectivity—must contain two elements. The first of these is a critique of heteronormativity, of the normative status of heterosexuality which renders any other sexualities as "other" and marginal. The second is a critique of what some have called "hetero-patriarchy" or "hetero-oppression" . . . in other words, heterosexuality as systematically male dominated.[30]

Just as Viagra's marketing is invested in heteronormativity, it sells heteronormative values to the drug's customers. Heteronormative values include traditional performances of both masculinity and femininity. Pfizer's target market is the heterosexual man with the "wife" as the default "partner" when the relational dynamics of ED are described. While she might be frustrated by her husband's erectile difficulties, she is patient and "stands by her man." Within relationships marked by traditional performances of masculine authority and feminine servility, it is the woman who feels the pressure to equalize the anxiety resulting from the compromised male ego and the unresponsive penis. As evidenced by the design of the Sexual Health Inventory for Men (SHIM), "intimacy" means penile-vaginal intercourse and "sex" stands in for male orgasm. Testimonies of masculinity contained in the news stories suggest a puerile and stagnant relationship between men and sexuality—one that Viagra preserves with its emphasis on subtlety, organic causes, and universal remedies. Both Pfizer's promotional materials and the news stories perpetuate traditional male sex roles by reproducing stereotypes of masculine behavior, beliefs, and values. Without these values the need for Viagra disappears, and the dominant socio/sexual order is threatened.

My critique of Viagra in this book answers Stevi Jackson's call because it questions both heteronormativity and the male-dominated system that supports it. To question the norms of heterosexuality—indeed, to question its "naturalness"—is deeply threatening.[31] Both the news stories and the promotional materials analyzed in this book promote Viagra through a rhetoric of heteronormativity. Viagra is portrayed as the champion to heterosexuality's Black Knight—the loss of intimacy, narrowly defined as penile-vaginal penetration. Furthermore, Viagra renders other sexualities marginal. Pfizer has yet to produce any educational or even promotional material for gay men. News stories—in their investigation of the risks surrounding Viagra—scapegoat gay men and other "queer" users of Viagra. Furthermore, through the use of a black male (i.e., "Joe") in its television advertising, Pfizer appropriates a mythos of hypersexuality in order to benefit the white, middle-class men whose use of Viagra supports racist and classist materials and social constructions. By maintaining that men have power over women and straight men have power over gay men, heteronormativity is an oppressive institution and one that operates by stigmatizing other ways of being men and women in the world. Heteronormativity is a vertical architecture.

The creation of attributes to be repaired has a long history in the love affair between manufacturing, advertising, and the constraints, prohibitions, and obligations of society. Erving Goffman writes that a stigma is "a special kind of relationship between attribute and stereotype."[32] The emergence of a stigma comes about through a delicate dependence of social norms and their interpretation. The emergence of advertising strategies coincides with the *creation* of attributes that, if untreated (as they presumably should be with the advertiser's products), contribute to the creation of stereotypes, namely, what Goffman calls the "discredited." Pitted against "normals" (who follow the instructions of the advertiser), the discredited (as stereotypes) represent a *danger* in their willingness to depart "from the particular expectations at issue."[33]

Questioning the values inherent in Viagra as cultural artifact means questioning patriarchy, a power structure that has a deep interest in its preservation.[34] If I refuse to recognize a disconnection between mind and body in health, then I must not lose sight of that refusal when it comes to the mind and body of a society. The mind in the body and the body in the mind are maintained both through ideology and architecture. Nationalists speak in terms of biology—of the nation as a living, breathing, and sexed entity—of founding fathers and the motherland. The heterosexual male body and its products are continually summoned as both current and future metaphors for the nation.[35] The knowledge of how bodies have been historically disciplined is valuable as a theoretical lens and a tool of activism. This knowledge draws analogies—both literal and figurative—without losing sight of the different subjectivities that have created and continue to create these conditions. In producing erections, Viagra reifies the metaphor of the virile male as the representative of the nation—ready, willing, and able.

Through this analysis of Viagra, my intention has been to find another way to meld artificially divided aspects of mind and body in the investigation of masculine sexuality and the dependence on/refusal of architecture. In the final section of this chapter, I advocate an architectural metaphor that endeavors to escape the trappings of hierarchy and the vertical thrust of architecture.

Wondering a Horizontal Architecture

In their introduction to *Gender and Architecture,* Louise Durning and Richard Wrigley suggest that architecture "structures and defines many of the social spaces in which gendered identities are rehearsed, performed and made visible as a form of shared private and public spectacle."[36] To this, Diana Agrest adds in her introduction to *The Sex of Architecture* that the "inscription of the sexualized body is a central and recurrent theme in Western architecture."[37]

Simultaneously structuring, defining, and inscribing bodies as buildings, the rhetoric of architecture has now entered the science of medicalized sexuality. This medicalization, however, pays little heed to the need for gender and sexuality to be transformed. Speaking in terms of architectural transformation in *Building Sex,* Aaron Betsky invites a change when he suggests that what the world needs is "an architecture of liberation that allows us all to re-create fantastically the world we have already made and make it our own."[38]

Viagra, as *the* remedy for erectile dysfunction, is a call for the reinstatement of a "traditional" and, I argue, dangerous value system reminiscent of an *imagined* American past that supposedly existed prior to the major advances made in equality among its people. Indeed, the debates surrounding the restructuring of the World Trade Center property following the destruction of 9/11 signifies this traditionalism in yet another metaphorical turn.

In a summary review of architectural theory, Carole Blair, Marsha Jeppeson, and Enrico Pucci constitute modern architecture as signifying the "dominance of technological innovation, rationality, and corporate power" with its beauty housed in function rather than form or style.[39] In addition, modernist architecture is devoid of contextual considerations such as the psychic or cultural needs of the public. As a discourse, "modern architecture's signs were almost purely self-referential and limited by a closed system of 'legitimate' signifiers."[40] Conversely, the authors explain, postmodern architecture is "disruptive" in its tendency to refuse universals, attending to context, and affecting a critical positionality in its understanding of the art form. Postmodern architects "adapt buildings to people."[41] I find in these definitions of modern and postmodern architecture an accommodating analogy that serves to challenge the current medical model of sexuality. Clearly, the one-pill-fits-all mentality promulgated by Pfizer (and now other pharmaceutical companies as well) is a modernist, more-is-better—indeed, a vertical—pursuit.

As Denise Riley's observation—"Only at times will the body impose itself or be arranged as that of a woman or a man"—implies, our perspectives are as easily changed as our capacity to pay attention "only at times." The rhetorical switch from impotence to erectile dysfunction illustrates the way in which "the normal and the stigmatized are not persons but rather perspectives."[42] As a man who has completed his fourth decade in this world and, as a result, entered into Pfizer's target market, I resist the implication that my once and future sexual individuality should be "fixed" either as a configuration of practices *or* by a universalized remedy. What we need is a postmodern architecture of sexuality—an egalitarian, horizontal architecture. I perceive this architecture to be comprised of four "active ingredients": education, communication, pleasure, and play.

In an age when men seek superior performance in all aspects of their lives—their jobs, their cars, their investments—sexual performance is no exception. As a result, Viagra is routinely used and abused by men of all ages (even those who have not been diagnosed with erectile dysfunction) to facilitate the ultimate sexual experience. Men use this drug to counteract or coincide with other recreational drugs, to improve the quality and longevity of an already adequate erection, or to shorten the physiologic refractory period between erections. Although there have been neither advertisements nor quantifiable evidence claiming improved erectile function in healthy men, the use of Viagra is believed to improve erectile longevity and rigidity.

It would seem that the search for improved sexual function would be better served by learning about arousal response and the type and amount of play that leads sexual partners to a mutual level of satisfaction. Improved knowledge of these physiologic processes might lead to improved sexual satisfaction between partners. But the rhetoric of "function" is culturally loaded, reinscribing the vertical impulse of mechanistic metaphors that rely on biomedical models of sex and the body.

Sex education can be an empowering tool to promote improved sexual satisfaction on the part of both partners. This educative process, however, should include more than sexual anatomy and physiology, normal (i.e., Masters and Johnson–endorsed) sexual response cycles for the sex of both partners, forms of stimulation that may lead to orgasm, and masturbation techniques.

Rather, sex education should begin with the information that orgasms, for men and women, are not dependent on an erect penis. And while I don't believe that orgasms should be the goal of sexual play (as they contribute to a hierarchical and linear model of sexual conduct), they can be felt in parts of the body other than the genitals. This kind of information may be new and surprising to patients seeking Viagra. Educators should be able to assess the individual's or couples' feelings about the information presented and acknowledge those feelings. In any event, it is important—and particularly incumbent upon the medical industry—to falsify the widespread belief that all sexual pleasure is derived solely from an erect penis. Obviously, this will *not* be news to many readers.

The goals of sexual intimacy and loveplay are highly individualistic and should be mutually agreed upon between partners. Communication is an essential element to improving sexual intimacy and satisfaction and partners must be able to dialogue freely about their feelings, pleasures, fantasies, likes, and dislikes regarding intimate loveplay. But communication must include more than the verbal expression of desire.

Socialist feminism suggests that the domination of women exists beyond the material definition of economy in that women are often asked to exchange both procreative and household labor for social validation. The trade-off for "success" as a female in society is often the suppression of individual desires. Socialist feminists seek to examine how capitalism and patriarchy impact each other to oppress women more glaringly than men. According to Juliet Mitchell, a woman's "place" is determined not only by her role in production and reproduction, but through her sexual collusion as well. Mitchell theorizes that attitudes toward women will never really change so long as female and male psychologies are dominated by the phallic symbol.[43]

In their effort to offer women alternatives to the medical model of sexuality, Heather Hartley and Leonore Tiefer advocate "the prevention of women's sexual problems through counteracting the sociocultural, political, and economic causes of these problems."[44] In *What Makes Women Sick: Gender and the Political Economy of Health,* Lesley Doyal points out how women, in particular, are not always "in a position to determine the nature of their sexual lives."[45] Men, too, can ultimately benefit from what socialist feminists have to say about women's sexuality. A feminist lens allows us to understand how sex is more than biological. A feminist lens demonstrates how sexual agency is not guaranteed to anyone. A feminist lens also resists the hold phallocentrism has on sex and pleasure. This is especially significant because questioning phallocentrism in sex necessarily encourages the exploration of alternatives for pleasure—something that requires communication (and a fair amount of trust) between partners.

Rather than something that requires communication in order to be "fixed," however, it is my belief that erectile dysfunction represents an opportunity for partners to engage in belated yet necessary dialogue about sexual variety and/or whether sex is something that is necessary in their relationship. It is important to acknowledge here the parallels between the components of my horizontal architecture model and those previously suggested by none other than Masters and Johnson, who suggest "sex education, nongenital and genital pleasuring, communication training, and variety of interventions designed to reduce performance anxiety."[46] What is different about my horizontal architecture approach, however, is that the components are not suggested in order to alleviate obstructions to "normal" heterosexual intercourse, for example, erectile dysfunction. Rather, they are suggested in order to yank sex from the functional domain of the biomedical model and into the playful domain of performance.

In both the news stories and the promotional materials I have examined there are repeated references to the "work" of sex and associated performance anxiety. The metaphors equating penis with machine (e.g., "hydraulics") further complicate this perspective. Without question, women often view sex as a responsibility and part of an economic exchange. I advocate for an alternative interpretation of the performance metaphor. Sex as "play"—as an improvisational and emergent activity that is not centered on the goals of penetration and ejaculation—can replace the sex as "work" model that currently dominates the rhetoric of sexual dysfunction. With a new metaphor in place, the possibilities for transcending the perceived sexual (and masculine identity) crisis of ED begins to extend beyond the pharmacy, "influencing," as Lynda Birke imagines in the epigram to this chapter, "our bodily workings." Even as I offer the metaphor of "play," I am aware of the heteronormative assumption in this vision. While the penetrative model is not relevant to all sexual partnerships, it is a hegemonic model and the model against which this critique is directed. Elizabeth Grosz argues that "there is an increasing discretion granted to the heterosexual couple, who, while remaining the pivot and frame of reference for the specification of . . . other sexualities, are less subject to scrutiny and intervention, are granted a form of discursive privacy."[47] My hope is that the improvisational nature of play helps transcend sexed bodies, not with the intention of advocating for equality (and thereby ignoring difference), but with the promise of freeing specific sexual "acts" from specific sexual "agents."

Theorists frequently turn to the phenomenology of play as a way of talking about cultural performances. Victor Turner credits Mihaly Csikszentmihaly with the observation that "the wheel of play reveals to us . . . the possibility of changing our goals and, therefore, the restructuring of what our culture states to be reality."[48] Performance theorist Richard Schechner similarly conceives of play as having the ability to create "its own multiple realities with porous and slippery boundaries."[49] It is important to acknowledge that Schechner recognizes seven approaches to play, including one that examines play as function. He asks,

> How [does play] affect individual and community learning, growth and creativity, distribute and express aggression, act out myths, fantasies, or values . . . or any number of possible "uses" play has? What are the economic consequences of any particular play act or genre of play?[50]

In these passages, Schechner both reveals the transformative potential of play and anticipates the ways in which play might contribute to a culture's systems of domination and exclusion.

Arguably, men are aligned with this functional, or efficacious, definition of play. The best example of this can be found in the baseball metaphors used to define sexual conquest. In the movement "around the base paths" of sexual conquest, boys and young men see the "accomplishment" of each stage as the logical precursor to the next. This compulsion to move forward inhibits pleasure for both partners. His pleasure is inhibited because he is too busy planning his next move. Her pleasure is inhibited by the fact that—fulfilling her cultural role—she must establish the rules. Since anything less than intercourse does not count as sex, he will someday equate his erectile dysfunction with a crisis in masculinity.

If the metaphor of "play" can better address this crisis at an individual level, "horizontal architecture" is the metaphor that addresses crisis at a cultural level. While we may find it problematic to think of architecture as anything other than work—and important work at that!—architecture can be playful, too. I, for one, was thrilled that the winning design for the World Trade Center site was a lively amalgam of aesthetically playful and colorful form, balanced by the demands of functional office space and memorial eloquence. Architecture can help us remember how sex—for good or for bad—structures our lives. Horizontal architecture can help us remember that sex is also play. As metaphor, horizontal architecture is a nonhierarchical form of sexual play that is focused not on a heterosexual model of penetration and male orgasm as the ultimate goals of sexual expression, but on the *horizon*, for possibilities and changes. Here "play" is improvisation. Risky? You bet. But as Mary Catherine Bateson reminds us, "improvisation is central to living in periods of change."[51]

Discussing safe sex in the age of HIV/AIDS, health communication scholar Mara Adelman maintains that the metaphor of play "can be understood not only in terms of its contribution to relational intimacy but also in furthering our understanding in mediating the tensions and obstacles to practicing safer sex."[52] The tensions and obstacles of changing bodies and changing desires can be similarly reconciled if we think about sex as play. Horizontal architecture advocates the positioning of communication and pleasure as equally significant and important aspects of intimacy, performed in an infinite variety of ways—in bed, in conversation, in play. Not only does this re-visioning hold great promise for the future of sex in the United States, it implies the possibility of a life beyond crisis—one that does not rely upon retaliation, oppression, separation, and exclusion. Both horizontal architecture and play are communicative, elaborative, improvisational, inclusive, and, ultimately, pleasurable.

Methodology

As consumers of texts, we seek out various media for guidance, frequently developing an attachment to those texts that validate our own experiences, often choosing not to interrogate them too closely. Anthony Giddens (1991) writes, "[I]ndividuals actively, although by no means consciously, selectively incorporate many elements of mediated experience into their daily conduct" (188). Kenneth Burke (1974) explains how mediated messages supply us with "equipment for living." Through this "secondary socialization," our social stock knowledge is created, bolstered, recreated, "re-ified" (Berger and Luckmann 1966). Most of the knowledge about health that we receive and use comes from the media (Johnson and Meischke 1993; Moyer et al. 1995; Stroot 1997; Wallack 1990).

Discourse analysis is a critical and "systematic method for describing, analyzing, interpreting, and evaluating" discursive messages (Frey et al. 2000:229). But according to Klaus Krippendorff (1991), individual researchers are far from unified regarding what these "systematic" methods entail (see Berg 2001; Frey et al. 2000; Infante et al. 1993; Silverman 2000; Stacks and Hocking 1992). Because my method is interpretive, I am more interested in investigating and critiquing the meanings associated with the texts, rather than with counting the number of times a particular word or phrase appears in a unit of analysis. With this in mind, I find Janet Cramer's (1998) definition of discourse analysis most applicable to this work:

> [In] discourse analysis, one seeks to uncover the codes, constructions, cultural assumptions, connotations, values, and beliefs embedded in the text by locating correspondences between a text and social structures and identities, noting recurring patterns, such as the repetition of certain themes, phrases, rhetoric, and so on in the discourse (13).

This type of analysis usually involves looking at a set of texts through a critical lens and so becomes a method that communication theorists call "critical rhetoric" (McGee 1990; McKerrow 1989; Ono and Sloop 1992). I employ a variety of critical lenses to accomplish my task, including feminist theory, dramatistic theory, and performance theory.

Feminist methodological and research practices are multiple. Shula Reinharz (1992) contends that these practices "must be recognized as a plurality" (4). Carolyn Sherif endorses a discipline-free approach to this kind of research when she writes,

> The study of sex and gender has to be cross-disciplinary if it is to be relevant to the goals of feminism . . . cross-disciplinary study is an essential antidote for the compartmentalized and de-humanizing definitions of contemporary disciplines (quoted in Reinharz 1992:10).

These multiple methods and disciplines are of significant value in the social sciences and humanities as they uncover "patterns and interrelationships and causes and effects and implications of questions that nonfeminists have not seen and still do not see" (Judith Lorber, quoted in Reinharz 1992:13). As a result, suggests Reinharz, "multiples methods enable feminist researchers to link past and present, 'data gathering' and action, and individual behavior with social frameworks" (197). This feminist plurality enables me to make connections between the discourse of sexual dysfunction and the larger societal implications for that discourse, by encouraging critique from several perspectives including critical theory, dramatistic analysis, and performance theory.

I will employ a feminist brand of critical theory that attempts "to discover and expose dominant ideologies, practices, and beliefs" (Humm 1995:50). According to Carolyn DiPalma (1999), Donna Haraway's *Primate Visions* is an example of such criticism. DiPalma demonstrates how Haraway applies Foucauldian discursive strategies of reversal, discontinuity, specificity, and exteriority in the effort to "agitate the dominant discourse" (55). Practitioners of feminist criticism often work to reveal the ways in which traditional portrayals of men and women perpetuate masculinist ideals. Specifically, I will utilize these strategies when I examine the metaphors, assumptions, and perspectives inherent in the texts I describe.

Also useful is the lens of Kenneth Burke's dramatistic criticism, which rests on the properties of communication as "symbolic action." The human situation is a dramatic one, Burke argues, and an analysis of the components of that drama can reveal the "important relationships between symbolic acts and the environment in which they occur" (Stewart et al. 1989:137). For Burke, this dramatic situation can best be understood by recognizing the five elements of his *dramatistic pentad* and identifying the dominant element(s). The five elements of the pentad are the agent (the "who" of the message), the scene (the "context," or the "where and when" of the message), the act (the "what" of the message), the agency (the "how" of the message), and the purpose (the "why" of the message). According to David Payne (1990) an appropriate use of Burke's dramatism will (1) determine whether a hierarchy is found in the discourse; (2) ascertain the vocabulary of motives; (3) uncover the presence of a scapegoat; and (4) reveal strategies of transcendence. Burke explains how the pentad element "act" promises "transcendence." In addition, Burke's use of dramatism recognizes how messages utilize "identification" processes and employ language "clusters." Identification is used by creators of persuasive messages to create a notion of shared reality for the recipients of a discursive strategy (Frey et al. 2000:234–235).

Finally, I will draw on performance theory by revealing the ways in which discursive events constitute sites for performance through the use of "sexual scripts" (Simon and Gagnon 1984), frames (Goffman 1959; Goffman 1974), and social dramas (Turner 1988). In so doing, I will be able to demonstrate how the texts I've chosen to analyze move subtly from personal issues of sexual health to the political terrain of healthcare.

For chapter 2's analysis of Viagra in the news, I chose the *New York Times, Newsweek,* and *U.S. News & World Report* as primary sites because they are well-established news sources, they are popular, they demonstrated a commitment to covering Viagra from the very beginning (and even before the beginning), and they are available in both print and electronic forms. Mass communications scholar and media critic Matthew McAllister (1992) has demonstrated how the relationship between the news media and medicine is a dangerous one. Both institutions value "verifiable objectivity" and authenticate the importance of each other: the news media "boils down" complex medical research, distributing it to an eager public while medical informants "make themselves available" as unquestioned authorities.

I selected articles from these well-known news sources by using the Lexis/Nexus database. This large academic database indexes many major magazines, journals, and newspapers, both from the United States and abroad. I entered the keywords "Viagra" and "erectile dysfunction" and/or "impotence" for each of the periodicals. I then eliminated those stories that were shorter than 475 words as well as those stories that mentioned Viagra only peripherally or as a pop culture reference. Very quickly, it seems, Viagra has entered the lexicon of American culture as a tongue-in-cheek metaphor for elevation and/or lifting (see, for example, Stuart Elliot's *New York Times* article "Viagra's fast climb to iconic status makes it a natural for a variety of campaigns," 1 September 1998; section C, page 2).

Therefore, the articles chosen for this section of my analysis have several characteristics: (1) they are at least 475 words in length; (2) they discuss Viagra and/or the medicalization of sexuality as a primary subject (rather than refer to Viagra by way of reference, humor, or analogy only); and (3) they are narrative reports (rather than interviews, comprehensive charts, or lists). I examined a total of fifty-two news stories matching these criteria: twenty-four from the *New York Times*, seventeen from *Newsweek*, and eleven from *U.S. News & World Report*. The dates of these fifty-two publications cover roughly six years—from September 1996 to October 2002 (for a complete list of these news stories, see Appendix B). Although many of these articles are accompanied by photographs, illustrations, and graphics, my analysis focuses specifically on the text of the stories.

With regard to article length, twenty-one of the fifty-two stories I survey contain between 1,000 and 2,000 words. Eight more are over 2,000 words. The longest article, by far, was Jack Hitt's *New York Times Magazine* feature titled "The Second Sexual Revolution" at 8,360 words. Thirteen articles are between 600 and 1,000 words, with the remaining ten stories containing between 475 and 599 words. The average article length is not quite 1,400 words. The mean is 1,378. These short, medium, long, and extra-long articles represent a tidy cross-section of popular press articles. (In the 1983 film *The Big Chill*, Jeff Goldblum's character is a writer for *People* magazine. He characterizes the readable length of popular press articles as being "no longer than the average person can read while taking a crap.")

In addition to representing a range of lengths, these articles also appear in a diversity of news sections. In the *New York Times*, for example, articles about Viagra appear in the Style section, the Business/Financial section, the Science section, and the Health and Fitness section with relatively equal distribution and on each and every day of the week. *Newsweek's* coverage of Viagra is evidenced in their Lifestyle, Society, Science, and Business sections, as well as the featured story several times as a Special Report. The *U.S. News and World Report* housed their coverage of Viagra stories in three sections: Health & Medicine, Science & Ideas, and Business & Technology.

For chapter 3's analysis of Pfizer Pharmaceutical's marketing materials, I collected a wide range of marketing materials. I recorded television commercials, stopped at urologists' offices to acquire educational videos and magazines, perused the *Journal of the American Medical Association* for print ads, called Pfizer directly or filled out questionnaires on their website in order to acquire more pamphlets and brochures, and relied on the generosity of my peers who continually stuffed my mailbox with Pfizer paraphernalia.

To say that Pfizer's promotional materials for Viagra are available in a variety of forms would be an understatement. The promotional videos, television commercials, brochures, and the Viagra magazine *LifeDrive* represent a significant commitment to marketing this product. Clearly—and this is probably the case with many food and drug products—Pfizer began the process of promoting Viagra long before it was approved by the FDA. In addition to advertising products aimed at the consumer, Pfizer produced a number of advertising premiums, items geared more toward those who would actually be prescribing the drug—urologists and general practitioners. I came across an interesting assortment of these premiums: leather briefbags, desk accessories bearing the image of the little blue pill (as well as of Rafael Palmeiro), coffee mugs, and pens and notepads by the score. As I was unsure how to credibly and actively analyze these materials, they are not part of the study. Nonetheless, these premiums indicate to me a commitment to success, despite the potential downside of the drug. In an informal interview with an Australian physician who had prescribed a number of erectile dysfunction drugs, I was told that "drug reps look after" physicians. I thought this to be an interesting turn of phrase.

I watched the television commercials and promotional videos repeatedly, focusing on different aspects each time. I also took note of production values, running times, camera angles, and the use of language in conjunction with images. Because the materials gathered—both Pfizer's promotional materials and the news articles—covered a period of over five years, I paid attention to changes in how the Viagra story was told.

I made choices, of course, about how to gather these texts. I did not, for example, contact Pfizer's advertising agency in the hope of securing commercials available in other parts of the country. With regard to the news stories, I could have chosen to review a wider *range* of sources. I did neither of these things because my goal was to analyze what I judged to be an average intake of commercials and news. Of course, future studies could pursue an analysis of other Viagra (or Cialis, or Levitra) "texts," especially those from other parts of the world.

With regard to the themes I uncover, I believe it is possible that another researcher looking at the same texts might find additional themes. What is important here is that the themes I did address are undeniably a part of the discourse. The value of the methodology I adopted is that it facilitates a critical reading of texts that tend to insinuate themselves into the public psyche without either resistance or the possibility for revision. As a researcher, the subjectivity of my analysis is also important. I am extremely privileged—a well-educated, straight, white male with no visible disability. My position as a member of Pfizer's target market, in combination with my education as a communication scholar with feminist mentoring, enables me to read these texts as both consumer and critic. Furthermore, I have participated in many conversations with men of all demographics concerning sexuality in general, and Viagra in particular. On more than one occasion, in the context of explaining how my research was critical of Viagra, I wondered if I was talking to someone who had taken, and believed in, the promise of the drug. Indeed, some men *did* confess more than a passing interest in experimenting with this drug. Such occasions evoked in me a need to soften my critique of consumers and sharpen my attention on the constructions of institutional discourse. These conversations provided me with significant insights for my analysis of these texts because I could see how readily appealing the promise of Viagra is to men of all backgrounds (and indeed, at times, to me). Thus, the subjectivity of my analysis is essential to the process of engaging with the texts both intellectually and emotionally—there is too much at stake to do otherwise.

Popular Press Articles

New York Times (24)

Author, title, newspaper, day, month, and year, edition, section number (if
    Sunday), page
Word count
Section—Day of the week

Anon. "Heart Groups Urge Caution on Viagra." *New York Times*, 21 August
    1998, late ed.: A16
573
National Desk—Friday

Arnold, Martin. "No Rush to Ride Viagra Coattails." *New York Times*, 7 May
    1998, late ed.: E3
1,038
Arts—Thursday

Brock, Fred. "Seniority: A Dose of Sense From Viagra's Spokesman." *New
    York Times*, 4 June 2000, late ed.: section 3, p. 14
951
Business/Financial Desk—Sunday

Brody, Jane E. "Sour Note in the Viagra Symphony." *New York Times*, 19
    May 1998, late ed.: F7
1,095
Science Desk/Health Page—Tuesday

Brody, Jane E. "Facing Viagra's Emotional Ripples." *New York Times,* 26
     May 1998, late ed.: F7
1,118
Science Desk/Health Page—Tuesday

Elliot, Stuart. "Viagra's Fast Climb to Iconic Status Makes It a Natural for a
     Variety of Campaigns." *New York Times,* 1 September 1998, late ed.:
     C2
1,024
Business/Financial Desk—Tuesday

Fisher, Ian. "$1 Million Gift for New Charity Case: The Viagra-Needy." *New
     York Times,* 10 June 1998, late ed.: B3
599
Metropolitan Desk—Wednesday

Goldberg, Carey. "Insurance for Viagra Spurs Coverage for Birth Control."
     New York Times, 30 June 1999, late ed.: A1
1,442
National Desk—Wednesday

Hitt, Jack. "The Second Sexual Revolution." *New York Times Magazine* 20
     February 2000, late ed.: section 6, p. 34
8,360
Magazine Desk—Sunday

Kirby, David. "Viagra Wants to Be (Taken) Alone." *New York Times,* 3 May
     1998, late ed.: section 14, p. 6
528
Neighborhood Report—Sunday

Kolata, Gina. "6 Taking Viagra Die, but the F.D.A. Draws No Conclusions."
     New York Times, 23 May 1998, late ed.: A8
505
National Desk—Saturday

Kuczynski, Alex. "Curious Women Are Seeing if Viagra Works Wonders for
     Them." *New York Times,* 17 May 1998, late ed.: section 9, p. 2
1,328
Style—Sunday

Martin, Douglas. "Thanks a Bunch, Viagra: The Pill That Revived Sex, Or at Least Talking About It." *New York Times*, 3 May 1998, late ed.: section 4, p. 3
1,199
Week in Review—Sunday

Nordheimer, Jon. "Some Couples Find Viagra a Home Wrecker." *New York Times*, 10 May 1998, late ed.: section 9, p. 2
1,758
Style—Sunday

Pear, Robert. "White House Plans Medicaid Coverage of Viagra by States." *New York Times*, 28 May 1998, late ed.: A1
1,069
National Desk—Thursday

Pear, Robert. "New York and Wisconsin Will Defy Federal Directive to Provide Viagra Through Medicaid." *New York Times*, 3 July 1998, late ed.: A12
961
National Desk—Friday

Peterson, Melody. "Pfizer, Facing Competition from Other Drug Makers, Looks for a Younger Market for Viagra." *New York Times*, 13 February 2002, late ed.: C10
1,005
Business/Financial Desk—Wednesday

Rich, Frank. "Electric Kool-Aid Viagra." *New York Times*, 12 August 1998, late ed.: A19
748
Editorial Desk—Wednesday

Riordan, Teresa. "Viagra's Success Has Brought to Light a Second Big Market for Sexual Dysfunction Therapies: Women." *New York Times*, 26 April 1999, late ed.: C6
775
Business/Financial Desk—Monday

Steinhauer, Jennifer. "Viagra's Other Side Effect: Upsets in Many a Marriage." *New York Times*, 23 June 1998, late ed.: F1
1,731
Science Desk—Tuesday

Tuller, David. "Experts Fear a Risky Recipe: Viagra, Drugs and H.I.V." *New York Times,* 16 October 2001, late ed.: F5
1,236
Health & Fitness—Tuesday

Tuller, David. "Competitors to Viagra Get Ready to Rumble." *New York Times,* 23 September 2002, late ed.: F7
699
Men's Health—Monday

Weinstein, Michael M. "Fallen Taboo: Frank Talk on Viagra Is About Cost." *New York Times,* 11 July 1998, late ed.: D1
1,118
Business/Financial Desk—Saturday

WuDunn, Sheryl. "Japan's Tale of Two Pills: Viagra and Birth Control." *New York Times,* 27 April 1999, late ed.: F1
1,438
Science Desk—Tuesday

Newsweek (17)

Author, title, magazine, day, month, and year, page
Word count
Section

Adler, Jerry. "Take a Pill and Call Me Tonight." *Newsweek,* 4 May 1998: 48
952
Business

Breslau, Karen. "The 'Sexstasy' Craze." *Newsweek,* 3 June 2002: 30
478
National

Cowley, Geoffrey. "Attention: Aging Men." *Newsweek,* 16 September 1996: 68
3,778
Lifestyle

Cowley, Geoffrey. "Rebuilding the Male Machine." *Newsweek,* 17 November 1997: 66
1,254
Lifestyle

Cowley, Geoffrey. "Is Sex a Necessity?" *Newsweek*, 11 May 1998: 62
928
Society

Cowley, Geoffrey. "Looking Beyond Viagra." *Newsweek*, 24 April 2000: 77
837
Health

Dogar, Rana. "Just How Safe Is Sex?" *Newsweek*, 22 June 1998: 42
528
Special Report

Itoi, Kay. "The Great Viagra Emergency." *Newsweek*, 8 February 1999: 39
974
International

Kalb, Claudia. "Still Sexy After All These Years." *Newsweek*, 3 April 2000: 74
516
Special Report

Leland, John. "A Pill for Impotence?" *Newsweek*, 17 November 1997: 62
2,228
Lifestyle

Leland, John. "Not Quite Viagra Nation." *Newsweek*, 26 October 1998: 68
726
Society

Leland, John. "Let's Talk About Sex." *Newsweek*, 4 January 1999: 62
2,029
Perspectives 1998/Story of the Year

Leland, John. "Bad News in the Bedroom." *Newsweek*, 22 February 1999:
47
726
Society

Leland, John, Claudia Kalb, and Nadine Joseph. "The Science of Women
Sex." *Newsweek*, 29 May 2000: 48
2,531
Science and Technology

McGinn, Daniel and Anjali Arora. "Viagra's Hothouse." *Newsweek*, 21
December 1998: 44
1,839
Business

Seibert, Sam. "The Culture of Viagra." *Newsweek,* 22 June 1998: 39
2,140
Special Report

Watson, Russell. "The Globe Is Gaga for Viagra." *Newsweek,* 22 June 1998:
    44
1,503
International

U.S. News & World Report (11)

Author, title, magazine, day, month, and year, page
Word count
Section

Brink, Susan. "The Drugs of Choice." *U.S. News & World Report,* 16
    November 1998: 82
785
Health

Brink, Susan. "A New Definition of Safe Sex?" *U.S. News & World Report,*
    11 January 1999: 66
534
Health

Brink, Susan. "The Do or Die Decade." *U.S. News & World Report,* 11
    March 2002: 60
3,524
Health & Medicine

Brophy Marcus, Mary. "Aging of AIDS." *U.S. News & World Report,* 12
    August 2002: 40
1,222
Health & Medicine

Brownlee, Shannon, Stacey Schultz, Sheila Kaplan, Gary Cohen, Penny
    Loeb, and Susan Brink. "Dying for Sex." *U.S. News & World Report,*
    11 January 1999: 62
2,962
Health

Comarow, Avery. "Viagra Tale." *U.S. News & World Report,* 4 May 1998:
    64
1,623
Health

Fischman, Josh. "Do Men Experience Menopause?" *U.S. News & World Report*, 30 July 2001: 47
475
Science & Ideas

Herbert, Wray. "Not Tonight, Dear." *U.S. News & World Report*, 22 February 1999: 57
1,643
Science & Ideas

Hobson, Katherine. "The Doctor's Got Your Goat." *U.S. News & World Report*, 26 August 2002: 63
891
Special Issue: Hoaxes

McGraw, Dan. "A Pink Viagra?" *U.S. News & World Report*, 5 October 1998: 54
475
Business & Technology

Schultz, Stacey. "When Sex Pales, Women May Need More Than Viagra." *U.S. News & World Report*, 26 June 2000: 64
1,259
Health

Pfizer's Promotional *Materials*

Television Commercials (4)

(1999) "Bob Dole."
(2001) "Mark Martin."
(2002) "Rafael Palmeiro."
(2002) "Joe."

Product Brochures and Pamphlets (8)

Pfizer. "The *New* Facts of Life," Brochure HX003X98, May 1998.
Pfizer. "Prime Time," Brochure HC178Y99, April 1999.
Pfizer. "Start Something All Over Again," Brochure HC180Y99, April 1999.
Pfizer. "What Every Man (and Woman) Should Know about Erectile Dysfunction," Brochure HX062Y99A, July 1999.
Pfizer. "Real People Real Results," Brochure HC616Y00, December 2000.
Pfizer. "Mark Martin Wants to Know . . . Are You Up to the Challenge?" Brochure HC152R01, April 2001.
Pfizer. "Step Up to the Plate," Brochure VG1110647A, April 2002.
Pfizer. "Viagra Stories," Brochure VG115896A, October 2002.

Viagra Magazine (4)

Pfizer. *Voices*. Magazine HC122A01, Spring/April 2001.
Pfizer. *LifeDrive*. Magazine HC369B01, Fall/August 2001.
Pfizer. *LifeDrive*. Magazine VG107535, Summer/April 2002.
Pfizer. *LifeDrive*. Magazine VG117615, Winter/October 2002.

Promotional Videos (3)

Pfizer. "The *New* Facts of Life," Promotional Video HX728F97, May 1998.
Pfizer. "What Every Man (and Woman) Should Know about Erectile Dysfunction," Promotional Video HX117Y99, March 1999.
Pfizer. "Real People Real Stories," Promotional Video HC613F00, December 2000.

Print Advertisements (4)

Pfizer. "Finally, Directions Your Patients Are Willing to Ask For," Advertisement VG103745, *JAMA*.
Pfizer. "How Did Viagra Become a Proven Standard in ED?" Advertisement *JAMA*.
Pfizer. "The One You Know," Advertisement VG115327, *JAMA*.
Pfizer. "Your Patients Are Looking for Your Help," Advertisement HC521A01; *JAMA*.

Advertising Premium (1)

Katzenstein, Larry. *Viagra: The Remarkable Story of the Discovery and Launch.* Book HX377R99. New York: CMD Publishing, 2001.

otes

Chapter 1

1. Advice can take many forms. In Act II, Scene 1 of Shakespeare's *Macbeth,* for example, a porter provides Macduff with the following admonition regarding alcohol and its affects on sexual function: "[I]t provokes desire, but it takes away the performance." In March 2004 at a photography exhibit at the Cultural Center of Chicago, I observed a piece of Fazal Sheikh's titled "To Cure Impotence." His photograph of a chicken is accompanied by the following text (supplied by Brazilian farmers):

   First catch a free range chicken. Cut the large claws from its back feet and roast them. Then, put the powdered claws into a liter of white wine. After nine days, serve a glass of wine to the person at lunch and again at dinner. Note: The person who is taking it should know what it is for.

2. Similar injectable drugs include papaverine and alprostadil. Alprostadil has since been developed in pellet form. The pellet, prescribed under the trade name Muse, is inserted into the urethra where it dissolves.
3. Actually, Pfizer's stock began to swell as early as the summer of 1997, in *anticipation* of Viagra's success.
4. Levitra (vardenafil) is manufactured by Bayer/GlaxoSmithKline and Cialis (tadalafil) is manufactured by Lilly Icos.
5. From the Pharma Marketing Network website: http://www.pharma-mkting.com/news/pmn34-article04.html. Retrieved July 8, 2004.
6. The generic name for Viagra is sildenafil citrate. When discussing its laboratory development, I'll use this generic name. But because the trade name Viagra has become a household word, I'm inclined to take advantage of that familiarity when referring to the drug generally.
7. And at a teaching workshop I attended, the facilitator was having difficulty stowing the projection screen after a PowerPoint presentation. "Does anybody know how to get this up?" she asked the group. "Try Viagra!" joked an enthusiastic participant,

thrilled by his ability to take part in the burgeoning cottage industry of erection humor.

8. The National Institute of Health Consensus Development Panel on Impotence proposed the name change in 1993. This will be explored more fully in chapter 4.

9. Harrison's paper, now considered a classic and frequently anthologized, was first published in a special issue of the *Journal of Social Issues,* 34, 1, Spring 1978.

10. Ingrid Waldron's work has been integral in illustrating how gender differences are responsible for the disparity in men's and women's health. With regard to the United States, Waldron (1983) has demonstrated that males as a group (1) have a higher mortality rate than women at all ages; (2) engage in more health-risking behaviors such as smoking and drinking; and (3) take more physical risks—as evidenced by poor driving habits (including a disparity in seatbelt use and participating in aggressive behavior known as "road rage"), the use of guns, and dangerous recreational activities. Furthermore, Waldron (1991) identified the greater exposure men have to occupational danger as a critical component in accounting for differences in men's and women's health experiences.

Will Courtenay (2000a) examines the factors that influence men's health. He concludes that men who adopt traditional beliefs about masculinity are at an increased risk for a variety of health problems. Citing poor health *behaviors* as the factors contributing to the disparity between American men and women in life expectancy, injury, and illness, Courtenay argues that most of these factors are both attributed to men's sex role socialization *and* modifiable. In another of his articles proposing a relational theory for men's health, Courtenay (2000b) concludes simply, "the social practices that undermine men's health are often signifiers for masculinity" (1385).

Toni Schofield et al. (2000) concur that "social disadvantages produce the margins of difference between men's and women's health patterns" (249). They advocate a "gender-relations approach to health." Such an approach emphasizes the way social environments contribute to the utilization of health resources for some while others find resources constraining and limiting.

Other contemporary research addressing men's health concerns focuses on how illness affects masculine identity (Charmaz 1995; Gerschick and Miller 1994; Watson 2000).

11. Gayle Rubin (1975) coined the term "the sex/gender system" to refer to the way societies organize the biological designations of male/female into social expectations labeled masculine/feminine. Teresa de Lauretis (1987) states emphatically that "the construction of gender is both the product and process of its representation" (5). In his summary of Judith Butler's (1989) *Gender Trouble,* communication studies scholar John Sloop (2000) remarks that "the project of a political genealogy of gender becomes one of noting the forces that turn contingent acts into naturalistic necessities" (131).

In this book, I use "masculine/masculinity" to refer to gendered behavior (performed by both people and institutions) that is problematically traditional, as well as a configuration of practices by male-assigned bodies. These practices may be performed consciously or unconsciously through interpersonal relationships and both physical and fiscal habits.

12. In a revised edition of his book *The New Male Sexuality* (1999), Bernie Zilbergeld includes an appendix that lists over *150* prescription drugs known to have detri-

mental effects on male sexual function. I wonder how many are manufactured by Pfizer?

13. *Guns, Germs, and Steel: The Fates of Human Societies* (1997).
14. "Constructing Normalcy: The Bell Curve, the Novel, and the Invention of the Disabled Body in the 19th Century" (1997).
15. Novelist John Irving offers this assessment in *The World According to Garp* (1976):

> He was still only half dressed—an attitude that was, perhaps . . . the most compromising for men: when they were not one thing and also not another. A woman half dressed seemed to have some power, but a man was simply not as handsome as when he was naked, and not as secure as when he was clothed (361).

16. *The Male Body: A New Look at Men in Public and in Private* (1998), p. 44.
17. For an analysis of male body image and male genitalia, including jokes and visual representation in Hollywood films, see Peter Lehman's *Running Scared: Masculinity and the Representation of the Male Body* (1993). Lehman suggests that, in a patriarchal culture, "dominant representations of phallic masculinity . . . depend on keeping the male body and the genitals out of the critical spotlight" (28). In a later essay (2001), Lehman argues that the polarity of male movie stars in popular films between "pitiable and/or comic collapse" (e.g., Woody Allen) and "phallic spectacle" (e.g., Arnold Schwarzeneggar) corresponds to soft/hard. Furthermore, in its structuring of masculine types, this representation is in some ways similar to the virgin/whore dichotomy women face.
18. The ways in which Pfizer has expanded the definition of "erectile dysfunction" is a primary focus of chapter 4.
19. *Men in Groups* (1969).
20. I provide an in-depth summary of masculinity studies and male roles and stereotypes in chapter 2.
21. *Sexuality and the Field of Vision* (1986).
22. "The Social Construction of Normality" (1999).
23. Gayle Rubin writes, "Disputes over sexual behavior often become vehicles for displacing social anxieties" (quoted in Parker and Aggleton 1999, p. 143).
24. *Sex Is Not a Natural Act* (1995).
25. *Stigma* (1963), p. 5.
26. The use of the term "scripts" to describe how humans enact sexual conduct is adopted from symbolic interactionist sociologists William Simon and John Gagnon (1984).
27. *Human Sexuality: Feelings and Functions* (1979).
28. *Gender Trouble: Feminism and the Subversion of Identity* (1990) and *Bodies That Matter: On the Discursive Limits of "Sex"* (1993).
29. *Presence and Desire: Essays on Gender, Sexuality, Performance* (1993), p. 6.
30. "Performance as Metaphor" (1996), p. 2.
31. More specifically, Haraway writes, "Their *boundaries* materialize in social interaction. Boundaries are drawn by mapping practices; 'objects' do not preexist as such" (595, emphasis original). In "Situated Knowledges: The Science Question in Feminism and the Privilege of Partial Perspective" (1988).
32. "Beyond the Text: Toward a Performative Cultural Politics," (1995). For a useful summary, see also Elizabeth Bell's essay "Weddings and Pornography" (1999).

33. *The Presentation of Self in Everyday Life* (1959).
34. *The Presentation of Self in Everyday Life* (1959), p. 15.
35. See especially Pollock (1995) and Sayre (1990).
36. Victor Turner's analysis of the social drama is especially concerned with "making." Using ritual as his primary element of investigation, Turner pays particular attention to liminal space, the interstices that mark the place of transformation of identity, whether individual or collective. Turner's model of the social drama is composed of four developmental stages: (1) the *breach* is signaled by the interruption of normal life by a violation of expectations; (2) the *crisis* follows when the complexity of the breach is identified; (3) the *redress* is an attempt at sense-making and typically includes some sort of ritualized response that serves to temper the peculiarities of the crisis; and (4) resolution is sought by way of (a) reintegration of opposing forces or (b) irreparable schism—a recognition of permanent detachment from the way things were. It is the redressive stage that Turner identifies as the liminal space "that has the most to do with the genesis and sustentation of cultural dramas" (quoted in Conquergood 1983). While Turner's notion of performance from a cultural perspective helps bridge the gap between individual sense-making and the larger societal outcomes individual practice reflects, it is beyond the scope of this study to include those connections here. My use of performance in this study is primarily concerned with a Goffmanian "doing" in everyday life. Nonetheless, it is worth pointing out the tiresome descriptor of perpetual male angst—"crisis"—operates in Turner's drama in a significant way. What Viagra promises is a redressive action that everlastingly postpones a resolution.
37. *Presence and Desire: Essays on Gender, Sexuality, Performance* (1993), p. 95.
38. *Performance Studies* (2003).
39. "Foreword" (1998), p. xxv.
40. In a popular undergraduate course I teach titled "Communication, Gender, and Identity," I have my students ask their parents to describe how masculinity and femininity were performed in previous generations and in other parts of the United States (and around the world). Responses point to favorite activities, clothing choices, hairstyles, and a range of other behaviors and demonstrate not only how definitions of gender are constantly changing and are (frequently) culturally specific, but also how these definitions are marked on the body. Resonant examples are, of course, tattooing and piercing. I find it fascinating how both the artwork itself and its placement on the body have very specific "rules" for masculinity and femininity, rules that will no doubt change.
41. *Unmaking Mimesis* (1997), p. 47.
42. "Performativity, Parody, Politics" (1999), p. 201.
43. "Bodies and Biology" (1999), p. 47.
44. "Bodies, Identities, Feminisms" (1999), p. 201.
45. *A Mind of Its Own* (2001), p. 256.
46. Leonore Tiefer (1979) explains:

A major source of misinformation has to do with what is considered "normal," in terms of frequency of sexual activity, techniques used, presence of fantasy, differences between men and women, and what are thought to be unconventional practices. . . . The guilt and fear associated with desiring or engaging in unconventional sexual activity probably does far more harm than any of the acts themselves. Educating people about the range of sexual possibilities, the cultural differences in definitions of normalcy and the inadequacy of definitive data on these matters usually has a positive effect (101).

47. *An Archaeology of Knowledge* (1972).
48. *Slow Motion: Changing Masculinities, Changing Men* (1990), pp. 92–93.
49. *Women and Men Speaking* (1981).
50. *Keywords: A Vocabulary of Culture and Society* (1976), p. 13.
51. I chose advertising to consumers for two reasons: (1) the method of advertising pharmaceuticals directly to the target market (as opposed to targeting the physicians who write prescriptions which does, of course, continue) is still in its infancy; and (2) advertising reveals a great deal about what the dominant discourse of medicine presumes the public knows/wants to know about sexual health.
52. I chose to analyze the information Pfizer intends for those healthcare providers who ultimately prescribe Viagra because this "backstage" material reveals all kinds of expectations and assumptions regarding the doctor–patient relationship.
53. *Revisioning Women, Health, and Healing* (1999), p. 18.

Chapter 2

1. For the formative text see Peter Berger and Thomas Luckmann's *The Social Construction of Reality* (1966).
2. Drawing from structural linguistics, Michel Foucault's work argues for the recognition that material bodies, too, are subject to discursively constructed systems of power. *Discipline and Punish* (1977) explains how bodies become "docile" through the discursive structures that impose "constraints, prohibitions, or obligations" (136). For Foucault (1980), discursive systems operate as "regimes of truth," establishing mechanisms by which members of a particular society (1) recognize some discourses as true and others as false; (2) identify acceptable methods of discovery while others are labeled suspect; and (3) grant status to certain individuals and institutions even as others are denied voice and credibility. In our society, scientific discourse is valued above all others.
3. This term is from Anthony Gidden's *The Constitution of Society* (1984), p. 43.
4. Social problems and sexual problems are socially constructed in terms of how causality is attributed and what solutions are recommended. It should be noted that among social constructionists, opinions differ on what phenomena might be socially constructed (Vance 1995). Moreover, Ian Hacking (1999) asks that we examine what is done when phenomena are labeled social constructions—how do we go about disrupting assumptions and routines? The theory of social construction insists that we acknowledge human "authorship" in the construction of institutions and the knowledge(s) they create. Investigations over the last twenty years of the phenomenon known as "intersexed" births have questioned even the previously immutable biological "realities" of male and female. Indeed, one in two thousand babies are born with ambiguous or abnormal genitalia. As newborns, they are subjected to surgery in order to better fit them into our societal classifications of male and female (Phillips 2001). Although survivors of this neonatal surgery raise compelling questions as to the ethics of this practice, the ideology apparent in both the clinical management of the intersexed and biomedical sexology is vainly essentialist (Fausto-Sterling 1995; Irvine 1990).

5. *Stigma* (1963), p. 128.
6. Several important studies surfaced even earlier. Lionel Tiger's *Men in Groups* (1969) looked at the group processes and social behavior of men as collectives, suggesting that what compels some men to violent competition, defense, and attack stems from evolutionary origins. Warren Farrell's *The Liberated Man* (1974) was a look at the dynamics of male–female relationships as informed by the persistence of economic, physical, and emotional burdens defining masculinity. Joseph Pleck's *The Myth of Masculinity* (1981) critiqued the myth of the traditional male sex role and advanced instead the idea of a nonnormative masculine self. These two options, Pleck explains, are inextricably related. The very expectations of society—articulated or imagined—"[prevent] individuals who violate the traditional role for their sex from challenging it" (160).
7. See also Kohn (1986).
8. See, for example, Nancy Chodorow, *The Reproduction of Mothering: Psychoanalysis and the Sociology of Gender* (1978).
9. *Sex Is Not a Natural Act* (1995), p. 141.
10. *Masculinities* (1995).
11. *Contingency, Hegemony, Universality* (2000).
12. For example, in the comedy *Meet the Parents* (2002), Ben Stiller's character is subjected to the scrutiny of his fiancée's family when he reveals that nursing is his career choice.
13. Candace West and Sarah Fenstermaker (1995) follow up previous work on gender as "interactional" and "emergent" by developing a perspective of gender that includes considerations of race and class as organizing principles and "mechanisms for producing social inequality" (9). In an earlier essay, West and Don Zimmerman (1987) demonstrate the contingent quality of "doing gender" by describing it as "the activity of managing situated conduct in light of normative conceptions and attitudes and activities appropriate for one's sex category" (14). The quality of this definition suggests an aspect of Michel Foucault's (1977) model of the panopticon: we police our behavior in anticipation of societal approval whether or not there is evidence of a watchful eye. Theoretical descriptions of oppression as multiple and interlocking lead West and Fenstermaker to amend earlier arguments of gender as "situated." As they attempt to avoid privileging one form of oppression over another, however, they privilege "*all three* systems of domination" (my emphasis)— gender, race, and class—without regard to any and all other forms of oppression such as physical ability, age, education, sexual preference, and language barriers. They do, however, construct a model that can accommodate an unlimited inventory of conditions. This experiential framework can begin to account for how these variables are perceived and attributed by different people at different times in different places. This is a far more useful tool than creating a Venn diagram of demographic types that assumes all people falling in the same intersecting circles have similar responses to inequality or privilege (or desires or fantasies or exigencies).
14. "Identity Dilemmas of Chronically Ill Men" (1995).
15. "The Social Construction of Sexuality" (1995), p. 42.
16. *Discipline and Punish* (1977).
17. Susan Bordo (1999b) elucidates the point:

When I first read Foucault, I remember thinking: "finally, a male theorist who understands Western culture as neither a conversation among talking heads nor a series of military adventures, but as a history of the body!" . . . for Foucault, modern power (as opposed to sovereign power) is non-authoritarian, non-conspiratorial, and indeed non-orchestrated; yet it nonetheless produces and normalizes bodies to serve prevailing relations of dominance and subordination. (250)

18. A homosexual "identity," according to some theorists (Weeks 1977; D'Emilio and Freedman 1988), has evolved only since the late nineteenth century. Other theorists (Boswell 1994; Whitam 1983) suspect that identities other than what we in the twenty-first century consider to be traditional heterosexuality have always existed, across cultures.

19. *The Gender of Sexuality* (1998), p. 24.

20. *The Gender of Sexuality* (1998), p. 25.

21. In *Manhood in America* (1996) Michael Kimmel points out how, in the nineteenth century, succumbing to the temptation of masturbation was considered a weakness. According to medical experts of the time, writes Kimmel, "conservation of sperm was the single best way to conserve energy for other, more productive uses" (45). A similar understanding of ejaculation as a "loss of control" persists in many cultures. A Dire Straits song, "Lady Writer," has always signaled a different kind of "loss" for me: "Just the way that her hair fell down around her face/and I recall my fall from grace."

22. *Disorders of Desire* (1990).

23. Quoted in Irvine (1990), pp. 60–61.

24. *Disorders of Desire* (1990), p. 54.

25. *Disorders of Desire* (1990), p. 76.

26. *Disorders of Desire* (1990), p. 91.

27. *Disorders of Desire* (1990), p. 128.

28. An important component in Irvine's critique is her analysis of sex therapists William Hartman and Marilyn Fithian. Representing the humanist branch of sexology, therapists like Hartman and Fithian employed a great deal of "experiential and experimental technique," opening the door for criticism by scientific sexologists who objected to the surrogates, nudity, and touch between therapist and client that some humanist sexologists utilized in their practice (120–124). Without regard to claims of effectiveness, the objections held by scientific sexologists in this area were likely representative of a self-defined commitment to respectability. And feminists are quick to point out that in these scenarios, the peer pressure and "vulnerability to expert authority" is rife with questions about power and its abuses. In the humanist sexologist's domain, contends Irvine, "sexism and exploitation can masquerade as sexual liberation" (124–126).

29. Indeed, the search for a "third" approach is necessary and consistent with much of feminist theory's project of questioning the existence of binaries.

30. *Disorders of Desire* (1990), p. 137.

31. *Disorders of Desire* (1990), p. 136.

32. *Disorders of Desire* (1990), p. 139.

33. *Disorders of Desire* (1990), p. 141.

34. "Melancholy Gender" (1995), p. 24.

35. *Sex Is Not a Natural Act* (1995).

36. *Sex Is Not a Natural Act* (1995), p. 109.

37. See, for example, Ludmilla Jordanova, *Sexual Visions: Images of Gender in Science and Medicine between the Eighteenth and Twentieth Centuries* (1989).
38. Donna Haraway (1988) writes, "Feminist objectivity is about limited location and situated knowledge, not about transcendence and splitting of subject and object. It allows us to become answerable for what we learn how to see" (583).
39. *Sex Is Not a Natural Act* (1995), pp. 99–100.
40. *The Hite Report* (1976).
41. *Sex Is Not a Natural Act* (1995), p. 138.
42. *Sex Is Not a Natural Act* (1995), p. 136.
43. *Sex Is Not a Natural Act* (1995), p. 136.
44. *Sex Is Not a Natural Act* (1995), p. 114.
45. *Sex Is Not a Natural Act* (1995), p. 141.
46. *Sex Is Not a Natural Act* (1995), p. 141.
47. *Sex Is Not a Natural Act* (1995), p. 144.
48. *Sex Is Not a Natural Act* (1995), p. 142.
49. *Sex Is Not a Natural Act* (1995), p. 199.
50. *Sex Is Not a Natural Act* (1995), p. 143.
51. Londa Schiebinger (1989) chronicles the historical development of anatomical theories of the body to demonstrate how female bodies were classified as inferior to normalized male bodies. Barbara Ehrenreich and Deirdre English (1978) criticize biomedicine's standards for defining normalcy in health through the generic patient "he." In these and other studies, the idea of a universal body was criticized as reductionist and problematically rudimentary. As a result, it wasn't long before proponents of the new men's studies also looked at how a homogenetic approach to bodies and medicine could compromise individual notions of health and well-being. And while it is important to recognize that most medical research before 1970 focused almost exclusively on a universal male body, contemporary research on men's health from a gender-relations perspective remains scarce (Riska 2002).
52. "Reconstructing Masculinity and Sexuality" (2001), p. 301.
53. *Slow Motion* (1990), p. 212.
54. *Slow Motion* (1990), p. 219.
55. *Sex Is Not a Natural Act* (1995), p. 156.
56. *The Magic Mountain* (1927/1969), p. 179.
57. "Identifying Ideological Seams" (1986), p. 109.
58. *Disease and Representation* (1988), p. 4.
59. *Men's Health and Illness* (1995).
60. See especially Daly (1978) and Ehrenreich and English (1974).
61. National Organization for Men Against Sexism, "Statement of Principles" (1991).
62. Lynn Segal, *Slow Motion* (1990), and Robert Connell, *Masculinities* (1995).
63. See especially Kimmel (1990), Klein (1986), Messner (1987), and Sabo (1985).
64. See Sabo and Gordon (1995).
65. *Men's Health and Illness* (1995).
66. Conversely, Elaine Cameron and Jon Bernardes (1998) ask why these traditional male sex roles are not an advantage to men in the U.S. healthcare system. That is, couldn't traditional roles for masculinity be a *resource* in negotiating health?
67. "From Type A Man to Hardy Man" (2002).
68. The clinical trials Pfizer Pharmaceuticals conducted for Viagra also *required* a stable heterosexual relationship as a requirement for participation.

69. See especially Messerschmidt (2000), Savran (1998), Staples (1995), and Waldron (1995).
70. *Sex Is Not a Natural Act* (1995), pp. 162–163.
71. "Body Matters" (1999), p. 107.
72. "Ideology and Ideological State Apparatuses" (1970).
73. "Performativity, Parody, Politics" (1999), p. 195.

Chapter 3

1. For the specific criteria I established for choosing these stories, see Appendix A. For a complete list of these news stories, see Appendix B.
2. Cowley, Geoffrey. "Attention, Aging Men," *Newsweek* 16 September 1996; p. 68.
3. Martin, Douglas. "Thanks a Bunch, Viagra; The Pill That Revived Sex, Or at Least Talking About It," *New York Times* 3 May 1998; Section 4; p. 3; Column 1.
4. Steinhauer, Jennifer. "Viagra's Other Side Effect," *New York Times* 23 June 1998; Section F; p. 1; Column 1.
5. Rich, Frank. "Electric Kool-Aid Viagra," *New York Times* 12 August 1998; Section A; p. 19; Column 1.
6. Itoi, Kay. "The Great Viagra Emergency," *Newsweek* 8 February 1999; p. 68.
7. Herbert, Wray. "Not Tonight, Dear," *U.S. News & World Report* 22 February 1999; p. 57.
8. Nelkin, Dorothy. *Selling Science: How the Press Covers Science and Technology* (1995).
9. And yet these sobriquets of technologized sexuality are not new. Literature and film had anticipated the modernization of intimacy in a variety of forms. Aldous Huxley gave us the soma tablet in *Brave New World* (1946/1962), Roger Vadim's *Barbarella* (1968) suggested the exaltation transference pill, and Woody Allen's *Sleeper* (1973) introduced the orgasmatron. More recently, Margaret Atwood reveals the orgy pill "BlyssPluss" in her dystopia *Oryx and Crake* (2003). Furthermore, cartoon characters—Underdog and Popeye, for example—have relied on both chemical and organic supplements ("super energy pills" and spinach, respectively) in order to augment their physical strength, which, in our culture, translates into sexual capital among males. In order to transform into Underdog (and save the world from Simon Bar Sinister), Shoeshine Boy needed a boost:

> The secret compartment of my ring I fill
> With my Underdog super energy pill
> When Sweet Polly's in trouble I am not slow
> It's hip, hip, hip and away I go

As a faithful fan of Underdog (whose voice was supplied by none other than Wally Cox!), I readily gleaned that if a blue-collar bootblack like Shoeshine Boy was to garner the affections of ace television reporter Sweet Polly Purebread, he would surely need chemical enhancement. Likewise, Popeye the Sailor—although his method was more organic—required larger muscles to counter the appeal of Bluto in his quest for Olive Oyl. Not only do these fictional surrogates for traditional desire make statements about the plusses and minuses of a medicalized future, they have arguably influenced both the pharmaceutical industry's impulse toward medically enhanced sexual relations and the public's acceptance of them.

10. "The *New York Times* Looks at One Block in Harlem" (1998), p. 239.
11. Gitlin, Todd. *The Whole World Is Watching: Mass Media in the Making and Unmaking of the New Left* (1980).
12. The research of media analysts Eleanor Singer and Phyllis Endreny (1993) is particularly valuable in pointing this out.
13. *Gendered Lives: Communication, Gender, and Culture* (1999), p. 322.
14. *Communicating About Health: Current Issues and Perspectives* (2000).
15. *Sex Is Not a Natural Act* (1995).
16. *The Man Question: Visions of Subjectivity in Feminist Theory* (1993), pp. 25–27.
17. Cowley, Geoffrey. "Attention, Aging Men," *Newsweek* 16 September 1996; p. 68.
18. Leland, John. "A Pill for Impotence," *Newsweek* 17 November 1997; p. 62.
19. Martin, Douglas. "Thanks a Bunch Viagra; The Pill That Revived Sex, Or at Least Talking About It," *New York Times* 3 May 1998; Section 4; p. 3; Column 1.
20. Comarow, Avery and Mary Brophy Marcus. "Viagra Tale," *U.S. News & World Report* 4 May 1998; p. 64.
21. Brody, Jane E. "Sour Note in the Viagra Symphony," *New York Times* 19 May 1998; Section F; p. 7; Column 4.
22. Two other companies have tapped into this idea of "natural" to hawk their products on cable television. One is called "Enzyte" and features a grinning idiot named "Bob" who promotes a pill that promises "natural male enhancement." Of course it is not immediately clear what "enhancement" refers to—only that since Bob started taking it, he's "steppin' large and laughin' easy." The Enzyte commercials appear constantly on Comedy Central. By comparison, I first saw the ads for "Avlimil" on the Lifetime Channel. A nonpharmaceutical like Enzyte, Avlimil promises to "help restore a woman's natural balance." The implication behind the commercial is that today's women, overworked and underappreciated, can become "refreshed and alert" simply by taking Avlimil daily, allowing them to better "enjoy the physical and emotional pleasures of being with their partners." Unlike Viagra, which is taken an hour before sexual activity, Avlimil is taken daily—suggesting that women *always* need to be ready for sex in case their partners (read "husbands") are. As expected, *Saturday Night Live* targeted all of these commercials (but especially Viagra) with Amy Poehler's parody, "Dr. Porkenheimer's Boner Juice," which aired October 4, 2004 on NBC.
23. In fact, it was *because of* implant surgery that researchers acquired the penile tissue needed to develop a better understanding of how blood is absorbed by the penis at the time of erection (see Friedman 2001).
24. *Philosophy of Literary Form* (1973), p. 174.
25. *Philosophy of Literary Form* (1973), p. 171.
26. Leland, John. "A Pill for Impotence," *Newsweek* 17 November 1997; p. 62.
27. Comarow, Avery and Mary Brophy Marcus. "Viagra Tale," *U.S. News & World Report* 4 May 1998; p. 64.
28. See especially Douglas Martin, "Thanks a Bunch Viagra; The Pill That Revived Sex, Or at Least Talking About It," *New York Times* 3 May 1998; Section 4; Page 3; Column 1; and Stacey Schultz, "When Sex Pales, Women May Need More Than Viagra," *U.S. News & World Report* 26 June 2000; p. 64.
29. Steinhauer, Jennifer. "Viagra's Other Side Effect," *New York Times* 23 June 1998; Section F; p. 1; Column 1.
30. Brody, Jane E. "Sour Note in the Viagra Symphony," *New York Times* 19 May 1998; Section F; p. 7; Column 4.

In Ernest Hemingway's *The Sun Also Rises,* protagonist Jake Barnes has sustained a war wound that has rendered him impotent. This following excerpt demonstrates his reluctance for any sort of intimacy in the way described in the news stories above:

> She cuddled against me and I put my arm around her. She looked up to be kissed. She touched me with one hand and I put her hand away.
> "Never mind."
> "What's the matter? You sick?"
> "Yes."
> "Everybody's sick. I'm sick, too" (15–16).

31. *Stigma* (1963).
32. *Stigma* (1963), p. 94.
33. Or less. The section of this chapter focusing on political economy reveals the ease with which Viagra can be obtained online.
34. Leland, John. "A Pill for Impotence," *Newsweek* 17 November 1997; p. 62.
35. Herbert, Wray. "Not Tonight, Dear," *U.S. News & World Report* 22 February 1999; p. 57.
36. Leland, John. "A Pill for Impotence," *Newsweek* 17 November 1997; p. 62.
37. Leland, John. "Bad News in the Bedroom," *Newsweek* 22 February 1999; p. 47.
38. Leland, John. "The Science of Women Sex," *Newsweek* 29 May 2000; p. 48.
39. Leland, John. "The Science of Women Sex," *Newsweek* 29 May 2000; p. 48.
40. See, for example, Meyers and Seibold (1985), Ragsdale (1996), and Tannen (1990).
41. See Laumann et al. (1994).
42. See Shapiro and Kroeger (1991).
43. Schultz, Stacey. "When Sex Pales, Women May Need More Than Viagra," *U.S. News & World Report* 26 June 2000; p. 64.
44. Martin, Douglas. "Thanks a Bunch Viagra; The Pill That Revided Sex, Or at Least Talking About It," *New York Times* 3 May 1998; Section 4; p. 3; Column 1.
45. 1,758 words.
46. Nordheimer, John. "Some Couples May Find Viagra a Home Wrecker," *New York Times* 10 May 1998; Section 9; p. 2; Column 1.
47. "Struggling for a Self: Identity Levels of the Chronically Ill."
48. Annie Potts et al. (2003) examine how Viagra impacts women in their qualitative study involving in-depth interviews. The study reveals "experiences and concerns" of women whose partners use Viagra. This particular frame is developed as well in the following chapter, where I look at Pfizer's marketing materials.
49. Watson, Russell. "The Globe Is Gaga for Viagra," *Newsweek* 22 June 1998; p. 44.
50. Jennifer Fishman and Laura Mamo (2002) point out that when Bob Dole was pitching Viagra and used the term "partner" he was chastised by representatives from family values groups for raising the possibility of "alternative" users.
51. "In the Same Boat? The Gendered (In)experience of First Heterosex" (1996).
52. French feminist Luce Irigary, on the other hand, rightly points out in *The Speculum of the Other Woman* (1974) how the need to name a child after the male is in response to the *uncertainty* of fatherhood.
53. We meet nearly three dozen men in these articles who talk about their experience with erectile dysfunction and/or their experience taking Viagra. The average age of

these men is fifty-five; six men are under forty. They are, almost without exception, heterosexual. They are—when specifics are provided—overwhelmingly white-collar professionals. And if pseudonyms are supposed to reflect the spirit of the actual name, they seem to be overwhelmingly white. The aliases are, for example, Ron, Steve, Bob, Bill, Jack, John, Adam, and Mike.

54. See, for example, Kramarae (1981), Tannen (1990), and Wood (1999).
55. Tannen (1990), p. 77.
56. Hitt, Jack. "The Second Sexual Revolution," *New York Times Magazine* 20 February 2000; Section 6; pp. 36–37.
57. Cowley, Geoffrey. "Attention, Aging Men," *Newsweek* 16 September 1996; p. 68.
58. This theme continues in the rhetoric of Pfizer's publications and videos.
59. See Doyle (1983).
60. Nordheimer, John. "Some Couples May Find Viagra a Home Wrecker," *New York Times* 10 May 1998; Section 9; p. 2; Column 1.
61. Nordheimer, John. "Some Couples May Find Viagra a Home Wrecker," *New York Times* 10 May 1998; Section 9; p. 2; Column 1.
62. Steinhauer, Jennifer. "Viagra's Other Side Effect," *New York Times* 23 June 1998; Section F; p. 1; Column 1.
63. Steinhauer, Jennifer. "Viagra's Other Side Effect," *New York Times* 23 June 1998; Section F; p. 1; Column 1.
64. Leland, John. "A Pill for Impotence," *Newsweek* 17 November 1997; p. 62.
65. Hobson, Katherine. "The Doctor's Got Your Goat," *U.S. News & World Report* 26 August 2002; p. 63.
66. Steinhauer, Jennifer. "Viagra's Other Side Effect," *New York Times* 23 June 1998; Section F; p. 1; Column 1.
67. Brink, Susan. "The Do or Die Decade," *U.S. News & World Report* 11 March 2002; p. 60.
68. Martin, Douglas. "Thanks a Bunch Viagra; The Pill That Revived Sex, Or at Least Talking About It," *New York Times* 3 May 1998; Section 4; p. 3; Column 1.
69. Comarow, Avery and Mary Brophy Marcus. "Viagra Tale," *U.S. News & World Report* 4 May 1998; p. 64.
70. Martin, Douglas. "Thanks a Bunch Viagra; The Pill That Revived Sex, Or at Least Talking About It," *New York Times* 3 March 1998; Section 4; p. 3; Column 1.
71. Hitt, Jack. "The Second Sexual Revolution," *New York Times Magazine* 20 February 2000; Section 6; p. 36; Column 2.
72. *Studs, Tools, and the Family Jewels* (2001), p. 31.
73. WuDunn, Sheryl. "Japan's Tale of Two Pills: Viagra and Birth Control," *The New York Times* 27 April 1999, late ed.; p. F1.
74. Hitt, Jack. "The Second Sexual Revolution," *The New York Times* 20 February 2000, late ed.; Section 6; p. 34.
75. See, for example, Emily Martin, *The Woman in the Body: A Cultural Analysis of Reproduction* (1987).
76. See Josh Fishman's article in *U.S. News & World Report* (30 July 2001) and Geoffrey Cowley's article in *Newsweek* (16 September 1996). These articles also refer to Sheehy's "the unspeakable passage" and Diamond's "Male Menopause."
77. Steinhauer, Jennifer. "Viagra's Other Side Effect: Upsets in Many a Marriage," *The New York Times* 23 June 1998, late ed.; p. F1.
78. Cowley, Geoffrey. "Is Sex a Necessity?" *Newsweek* 11 May 1998; p. 62.

79. Brink, Susan. "The Do or Die Decade," *U.S. News & World Report* 11 March 2002; p. 60.

80. Doyle (1983).

81. Brink, Susan. "The Do or Die Decade," *U.S. News & World Report* 11 March 2002; p. 60.

82. *Slow Motion: Changing Masculinities, Changing Men* (1990), p. 61.

83. While general health costs of a "hypermasculine construction" (Courtenay 2000b) were discussed in chapter 2, this section examines specific costs and theorizes the driving force behind the construction of "risk" in news accounts.

84. With regard to less serious side effects, I find Pfizer's rhetoric in its promotional videos quite interesting. After listing the side effects (blue vision, nausea, headaches), the narrators chide, "Most men weren't bothered by the side effects enough to stop taking Viagra," as if to say, "If you were a *real* man you wouldn't let a little headache get in the way of your erection."

85. Brownlee, Shannon. "Dying for Sex," *U.S. News & World Report* 11 January 1999; p. 62.

86. McGinn, Daniel. "Viagra's Hothouse," *Newsweek* 21 December 1998; p. 44.

87. Martin, Douglas. "Thanks a Bunch Viagra; The Pill That Revived Sex, Or at Least Talking About It," *New York Times* 3 March 1998; Section 4; p. 3; Column 1.

88. Brody, Jane. "Sour Note in the Viagra Symphony," *New York Times* 19 May 1998; Section F; p. 7; Column 4.

89. Brownlee, Shannon. "Dying for Sex," *U.S. News & World Report* 11 January 1999; p. 62.

90. From the FDA website: http://www.fda.gov/cder/consumerinfo/viagra/ safety3.htm. Retrieved May 14, 2003:

    From the marketing of sildenafil citrate (Viagra) in late March through mid-November 1998, during which more than 6 million outpatient prescriptions (representing about 50 million tablets) were dispensed, the FDA received reports of 130 U.S. patients who died after having been prescribed this drug. Excluded were reports of 55 foreign patients, 35 with unverifiable information (from hearsay, rumor, the media, or unidentifiable reporters), and 22 with unconfirmed Viagra use.

91. Brownlee, Shannon. "Dying for Sex," *U.S. News & World Report* 11 January 1999; p. 62.

92. Brownlee, Shannon. "Dying for Sex," *U.S. News & World Report* 11 January 1999; p. 62.

93. Brownlee, Shannon. "Dying for Sex," *U.S. News & World Report* 11 January 1999; p. 62.

94. Brownlee, Shannon. "Dying for Sex," *U.S. News & World Report* 11 January 1999; p. 62.

95. Dogar, Rana. "Just How Safe Is Sex?" *Newsweek* 22 June 1998; p. 42.

96. Kolata, Gina. "6 Taking Viagra Die, but the FDA Draws No Conclusions," *New York Times* 23 May 1998; Section A; p. 8; Column 1.

97. Leland, John. "Not Quite Viagra Nation," *Newsweek* 26 October 1998; p. 68.

98. "Introduction," p. xxxix.

99. *The Rhetoric of Religion* (1970), pp. 44–46.

100. "Weddings and Pornography" (1999), p. 178.

101. The cultural cognizance of this risk was made clear in the 2003 film *Something's Gotta Give,* starring Jack Nicholson, Diane Keaton, Keanu Reeves, Frances McDormand, and Amanda Peet. In this film, Nicholson's character (a music industry executive) is romantically involved with a much younger woman (Peet). At the onset of an afternoon love-making session, Nicholson suffers a heart attack. In the emergency room, the physician (Reeves) asks Nicholson if he has "taken any Viagra today." Glancing over at Keaton, McDormand, and Peet, Nicholson responds, "I don't need Viagra." Reeves says that he needs to know because he has just started a nitrate drip which, in combination with Viagra, can be fatal. Nicholson responds to this news by violently yanking the IV from his arm. Although this scene was played for laughs, I wonder how it was received by those in the audience who *had* experienced problems with this combination. *Hollywood Homicide* (2003), starring Harrison Ford, also relies on the public's knowledge of Viagra.

102. Kirby, David. "Viagra Wants to Be (Taken) Alone," *New York Times* 3 May 1998; Section 14; p. 6; Column 4.

103. Kirby, David. "Viagra Wants to Be (Taken) Alone," *New York Times* 3 May 1998; Section 14; p. 6; Column 4.

104. Kirby, David. "Viagra Wants to Be (Taken) Alone," *New York Times* 3 May 1998; Section 14; p. 6; Column 4.

105. Tuller, David. "Experts Fear a Risky Recipe: Viagra, Drugs and HIV," *New York Times* 16 October 2001; Section F; p. 5; Column 2.

106. Tuller, David. "Experts Fear a Risky Recipe: Viagra, Drugs and HIV," *New York Times* 16 October 2001; Section F; p. 5; Column 2.

107. Tuller, David. "Experts Fear a Risky Recipe: Viagra, Drugs and HIV," *New York Times* 16 October 2001; Section F; p. 5; Column 2.

108. That Viagra is also contraindicated by protease inhibitors is almost lost here. Protease inhibitors are prescription drugs used to aggressively fight HIV. Quite simply, I am concerned that Pfizer develops a treatment for erectile dysfunction that disregards certain particular health needs of gay men (and others) *and* makes public statements that blatantly expose their assumptions about (and contempt for) gay sexual proclivities. Let's face it, Pfizer would never have let Viagra reach the market if it was contraindicated with, say, Lipitor.

109. Hitt, Jack. "The Second Sexual Revolution," *New York Times Magazine* 20 February 2000; Section 6; p. 50.

110. Breslau, Karen. "The 'Sexstasy' Craze," *Newsweek* 3 June 2002; p. 30.

111. Seibert, Sam. "The Culture of Viagra," *Newsweek* 22 June 1998; p. 39.

112. Watson, Russell. "The Globe Is Gaga for Viagra," *Newsweek* 22 June 1998; p. 44.

113. When the competing drug Cialis hit the market, I found it fascinating that Lilly Icos included a warning about priapism in its one-minute television commercial for the drug. Specifically, I think cautioning men about the possibility of a four-hour erection can be read two ways: as a caveat or as an enticement!

114. Seibert, Sam. "The Culture of Viagra," *Newsweek* 22 June 1998; p. 39.

115. Hitt, Jack. "The Second Sexual Revolution," *New York Times Magazine* 20 February 2000; Section 6; p. 50.

116. Brink, Susan. "The Do or Die Decade," *U.S. News & World Report* 11 March 2002; p. 60.

117. My sincere thanks to up-and-coming Burke scholar Angela Marie Day for insightful observations regarding hierarchy and guilt.

118. This topic will be covered in chapter 4.

119. Pfizer. "Start Something All Over Again," Pfizer HC180Y99 (April 1999); p. 9.

120. One might call Osterloh's version a "cock-and-bull" story. Interestingly, Leonore Tiefer makes similar claims about the hypercautious selection process that characterized the landmark studies of Masters and Johnson.

121. While the actual percentage of boys that play high school football is relatively small, football players do tend to represent hegemonic masculinity among the fourteen- to eighteen-year-old demographic. Among fourteen- to eighteen-year-old girls, however, those who cheer for football players—rather than those girls who are top athletes themselves—frequently signify the top of the girl's hierarchy.

122. Mitka, Mike. "Some Men Who Take Viagra Die—Why?" *Journal of the American Medical Association*. February 2, 2000; v. 283, n. 5, pp. 590, 593.

123. "Thrombosis: Viagra Deaths Explained by New Understanding of Platelet Clumping," *Heart Disease Weekly*. February 2, 2003; p. 24.
    The primary article was published in the journal *Cell*. See Li et al. (2003).

124. Leland, John. "Let's Talk About Sex," *Newsweek* 4 January 1999; p. 62.

125. I am indebted to feminist discourse theorist Kim Golombisky for pointing out to me *early* in this research process how Viagra and birth control are *not* parallel.

126. Singer-songwriter Alanis Morrisette employs a version of this metaphor when she suggests that we "swallow it down, the Jagged Little Pill" to deal with life's uncertainties.

127. Susan Brink reports in *U.S. News & World Report* (16 November 1998) that in the United States "2.4 billion prescriptions were dispensed in 1997, up 400 million prescriptions from 1993" (82).

128. Steinhauer, Jennifer. "Viagra's Other Side Effect: Upsets in Many a Marriage." *The New York Times* 23 June 1998; p. F1.

129. Hobson, Katherine. "The Doctor's Got Your Goat," *U.S. News & World Report* 26 August 2002; p. 63.

130. Brody, Jane. "Sour Note in the Viagra Symphony," *New York Times* 19 May 1998, late ed.; Section F; p. 7; Column 4.

131. Comarow, Avery. "Viagra Tale," *U.S. News & World Report* 4 May 1998; p. 64.

132. Adler, Jerry. "Take a Pill and Call Me Tonight," *Newsweek* 4 May 1998; p. 48.

133. Seibert, Sam. "The Culture of Viagra," *Newsweek* 22 June 1998; p. 39.

134. Brownlee, Shannon. "Dying for Sex," *U.S. News & World Report* 11 January 1999; p. 62.

135. Hitt, Jack. "The Second Sexual Revolution," *New York Times Magazine* 20 February 2000, late ed.; Section 6; p. 36.

136. Cowley, Geoffrey. "Is Sex a Necessity?" *Newsweek* 11 May 1998; p. 62.

137. Kalb, Claudia. "Still Sexy After All These Years," *Newsweek* 2 April 2000; p. 74.

138. McGinn, Daniel. "Viagra's Hothouse," *Newsweek* 21 December 1998; p. 44; and Cowley, Geoffrey. "Is Sex a Necessity?" *Newsweek* 11 May 1998; p. 62.

139. Pear, Robert. "White House Plans Medicaid Coverage of Viagra by States," *New York Times* 28 May 1998, late ed.; Section A; p. 1; Column 1.

140. Pear, Robert. "White House Plans Medicaid Coverage of Viagra by States," *New York Times* 28 May 1998, late ed.; Section A; p. 1; Column 1 .

141. Pear, Robert. "New York and Wisconsin Will Defy Federal Directive to Provide Viagra Through Medicaid," *New York Times* 3 July 1998, late ed.; Section A; p. 12; Column 1.

142. Weinstein, Michael. "Fallen Taboo: Frank Talk on Viagra Is About Cost," *New York Times* 11 July 1998, late ed.; Section D; p. 1; Column 5.

143. Weinstein, Michael. "Fallen Taboo: Frank Talk on Viagra Is About Cost," *New York Times* 11 July 1998, late ed.; Section D; p. 1; Column 5.

144. Weinstein, Michael. "Fallen Taboo: Frank Talk on Viagra Is About Cost," *New York Times* 11 July 1998, late ed.; Section D; p. 1; Column 5.

145. Weinstein, Michael. "Fallen Taboo: Frank Talk on Viagra Is About Cost," *New York Times* 11 July 1998, late ed.; Section D; p. 1; Column 5.

146. "Viagra Is a $50 Million Pentagon Budget Item," *New York Times* 4 October 1998, late ed.; Section 1; p. 38; Column 4.

147. "Viagra Is a $50 Million Pentagon Budget Item," *New York Times* 4 October 1998, late ed.; Section 1; p. 38; Column 4.

148. Pear, Robert. "White House Plans Medicaid Coverage of Viagra by States," *New York Times* 28 May 1998, late ed.; Section A; p. 1; Column 1.

149. McGinn, Daniel. "Viagra's Hothouse," *Newsweek* 21 December 1998; p. 44.

150. Cowley, Geoffrey. "Is Sex a Necessity?" *Newsweek* 11 May 1998; p. 62.

151. Weinstein, Michael. "Fallen Taboo: Frank Talk on Viagra Is About Cost," *New York Times* 11 July 1998, late ed.; Section D; p. 1; Column 5.

152. Pear, Robert. "New York and Wisconsin Will Defy Federal Directive to Provide Viagra Through Medicaid," *New York Times* 3 July 1998, late ed.; Section A; p. 12; Column 1.

153. Cowley, Geoffrey. "Is Sex a Necessity?" *Newsweek* 11 May 1998; p. 62.

154. Pear, Robert. "New York and Wisconsin Will Defy Federal Directive to Provide Viagra Through Medicaid," *New York Times* 3 July 1998, late ed.; Section A; p. 12; Column 1.

155. "Viagra Is a $50 Million Pentagon Budget Item," *New York Times* 4 October 1998, late ed.; Section 1; p. 38; Column 4.

156. Pear, Robert. "New York and Wisconsin Will Defy Federal Directive to Provide Viagra Through Medicaid," *New York Times* 3 July 1998, late ed.; Section A; p. 12; Column 1.

157. Goldberg, Carey. "Insurance for Viagra Spurs Coverage for Birth Control," *New York Times* 30 June 1999, late ed.; Section A; p. 1; Column 5.

158. Goldberg, Carey. "Insurance for Viagra Spurs Coverage for Birth Control," *New York Times* 30 June 1999, late ed.; Section A; p. 1; Column 5.

159. Bryant, Adam. "A Birth-control Ruling Signals a Shift for Women," *Newsweek* 25 June 2001; p. 38.

160. Bryant, Adam. "A Birth-control Ruling Signals a Shift for Women," *Newsweek* 25 June 2001; p. 38.

161. Sheryl WuDunn's article in the *New York Times,* "Japan's Tale of Two Pills," demonstrated that this controversy wasn't limited to the United States, let alone Western thinking. In Japan, the modern version of the birth control pill had not yet been approved, while it took only six months for Viagra to be approved by the Ministry of Health and Welfare. In addition, since condoms had been the established method of birth control in Japan for decades, there was a great deal of fear that the elimination of condoms in favor of birth control pills would result in an increase in HIV cases.

162. Brink, Susan. "The Do or Die Decade," *U.S. News & World Report* 11 March 2002; p. 60.

163. Brink, Susan. "The Do or Die Decade," *U.S. News & World Report* 11 March 2002; p. 60.

164. Brock, Fred. "A Dose of Sense from Viagra's Spokesman," *New York Times* 4 June 2000, late ed.; Section 3; p. 14; Column 3.

165. McGinn, Dan, "Viagra's Hothouse," *Newsweek* 21 December 1998; p. 44.

166. Not only is this the message at kwikmed.com (retrieved June 13, 2003) but at no less than a dozen other online pharmacies. While it is tempting to delve into a discussion of the Viagra-as-SPAM issue, it is beyond the scope of this project. Nonetheless, I have been intrigued by the lengths sellers of Viagra and similar medications will go in order to sell these products. My favorite subject line in an e-mail message for Viagra stated: "harden your johnny."

167. Rich, Frank. "Electric Kool-Aid Viagra," *New York Times* 12 August 1999, late ed.; Section A; p. 19; Column 1.

168. Hitt, Jack. "The Second Sexual Revolution," *New York Times Magazine* 20 February 2000, late ed.; Section 6; pp. 50, 68.

169. "Buying Viagra on the Internet," *U.S. News & World Report* 11 January 1999.

170. Adler, Jerry. "Take a Pill and Call Me Tonight," *Newsweek* 4 May 1998; p. 48.

171. Adler, Jerry. "Take a Pill and Call Me Tonight," *Newsweek* 4 May 1998; p. 48.

172. Mazur (2003), pp. 44–45.

173. Stolberg, Sheryl Gay. "Virtual Druggists: Internet Prescriptions Boom in the 'Wild West' of the Web," *New York Times* 27 June 1999, late ed.; Section 1; p. 1; Column 4.

Chapter 4

1. See Fried (1999) and Hilts (2003).

2. See Mazur (2003).

3. See Mazur (2003).

4. "Potency in All the Right Places" (2001), p. 14.

5. Both Viagra and erectile dysfunction *have* made their way into contemporary critical theory. Elizabeth Haiken (2000) questions how "medicine makes the man." Annie Potts (2000) examines the ways in which erectile dysfunction has come to be culturally constructed. In addition, Potts et al. (2003) interview women whose partners use Viagra. Barbara Marshall and Stephen Katz (2002) investigate the cultural requirements of sexual fitness among aging men. Marshall (2002) also considers how Viagra impacts the construction of gender in the claims made by "hard science."

6. "The Hard Sell: Advertising in America" (1994).

7. Bryson explains, "In the sense of persuading members of the public to acquire items they might not otherwise think of buying—items they didn't know they needed—advertising is a phenomenon of the modern age" (336).

8. "The Hard Sell: Advertising in America" (1994), p. 337.

9. "The Perils of Prevention" (2003), p. 54.

10. "Prime Time Pushers," (2001), p. 30.

11. "Prime Time Pushers," (2001), p. 36.

12. "Prime Time Pushers," (2001), p. 32.

13. Furthermore, 90 percent of these one- and two-page Viagra ads were positioned in the desirable first twelve pages of each issue. From reading the "Index to Advertisers" in the back of each issue, I discerned that *additional* promotional materials—in the form of detachable inserts—were included in twenty-one of the

seventy issues. Unfortunately, these inserts had been detached and could not be included in my analysis.

14. *Discipline and Punish* (1977), p. 137.
15. See Vestergaard (1985).
16. "A Study in Reproductive Technologies," (1999), p. 254.
17. See Tiefer (1979).
18. World Health Organization. (1975). *Education and Treatment in Human Sexuality: The Training of Health Professionals.* World Health Organization: Geneva, Switzerland, Technical Report Series, No. 572.
19. NIH Consensus Development Panel. "Impotence," *Journal of the American Medical Association.* July 7, 1993; v. 270, n. 1, pp. 83–90.
20. Feldman, Henry et al. (1994). "Impotence and Its Medical and Psychological Correlates: Results of the Massachusetts Male Aging Study," *The Journal of Urology* 151, 1, pp. 54–61.
21. Statistically speaking, the size of the sample is less problematic than the fact that it was not a random national sample. If it were a random sample of the U.S. population, then 1,300 is a quite respectable sample size.
22. *The Male Body* (1999), p. 59.
23. Unfortunately, it *does* seem to describe the way many women experience sex with men.
24. Katzenstein, Larry. *Viagra: The Remarkable Story of the Discovery and Launch* (2001). Pfizer HX377R99; p. 21.
25. Katzenstein, Larry. *Viagra: The Remarkable Story of the Discovery and Launch* (2001). Pfizer HX377R99; p. 11.
26. Katzenstein, Larry. *Viagra: The Remarkable Story of the Discovery and Launch* (2001). Pfizer HX377R99; p. 17.
27. The name was soon changed to *LifeDrive*—*Voices* probably carried too much of a psychological connotation.
28. Pfizer. "Myths and Facts," *Voices.* Pfizer HC122A01 (Spring 2001); p.12.
29. Pfizer. "Prime Time," Pfizer HC178Y99 (April 1999); p. 9.
30. Pfizer. "Take the Pfizer Health Challenge," Pfizer HC152R01 (April 2001); p. 6.
31. In his 1997 bestseller *I Don't Want to Talk about It: Overcoming the Secret Legacy of Male Depression,* psychotherapist Terrence Real suggests, however, that "not only the general public but even the medical and psychiatric community give credence to depression in only its most obvious and most severe form" (34). Pfizer has endeavored to make sure this is not a problem with erectile dysfunction.
32. While the use of the term "partner" throughout this brochure is most likely intended to bridge divides of sexual expression, twenty-three photographs attest to five racially diverse heterosexual couples.
33. Pfizer. "Start Something All Over Again," Pfizer HC180Y99 (April 1999); p. 5.
34. Pfizer. "Start Something All Over Again," Pfizer HC180Y99 (April 1999); p. 3.
35. Pfizer. "Start Something All Over Again," Pfizer HC180Y99 (April 1999); p. 1.
36. Pfizer. "Start Something All Over Again," Pfizer HC180Y99 (April 1999); p. 5.
37. Pfizer. "Start Something All Over Again," Pfizer HC180Y99 (April 1999); p. 7.
38. Pfizer. "Start Something All Over Again," Pfizer HC180Y99 (April 1999); p. 7.
39. Pfizer. "Start Something All Over Again," Pfizer HC180Y99 (April 1999); p. 3.
40. Pfizer. "The *New* Facts of Life," Pfizer HX728F97 (May 1998).
41. Pfizer. "What Every Man (and Woman) Should Know about Erectile Dysfunction," Pfizer HX117Y99 (March 1999).

42. Pfizer. "Real People/Real Stories: A World of Difference," Pfizer HC613F00 (December 2000).
43. "Forever Functional: Sexual Fitness and the Ageing Male Body" (2002); p. 59.
44. Pfizer. "What Every Man (and Woman) Should Know about Erectile Dysfunction," Pfizer HX117Y99 (March 1999).
45. Pfizer. "Start Something All Over Again," Pfizer HC180Y99 (April 1999); p. 11.
46. Katzenstein, Larry. *Viagra: The Remarkable Story of the Discovery and Launch* (2001). Pfizer HX377R99; p. 5.
47. Pfizer. "Take the Pfizer Health Challenge," Pfizer HC152R01 (April 2001); p. 6.
48. Pfizer. "Myths and Facts," *Voices.* Pfizer HC122A01 (Spring 2001); p. 13.
49. Pfizer. "Good Medicine," *LifeDrive.* Pfizer VG117615 (October 2002); p. 25.
50. Pfizer. "Good Medicine," *LifeDrive.* Pfizer VG117615 (October 2002); p. 25.
51. Moynihan, Ray. "Urologist Recommends Daily Viagra to Prevent Impotence," *British Medical Journal.* January 4, 2003; v. 326, n. 7379, p. 9.
52. NIH Consensus Development Panel. "Impotence," *Journal of the American Medical Association.* July 7, 1993; v. 270, n. 1, p. 84.
53. NIH Consensus Development Panel. "Impotence," *Journal of the American Medical Association.* July 7, 1993; v. 270, n. 1, p. 84.
54. NIH Consensus Development Panel. "Impotence," *Journal of the American Medical Association.* July 7, 1993; v. 270, n. 1, p. 84.
55. Feldman, Henry et al. "Impotence and Its Medical and Psychological Correlates: Results of the Massachusetts Males Aging Study," *Journal of Urology,* 151, 1 (1994); p. 55.
56. "Potency in All the Right Places: Viagra as a Technology of the Gendered Body," (2001); p. 24.
57. "Potency in All the Right Places: Viagra as a Technology of the Gendered Body," (2001); p. 25.
58. Katzenstein, Larry. *Viagra: The Remarkable Story of the Discovery and Launch* (2001). Pfizer HX377R99; p. 3.
59. Feldman, Henry et al. "Impotence and Its Medical and Psychological Correlates: Results of the Massachusetts Males Aging Study," *Journal of Urology* 151, 1 (1994); p. 54.
60. Feldman, Henry et al. "Impotence and its Medical and Psychological Correlates: Results of the Massachusetts Males Aging Study," *Journal of Urology* 151, 1 (1994); pp. 54–61.
61. Rosen, Raymond et al. "The International Index of Erectile Dysfunction (IIEF): A Multidimensional Scale for Assessment of Erectile Dysfunction," *Urology* 49, 6, (1997); pp. 822–830.
62. Rosen, Raymond et al. "The International Index of Erectile Dysfunction (IIEF): A Multidimensional Scale for Assessment of Erectile Dysfunction," *Urology* 49, 6, (1997); pp. 822–830.
63. *Understanding Men's Passages* (1999), p. 195.
64. Katzenstein, Larry. *Viagra: The Remarkable Story of the Discovery and Launch* (2001). Pfizer HX377R99; p. 3.
65. Feldman, Henry et al. "Impotence and Its Medical and Psychological Correlates: Results of the Massachusetts Males Aging Study," *Journal of Urology,* 151, 1 (1994); p 54.

66. Rosen, Raymond et al. "The International Index of Erectile Dysfunction (IIEF): A Multidimensional Scale for Assessment of Erectile Dysfunction," *Urology* 49, 6 (1997); p. 823.
67. NIH Consensus Development Panel. "Impotence," *Journal of the American Medical Association*. July 7, 1993; v. 270, n. 1, p. 83.
68. *The Male Body* (1999), p. 60.
69. *Gender and the Social Construction of Illness* (2002), p. 8.
70. See Burstyn (1999).
71. This is (sad to say) only partially true. As a former left-handed pitcher with pinpoint control, I still halfheartedly entertain the fantasy of being "discovered."
72. Two other products for middle-aged men use former baseball stars as spokesmen. A treatment for medical hair restoration at the Yahoo games website featured self-proclaimed "sex addict" and former batting champion Wade Boggs. The copy reads, "Even though he retired in 1999 he's now back in the game." And a television commercial promoting a product that colors facial hair employs former New York Mets first baseman Keith Hernandez calling the "play-by-play" in a sports bar. A gray-bearded man gets rejected by a much younger woman, then "scores" after using the product.
73. Well, maybe it's not just teenagers. The May 2003 issue of *Playboy* contains an advertisement for a company called NC17 Clothing. The "Second Base camisole" and "Home Run thong" are evidently hot sellers. And on an episode of *Seinfeld*, Keith Hernandez (playing himself) tries to seduce Elaine using the baseball analogy:

    Hernandez: Elaine. You don't know the first thing about first base.
    Elaine: Well I know something about getting to first base. And I know you'll never be there.
    Hernandez: The way I figure it I've already been there and I plan on rounding second tonight at around eleven o'clock.
    Elaine: Well, uh, I'd watch the third base coach if I were you 'cause I don't think he's waving you in.

74. In the 1992 film *A League of Their Own* (a semifictional account of the All-American Girls' Professional Baseball League of the 1930s and 1940s), pop singer Madonna plays the center fielder "All the Way" Mae Mordabito, a brash ballplayer with a heart of gold.
75. "Baseball and the Reconstitution of American Masculinity: 1880–1920" (1990), p. 56.
76. "Baseball and the Reconstitution of American Masculinity: 1880–1920" (1990), pp. 57–58.
77. "An Iron Man: The Body and Some Contradictions of Hegemonic Masculinity" (1990).
78. *Fathers Playing Catch With Sons* (1985), p. 49.
79. *The Rites of Men: Manhood, Politics, and the Culture of Sport* (1999), p. 233. See also Jackson Katz's (2000) *Tough Guise: Violence, Media, and the Crisis of Masculinity*.
80. In the process of writing this chapter, I happened to meet Tony Gwynn. On my way to an academic conference in May 2003, I had to change planes in Albuquerque where I boarded the plane for San Diego along with the SDSU baseball team and their celebrity coach. As I passed Mr. Gwynn and took my seat several

rows behind him, it occurred to me that I had in my possession the *LifeDrive* magazine with him on the cover. I approached him with the magazine opened to a full-color action picture and asked him for his autograph. After digging briefly in his carry-on bag for a Sharpie marker, he took the magazine from me, glanced at the image I had chosen for him to autograph, and casually flipped to the cover. Upon the discovery that what he was about to sign was *not* the usual Sports Illustrated or San Diego Padres program, but a long-forgotten article in a magazine for Viagra patients, he looked up at me and asked, "Do you just carry this around with you?" After spending about ten seconds nervously fumbling about my research, I thanked him for the autograph and returned to my seat.

81. Both of Viagra's competitors—Cialis and Levitra—utilize the sports metaphor in their advertising as well. In one of its television commercials, Levitra symbolizes successful erectile function by showing a man throw a football through a swinging tire (after several misses) as his proud wife looks on. On the drug's website, former Chicago Bears coach Mike Ditka asks you to take the Levitra challenge. And during the 2004 Olympics, Levitra television commercials beguiled viewers to "light the flame." Cialis asks, "When the moment is right, will you be ready?"

82. By naming this character "Joe," it is my belief that Pfizer is opting for a sort of diverse "everyman" strategy: Joe as in "He's a good Joe" or "Joe Sixpack."

83. The first time I saw this commercial, I was reminded of the Jimi Hendrix lyric "Hey Joe, where you goin' with that gun in your hand."

84. In a similar television commercial which I'll call the "Multicultural Cocktail Party," a white man in his early forties arrives at a party and is bombarded by similar questions from men and women of all races. He finally reaches his female partner at the far end of the room and she too notices a "change." Smirking, he tells her, "I saw the doctor today." In this commercial, just seeing the doctor has made him more of a stud. Why *she* is so excited about this transformation, I can't begin to guess.

85. The promotional video "Real People/Real Stories," produced in December 2000, does, in fact, include the testimony of a racially mixed couple.

86. *Technologies of the Gendered Body* (1996), p. 9.

87. *Slow Motion* (1990), p. 176.

88. "Stereotypes of Black Male Sexuality" (1998), p. 467.

89. Cultural critic bell hooks writes in her book about black men and masculinity, *We Real Cool* (2004), "the convergence of racist thinking about the black body . . . has always projected onto the black body a hypersexuality" (67). For a curious conflation of Viagra, virility, and black male sexuality, see Spike Lee's *She Hate Me* (2004).

90. "The Lacanian Phallus" (1992).

91. *Understanding Men's Passages* (1999), p. 32.

92. Pfizer. "What Every Man (and Woman) Should Know about Erectile Dysfunction," Pfizer HX062Y99A (July 1999); p. 12.

93. Pfizer. "Step Up to the Plate," Pfizer VG110647A (April 2002).

94. More recent issues of *LifeDrive* have changed this to "Start Talking."

95. *LifeDrive* magazine.

96. Pfizer. *LifeDrive*. HC369B01 (Fall 2001); pp. 2–3.

97. Lucky 7?

98. Pfizer. *LifeDrive*. HC369B01 (Fall 2001); p. 32.

99. Pfizer. *LifeDrive*. HC122A01 (Spring 2001); p. 32.

100. *Decoding Advertisements* (1978), p. 12.

101. *Decoding Advertisements* (1978), p. 19.

102. In a spring 2004 Viagra television ad that features the rock anthem "We Are the Champions" by Queen (!), men burst from their homes on a suburban street, unable to constrain their joy of being delivered by Viagra, dancing and high-fiving each other. Most relevant for this section are the penis-shaped (white) picket fences that mark each "castle."
103. Pfizer. *LifeDrive*. HC122A01 (Spring 2001); p. 32.
104. Pfizer. *LifeDrive*. HC122A01 (Spring 2001); p. 25.
105. Pfizer. "Prime Time," Pfizer HC178Y99 (April 1999); p. 12.
106. Pfizer. "What Every Man (and Woman) Should Know about Erectile Dysfunction," Pfizer HX117Y99 (March 1999).
107. Pfizer. *LifeDrive*. HC369B01 (Fall 2001); p. 28.
108. Pfizer. *LifeDrive*. VG107535 (Summer 2002); p. 17.
109. *The Rhetoric of Religion* (1970).
110. *Interplay: The Process of Interpersonal Communication* (1995), p. 300.
111. From an online etymological dictionary: www.etymonline.com/i3etym.htm. Retrieved July 2, 2003.
112. Katzenstein, Larry. *Viagra: The Remarkable Story of the Discovery and Launch* (2001). Pfizer HX377R99; p. 15.
113. Katzenstein, Larry. *Viagra: The Remarkable Story of the Discovery and Launch* (2001). Pfizer HX377R99; p. 16.
114. Dierdre Does Devonshire?
115. "Anticlimax Dept." (1998).
116. Rosen, Raymond et al. "The International Index of Erectile Dysfunction (IIEF): A Multidimensional Scale for Assessment of Erectile Dysfunction," *Urology* 49, 6 (1997); pp. 822–830.
117. "Anticlimax Dept." (1998), p. 26.
118. "Anticlimax Dept." (1998), p. 26.
119. Pfizer. "The *New* Facts of Life," HX728F97 (May 1998).
120. *Interplay: The Process of Interpersonal Communication* (1995).
121. I am also struck by the way in which "ED" (Eddie) seems to represent, like "Joe," an average American man.
122. AP, "A Medical Journal Eases Conflict Rule," *New York Times* 13 June 2002, Section A; p. 26; Column 1.

Chapter 5

1. Fineout, Gary. "Governor Bush Has Chaotic Day, Declares State of Emergency," *Lakeland Ledger* 12 September 2001; p. A3.
2. Tomkins (2001).
3. Muschamp (2002), p. A15.
4. "Tribute in Light" was the second architectural project developed as a sense-making mechanism for the citizens of the New York metropolitan area. In December 2001, a viewing platform allowed observers to gaze into the void created by the destruction. While the platform necessitated a visit to Ground Zero, "Tribute in Light" was designed so that it could be seen from a distance. The artists and architects who designed the spectacle, however, observed that people were drawn to the source.
5. Goldberger (2002).
6. "Mirror Images" (1996).

7. *Space, Text, and Gender* (1987).

8. *The Sex of Architecture* (1996), p. 11.

9. Language, as well as architecture, connects spatial concepts with the feminine and masculine. Hierarchical organization is a predominant mode of thinking in our culture and its metaphors are dispersed through other events. George Lakoff (1992) examines how, in our Western culture, the journey upward represents growth. For example, "*climbing* the ladder" is a hierarchical metaphor, referring to career advancement. The "*top* candidate" implies an overall favorite. "Keeping *up* with the Joneses" signifies social accomplishment. The stock market's bar charts and our nation's interstate highway system utilize enumeration by ascending numbers west to east (left to right) and from south to north (bottom to top). In religion and spiritual practice, the body is a "temple" and the eyes are "windows" to the soul. As part of his definition of man (*sic*), Kenneth Burke (1966) proposes that we are "goaded by the spirit of hierarchy," or motivated by the promise of order and status. We are mystified by those who are at a different level than ourselves in the hierarchy and, as a result, in competition with them. "Those 'Up' are guilty of not being 'Down,'" writes Burke, "those 'Down' are certainly guilty of not being 'Up'" (15).

10. *Flexible Bodies* (1994).

11. *Telling Sexual Stories* (1995).

12. See Martin (1987).

13. The phrase is from Sandra Bartky (1998).

14. "Deconstructing the Dominant" (1996), p. 611.

15. "Cultural Studies: What's in a Name?" (1995), p. 250.

16. The phrase is from Charles Taylor (1992).

17. American attitudes about male sexuality (as if there is only one kind) and the concomitant strategies for securing its continued enjoyment through this single pharmacological approach reminds me of our nation's attitude toward those forces (whether concrete or ideological) that inhibit the penetration of our supreme authority: capitalism. This approach to conflict—in the metaphor of the body politic—is a physical one; as we increase our material presence, we dismiss the possibilities for communication, compromise, and connection.

18. *Natural Symbols* (1970), p. xiv.

19. *Permanence and Change* (1935).

20. *Language as Symbolic Action* (1966).

21. "Dramatistic Analysis," (1990), p. 349.

22. "Dramatistic Analysis," (1990), p. 351.

23. *Grammar of Motives* (1969), p. 113.

24. *Feminist Politics and Human Nature* (1983), p. 308.

25. This hypothesis was put forth by Susan Bordo in *The Male Body* (1999a).

26. See especially Eisenberg (1977), Kleinman (1980), and Morris (1998).

27. "Anthropology Rediscovers Sexuality" (1991), p. 47.

28. See Snyder and Smith (1982).

29. The phase is from Jean Lyotard (1984).

30. *Heterosexuality in Question* (1999), p. 163.

31. See Doyal (1995).

32. *Stigma* (1963), p. 4.

33. *Stigma* (1963), p. 5.

34. I agree with Sandra Bartky (1998), who writes, "[P]atriarchy, like racism, is a lethal, and, unless we act with some dispatch, quite possibly a terminal illness of the social body" (xi).

35. Gender and sexuality have long been employed as a way to establish boundaries of inclusiveness to go along with artificially constructed geographical boundaries; how they are defined is crucial to the definition of the political life of a society. George Mosse (1985) suggests that "the dynamic of modern nationalism was built on the ideal of manliness" (14). Tamar Mayer (2000) determines that masculinity and femininity cannot exist without each other and "without these twin constructions the nation as we know it would not exist either" (14). David Evans (1993) argues that "sexuality is inextricably tied to [American] capitalism's requirements for reproduced labor" (36). Anne McClintock (1995) theorizes that the nation is constructed as the hegemonic arena for both heterosexuality *and* masculinity and it is in that domain where gender differences have come to be institutionalized. Dana Nelson (1998) examines how "'white' manhood [has come] to 'stand' for nation [and] how it came to be idealized as a 'representative' identity in the United States" (28). Carole Vance (1995) writes, "the history of the construction of sexuality in modern, state-level society shows that sexuality is an actively contested political and symbolic terrain in which groups struggle to implement programs and alter sexual arrangements and ideologies" (42). These theorists identify gender and sexuality as carefully, systematically, and, frequently, *rhetorically* constructed mechanisms with specific ideological intent and powerful social consequences. And they often do so through the metaphor of architecture.

36. *Gender and Architecture* (2000), p. 1.

37. *The Sex of Architecture* (1996), p. 11.

38. *Building Sex* (1995), p. 201.

39. "Public Memorializing in Postmodernity," (1994), p. 354.

40. "Public Memorializing in Postmodernity," (1994), p. 354.

41. "Public Memorializing in Postmodernity," (1994), p. 357.

42. Goffman (1963), p. 138.

43. *Psychoanalysis and Feminism* (1974).

44. "Taking a Biological Turn," (2003), p. 50.

45. *What Makes Women Sick: Gender and the Political Economy of Health* (1995), p. 61.

46. Quoted in Gayle Beck's (1995) "Hypoactive Sexual Desire Disorder: An Overview," p. 923.

47. *Volatile Bodies: Toward a Corporeal Feminism* (1994), p. 153.

48. *From Ritual to Theatre* (1983), pp. 233–234.

49. *Performance Studies* (2002), p. 82.

50. *Performance Studies* (2002), p. 84.

51. "Joint Performance Across Cultures," (1993), p. 120.

52. "Healthy Passions: Safer Sex as Play," (1992), p. 76.

Bibliography

Adelman, Mara (1992). "Healthy Passions: Safer Sex as Play." In Timothy Edgar, Mary Anne Fitzpatrick, and Vicki Freimuth (Eds.), *AIDS: A Communication Perspective*. Hillsdale, NJ: Lawrence Erlbaum Associates.

Adler, Ronald, Lawrence Rosenfeld, and Neil Towne (1995). *Interplay: The Process of Interpersonal Communication* (6th ed.). Fort Worth, TX: Harcourt Brace.

Agrest, Diana, Patricia Conway, and Leslie Kanes Weisman (1996). "Introduction." In Diana Agrest, Patricia Conway, and Leslie Kanes Weisman (Eds.), *The Sex of Architecture*. New York: Harry N. Abrams Publishers.

Althusser, Louis (1971). "Ideology and Ideological State Apparatuses." In *Lenin and Philosophy and Other Essays*. London: New Left Books.

Arrington, Michael (2002). *Recreating Ourselves: Stigma, Identity Changes, and Narrative Reconstruction Among Prostate Cancer Survivors*. Unpublished doctoral dissertation, University of South Florida, Tampa, FL.

Atwood, Margaret (2003). *Oryx and Crake*. Doubleday: New York.

Balsamo, Anne (1996). *Technologies of the Gendered Body*. Durham, NC: Duke University Press.

Barbarella (1968). Roger Vadim (director), Terry Southern and Roger Vadim (screenplay, from the comic strip by Jean-Claude Forest). Dino de Laurentis Cinematographica.

Bartky, Sandra (1998). "Foreword." In Tom Digby (Ed.), *Men Doing Feminism*. New York: Routledge.

Bateson, Mary Catherine (1993). "Joint Performance Across Cultures: Improvisation in a Persian Garden," *Text and Performance Quarterly*, 13, 3, 113–121.

Beck, Gayle (1995). "Hypoactive Sexual Desire Disorder: An Overview." *Journal of Consulting and Clinical Psychology*, 63, 6, 919–928.

Belkin, Lisa (2001, March/April). "Prime Time Pushers." *Mother Jones*, 30–36.

Bell, Elizabeth (1999). "Weddings and Pornography: The Cultural Performance of Sex." *Text and Performance Quarterly*, 19, 3, 173–195.

Berg, Bruce (2001). *Qualitative Research Methods for the Social Sciences* (4th ed.). Boston: Allyn & Bacon.

Bergen, Ann (1996). "Female Fetish, Urban Form." In Diana Agrest, Patricia Conway, and Leslie Kanes Weisman (Eds.), *The Sex of Architecture*. New York: Harry N. Abrams Publishers.

Berger, Peter and Thomas Luckmann (1966). *The Social Construction of Reality*. New York: Doubleday.

Betsky, Aaron (1995). *Building Sex*. New York: William Morrow.

Bhabha, Homi (1995). "Are You a Man or a Mouse?" In Maurice Berger, Brian Wallis, and Simon Watson (Eds.), *Constructing Masculinity*. New York: Routledge.

The Big Chill (1982). Lawrence Kasdan (director and screenplay). Columbia Pictures.

Birke, Lynda (1999). "Bodies and Biology." In Janet Price and Margrit Shildrick (Eds.), *Feminist Theory and the Body*. New York: Routledge.

Blair, Carole, Marsha Jeppeson, and Enrico Pucci (1994). "Public Memorializing in Postmodernity: The Vietnam Veterans Memorial as Prototype." In William Nothstine, Carole Blair, and Gary Copeland (Eds.), *Critical Questions: Invention, Creativity, and the Criticism of Discourse and Media*. New York: St. Martin's Press.

Boogie Nights (1997). Paul Thomas Anderson (director and screenplay). New Line Studios.

Bordo, Susan (1999a). *The Male Body: A New Look at Men in Both Public and Private*. New York: Farrar, Straus & Giroux.

Bordo, Susan (1999b). "Feminism, Foucault, and the Politics of the Body." In Janet Price and Margrit Shildrick (Eds.), *Feminist Theory and the Body*. New York: Routledge.

Boswell, John (1994). *Same-Sex Unions in Pre-Modern Europe*. New York: Villard.

Brannon, Robert (1976). "Introduction." In Robert Brannon and Deborah David (Eds.), *The Forty-Nine Percent Majority*. Reading, MA: Addison-Wesley.

Brod, Harry (1987). *The Making of Masculinities*. Winchester, MA: Allen & Unwin.

Brownlee, Shannon (2003, March 16). "The Perils of Prevention." *New York Times Magazine*, 52–55.

Bryson, Bill (1994). "The Hard Sell: Advertising in America." In Paul Eschholz, Alfred Rosa, and Virginia Clark (Eds.), *Language Awareness*. New York: St. Martin's Press.

Burke, Kenneth (1935). *Permanence and Change*. Berkeley: University of California Press.

Burke, Kenneth (1960). *A Grammar of Motives*. Berkeley: University of California Press.

Burke, Kenneth (1966). *Language as Symbolic Action*. Berkeley: University of California Press.

Burke, Kenneth (1970). *The Rhetoric of Religion*. Berkeley: University of California Press.

Burke, Kenneth (1973). *Philosophy of Literary Form*. Berkeley: University of California Press.

Bursytn, Varda (1999). *The Rites of Men: Manhood, Politics, and the Culture of Sport*. Toronto: University of Toronto Press.

Butler, Judith (1989). *Gender Trouble: Feminism and the Subversion of Identity*. London: Routledge.

Butler, Judith (1993). *Bodies That Matter: On the Discursive Limits of "Sex."* London: Routledge.

Butler, Judith (1995). "Melancholy Gender/Refused Identification." In Maurice Berger, Brian Wallis, and Simon Watson (Eds.), *Constructing Masculinity*. New York: Routledge.

Califia, Pat (1994). *Public Sex: The Culture of Radical Sex*. Pittsburgh, PA: Cleis Press.

Cameron, Elaine and Jon Bernardes (1998). "Gender and Disadvantage in Health: Men's Health for a Change." *Sociology of Health and Illness*, 20, 5, 673–693.

Charmaz, Kathy (1987). "Struggling for a Self: Identity Levels of the Chronically Ill." In Julius Roth and Peter Conrad (Eds.), *Research in the Sociology of Health Care*. Greenwich, CT: JAI Press.

Charmaz, Kathy (1995). "Identity Dilemmas of Chronically Ill Men." In Donald Sabo and David Gordon (Eds.), *Men's Health and Illness*. Thousand Oaks, CA: Sage.

Chodorow, Nancy (1978). *The Reproduction of Mothering: Psychoanalysis and the Sociology of Gender*. Berkeley: University of California Press.

Clarke, Adele and Virginia Oleson (1999). "Revising, Diffracting, Acting." In Adele Clarke and Virginia Oleson (Eds.), *Revisioning Women, Health, and Healing: Feminist, Cultural, and Technoscience Perspectives*. New York: Routledge.

Cohen, Jon (1998, July 6). "Anticlimax Department." *The New Yorker*, 26.

Connell, Robert (1987). *Gender and Power*. Cambridge, UK: Polity Press.

Connell, Robert (1990). "An Iron Man: The Body and Some Contradictions of Hegemonic Masculinity." In Michael Messner and Donald Sabo (Eds.), *Sport, Men and the Gender Order*. Champaign, IL: Human Kinetics.

Connell, Robert (1995). *Masculinities*. Berkeley: University of California Press.

Conquergood, Dwight (1983). "Communication as Performance: Dramaturgical Dimensions in Everyday Life." In John Sisco (Ed.), *The Jensen Lectures: Contemporary Communication Studies*. Tampa: University of South Florida.

Conquergood, Dwight (1995, February 17). "Beyond the Text: Toward a Performative Cultural Politics." *Otis J. Aggerd Performance Festival: The Future of Performance Studies*. Terre Haute: Indiana State University.

Courtenay, Will (2000a). "Behavioral Factors Associated With Disease, Injury, and Death Among Men: Evidence and Implications for Prevention." *Journal of Men's Studies*, 9, 1, 81.

Courtenay, Will (2000b). "Constructions of Masculinity and Their Influence on Men's Well-Being: A Theory of Gender and Health." *Social Science and Medicine*, 50, 10, 1385–1401.

Cramer, Janet (1998). "Women as Citizen: Race, Class, and the Discourse of Women's Citizenship." *Journalism and Mass Communication Monographs*, 165, 13.

D'Emilio, John and Estelle Freedman (1988). *Intimate Matters: A History of Sexuality in America*. New York: Harper & Row.

Daly, Mary (1978). *Gyn/Ecology: The Metaethics of Radical Feminism*. Boston: Beacon Press.

Davis, Lennard (1997). "Constructing Normalcy: The Bell Curve, the Novel, and the Invention of the Disabled Body in the Nineteenth Century." In Lennard Davis (Ed.), *The Disabilities Studies Reader*. New York: Routledge.

Diamond, Elin (1997). *Unmaking Mimesis*. New York: Routledge.

Diamond, Jared (1997). *Guns, Germs, and Steel: The Fates of Human Societies*. New York: W. W. Norton.

DiPalma, Carolyn (1999). "Reading Donna Haraway: A Feminist Theoretical and Methodological Perspective." *Asian Journal of Women's Studies*, 5, 1, 50.

Dire Straits (1979). "Lady Writer." *Communique*. Warner Bros. Records.

Dr. Doolittle 2 (2001). Steve Carr (director). Larry Levin (screenplay). 20th Century Fox.

Dolan, Jill (1993). *Presence and Desire: Essays on Gender, Sexuality, Performance*. Ann Arbor: University of Michigan Press.

Douglas, Mary (1970). *Natural Symbols: Explorations in Cosmology*. New York: Random House.

Doyal, Lesley (1995). *What Makes Women Sick: Gender and the Political Economy of Health.* New Brunswick, NJ: Rutgers University Press.

Doyle, James (1983). *The Male Experience.* Dubuque, IA: W. C. Brown Publishers.

Durning, Louise and Richard Wrigley (2000). "Introduction." In Louise Durning and Richard Wrigley (Eds.), *Gender and Architecture.* Chichester, UK: Wiley Publishers.

de Lauretis, Teresa (1987). *Technologies of Gender.* Bloomington: Indiana University Press.

du Pré, Athena (2000). *Communicating About Health: Current Issues and Perspectives.* Mountain View, CA: Mayfield Press.

Ehrenreich, Barbara and Dierdre English (1974). *Witches, Midwives, and Nurses.* Old Westbury, NY: Feminist Press.

Ehrenreich, Barbara and Dierdre English (1978). *For Her Own Good: 150 Years of the Experts' Advice to Women.* Garden City, NY: Anchor.

Eisenberg, Leon (1977). "Disease and Illness: Distinctions Between Professional and Popular Ideas of Sickness." *Culture, Medicine, and Psychiatry,* 1, 11.

Evans, David (1993). *Sexual Citizenship: The Material Construction of Sexualities.* London: Routledge.

Faludi, Susan (1991). *Backlash: The Undeclared War Against American Women.* New York: Anchor.

Farrell, Warren (1974). *The Liberated Man.* New York: Random House.

Fausto-Sterling, Anne (1995). "How to Build a Man." In Maurice Berger, Brian Wallis, and Simon Watson (Eds.), *Constructing Masculinity.* New York: Routledge.

Feldman, Henry, Irwin Goldstein, Dimitrios Hatzichristou, Robert Krane, and John McKinlay (1994). "Impotence and Its Medical and Psychological Correlates: Results of the Massachusetts Male Aging Study," *The Journal of Urology,* 151, 1, 54–61.

Ferguson, Kathy (1993). *The Man Question: Visions of Subjectivity in Feminist Theory.* Berkeley: University of California Press.

Fight Club (1999). David Fincher (director), Jim Uhls (screenplay, from the novel by Chuck Palahniuk). Fox 2000 Pictures.

Fineout, Gary (2001). "Governor Bush Has Chaotic Day, Declares State of Emergency," *Lakeland Ledger.* A3.

Fishman, Jennifer and Laura Mamo (2002). "What's in a Disorder?: A Cultural Analysis of Medical and Pharmaceutical Constructions of Male and Female Sexual Dysfunction." *Women & Therapy.* 24, 1&2, 179–193.

Foucault, Michel (1972). *An Archaeology of Knowledge.* New York: Random House.

Foucault, Michel (1977). *Discipline and Punish.* New York: Vintage Books.

Foucault, Michel (1978). *History of Sexuality.* New York: Pantheon Books.

Foucault, Michel (1980). "Power/Knowledge." In Colin Gordon (Ed.), *Selected Interviews and Other Writings, 1972–1977.* New York: Pantheon Books.

Freud, Sophie (1999). "The Social Construction of Normality." *Families in Society,* 80, 4, 333–339.

Frey, Lawrence, Carl Botan, and Gary Kreps (2000). *Investigating Communication: An Introduction to Research Methods* (2nd ed.). Boston: Allyn & Bacon.

Fried, Stephen (1999). *Bitter Pills: Inside the Hazardous World of Legal Drugs.* New York: Bantam.

Friedman, David (2001). *A Mind of Its Own: A Cultural History of the Penis.* New York: Free Press.

Garber, Marjorie (1992). *Vested Interests: Cross-dressing and Cultural Anxiety.* New York: Routledge.

Garlick, Barbara, Suzanne Dixon, and Pauline Allen (1992). *Stereotypes of Women in Power: Historical Perspectives and Revisionist Views*. Westport, CT: Greenwood Press.

Gerschick, Thomas and Adam Stephen Miller (1994). "Coming to Terms: Masculinity and Physical Disability." *Masculinities*, 2, 1.

Giddens, Anthony (1984). *The Constitution of Society*. Berkeley: University of California Press.

Giddens, Anthony (1991). *Modernity and Self-Identity: Self and Society in the Late Modern Age*. Stanford, CA: Stanford University Press.

Gilman, Sander (1988). *Disease and Representation: Images of Illness from Madness to AIDS*. Ithaca, NY: Cornell University Press.

Gitlin, Todd (1980). *The Whole World Is Watching: Mass Media in the Making and Unmaking of the New Left*. Berkeley: University of California Press.

Goffman, Erving (1959). *The Presentation of Self in Everyday Life*. Garden City, NY: Doubleday.

Goffman, Erving (1963). *Stigma*. New York: Simon & Schuster.

Goffman, Erving (1974). *Frame Analysis*. New York: Harper & Row.

Goldberger, Paul (2002, April 15). "Horizon Department: Lights Out." *The New Yorker*, 34.

Grossberg, Lawrence (1995). "Cultural Studies: What's in a Name? (One More Time)." *Taboo*, 1, 1–37.

Grosz, Elizabeth (1994). *Volatile Bodies: Toward a Corporeal Feminism*. Bloomington: Indiana University Press.

Hacking, Ian (1995). "An Indeterminacy in the Past." In *Rewriting the Soul: Multiple Personality and the Sciences of Memory*. Princeton, NJ: Princeton University Press.

Hacking, Ian (1999). *The Social Construction of What?* Cambridge, MA: Harvard University Press.

Haiken, Elizabeth (2000). "Virtual Virility, or, Does Medicine Make the Man?" *Men and Masculinities*, 2, 4, 388–409.

Hall, Donald (1985). *Fathers Playing Catch With Sons*. San Francisco: North Point Press.

Haraway, Donna (1988). "Situated Knowledges: The Science Question in Feminism and the Privilege of Partial Perspective." *Feminist Studies*, 14, 3, 575–599.

Haraway, Donna (1989). *Primate Visions: Gender, Race, and Nature in the World of Modern Science*. New York: Routledge.

Harrison, James (1978). "Warning: The Male Sex Role May Be Dangerous to Your Health." *Journal of Social Issues*, 34, 1, 65–86.

Hartley, Heather and Leonore Tiefer (2003). "Taking a Biological Turn: The Push for a 'Female Viagra' and the Medicalization of Women's Sexual Problems." *Women's Studies Quarterly*, 1, 2, 42–54.

Hartouni, Valerie, "A Study in Reproductive Technologies" (1999). In Adele Clarke and Virginia Oleson (Eds.), *Revisioning Women, Health, and Healing*. New York: Routledge.

Hearn, Jeff (1996). "Deconstructing the Dominant: Making the One(s) the Other(s)." *Organization*, 3, 611–626.

Heart Disease Weekly (2003). "Thrombosis: Viagra Deaths Explained by New Understanding of Platelet Clumping," February 2, 24.

Hemingway, Ernest (1926/1954). *The Sun Also Rises*. New York: Macmillan.

Hendrix, Jimi (1967). "Hey Joe." *Are You Experienced?* Reprise.

Hilts, Philip (2003). *Protecting America's Health: The FDA, Business, and One Hundred Years of Regulation*. New York: Alfred A. Knopf.

Hite, Shere (1976). *The Hite Report: A Nationwide Study on Female Sexuality*. New York: Macmillan.

Holland, Janet, Caroline Ramzanoglu, and Rachel Thomson (1996). "In the Same Boat? The Gendered (In)experience of First Heterosex." In Diane Richardson (Ed.), *Theorising Heterosexuality*. Buckingham, UK: Open University Press.

Hollywood Homicide (2003). Ron Shelton (director), Robert Souza (screenplay). Columbia Pictures.

hooks, bell (2003). *We Real Cool: Black Men and Masculinity*. New York: Routledge.

Humm, Maggie (1995). *The Dictionary of Feminist Theory*. Columbus: Ohio State University Press.

Huxley, Aldous (1946/1962). *Brave New World*. New York: Harper.

Ian, Marcia (1996). "When Is a Body Not a Body? When It's a Building." In Joel Sanders (Ed.), *Stud: Architectures of Masculinity*. Princeton, NJ: Princeton Architectural Press.

Infante, Dominic, Andrew Rancer, and Deanna Womack (1993). *Building Communication Theory* (2nd ed.). Prospect Heights, IL: Waveland Press.

Irigary, Luce (1974). *The Speculum of the Other Woman*. Cornell, NY: Cornell University Press.

Irvine, Janice (1990). *Disorders of Desire: Sex and Gender in Modern American Sexology*. Philadelphia: Temple University Press.

Irving, John (1976). *The World According to Garp*. New York: Simon & Schuster.

Jackson, Stevi (1999). *Heterosexuality in Question*. London: Sage.

Jagger, Allison (1983). *Feminist Politics and Human Nature*. Totowa, NJ: Rowman & Allanheld.

Janis, Ian (1980). "The Influence of Television on Personal Decision-Making." In *Television and Social Behavior: Beyond Television and Children*. Hillman, NJ: Lawrence Erlbaum & Associates.

Johnson, J. David and Hendrika Meischke (1993). "A Comprehensive Model of Cancer Related Information Seeking Applied to Magazines." *Human Communication Research*, 19, 3, 343–367.

Jordanova, Ludmilla (1989). *Sexual Visions: Images of Gender in Science and Medicine Between the Eighteenth and Nineteenth Centuries*. Madison: University of Wisconsin Press.

Katz, Jackson (2000). *Tough Guise: Violence, Media, and the Crisis of Masculinity*. Northampton, MA: Media Education Foundation.

Kimmel, Michael (1990). "Baseball and the Reconstitution of American Masculinity: 1880–1920." In Michael Messner and Donald Sabo (Eds.), *Sport, Men, and the Gender Order: Critical Feminist Perspectives*. Champaign, IL: Human Kinetics.

Kimmel, Michael (1996). *Manhood in America*. New York: Free Press.

Klein, Alan (1986). "Pumping Irony: Crisis and Contradiction in Bodybuilding. *Sociology of Sport Journal*, 3, 1, 3–23.

Kleinman, Arthur (1980). *Patients and Healers in the Context of Culture: An Exploration of the Borderlands Between Anthropology, Medicine, and Psychiatry*. Berkeley: University of California Press.

Kohn, Alfie (1986). *No Contest: The Case Against Competition*. Boston: Houghton Mifflin.

Kramerae, Cheris (1981). *Women and Men Speaking*. Rowley, MA: Newbury House.

Krippendorf, Klaus (1991). "Reconstructing (Some) Communication Research Methods." In Frederic Steier (Ed.), *Research and Reflexivity*. London: Sage.

Laclau, Ernesto (2000). *Contingency, Hegemony, Universality*. London: Verso.

Lakoff, George (1992). "The Contemporary Theory of the Metaphor." In Andrew Ortony (Ed.), *Metaphor and Thought*. Cambridge, UK: Cambridge University Press.

Laumann, Edward, John Gagnon, Robert Michael, and Stuart Michaels (1994). *The Social Organization of Sexuality: Sexual Practices in the United States*. Chicago: University of Chicago Press.

A League of Their Own (1992). Penny Marshall (director), Lowell Ganz and Babaloo Mandel (screenplay, from the story by Kelly Candaele and Kim Wilson). Columbia/TriStar.

Lehman, Peter (1993). *Running Scared: Masculinity and the Representation of the Male Body*. Philadelphia: Temple University Press.

Lehman, Peter (2001). "Crying Over the Melodramatic Penis: Melodrama and Male Nudity in Films of the 90s." In Peter Lehman (Ed.), *Masculinity: Bodies, Movies, Culture*. New York: Routledge.

Li, Zhenyu, Xiaodong Xi, Minyi Gu, Robert Feil, Richard Ye, Martin Eigenthaler, Franz Hoffman, and Xiaoping Du (2003). "A Stimulatory Role for cGMP-dependent Protein Kinase in Platelet Activation." *Cell*, 112, 1, 77–86.

Lloyd, Moya (1999). "Performativity, Parody, Politics." *Theory, Culture, and Society*, 16, 2, 195–213.

Lorber, Judith and Lisa Jean Moore (2002). *Gender and the Social Construction of Illness* (2nd ed.). Walnut Creek, CA: Altamira Press.

Lyotard, Jean (1984). *The Postmodern Condition: A Report on Knowledge*. Minneapolis: University of Minnesota Press.

Mamo, Laura and Jennifer Fishman (2001). "Potency in All the Right Places: Viagra as a Technology of the Gendered Body." *Body and Society*, 7, 4, 13–35.

Mankoff, Robert (1999, November 22). "Now, That's Product Placement!" [cartoon]. *The New Yorker*, 60.

Mann, Thomas (1927/1969). *The Magic Mountain*. New York: Vintage Books.

Marshall, Barbara (2002). "'Hard Science': Gendered Constructions of Sexual Dysfunction in the 'Viagra Age.'" *Sexualities*, 5, 2, 131–158.

Marshall, Barbara and Stephen Katz (2002). "Forever Functional: Sexual Fitness and the Ageing Male Body." *Body & Society*, 8, 4, 43–70.

Martin, Emily (1987). *The Woman in the Body: A Cultural Analysis of Reproduction*. Boston: Beacon Press.

Martin, Emily (1994). *Flexible Bodies*. Boston: Beacon Press.

Mayer, Tamar (2000). "Gender Ironies of Nationalism: Setting the Stage." In Tamar Mayer (Ed.), *Gender Ironies of Nationalism: Sexing the Nation*. London: Routledge.

Mazur, Dennis (2003). *The New Medical Conversation: Media, Patients, Doctors, and the Ethics of Scientific Communication*. London: Rowman & Littlefield.

McAllister, Matthew (1992). "AIDS, Medicalization, and the New Media." In Timothy Edgar, Mary Anne Fitzpatrick, and Vicki Freimuth (Eds.), *AIDS: A Communication Perspective*. Hillsdale, NJ: Lawrence Erlbaum Associates.

McClintock, Anne (1995). *Imperial Leather: Race, Gender, and Sexuality in the Colonial Contest*. New York: Routledge.

McGee, Michael Calvin (1990). "Text, Context, and the Fragmentation of Contemporary Culture." *Western Journal of Speech Communication*, 54, 3, 274–289.

McKerrow, Raymie (1989). "Critical Rhetoric: Theory and Praxis." *Communication Monographs*, 56, 2, 91–111.

Meet the Parents (2000). Jay Roach (director), Greg Glienna and Mary Ruth Clarke (screenplay). Universal.

Messerschmidt, James (2000). *Nine Lives: Adolescent Masculinities, the Body, and Violence.* Boulder, CO: Westview Press.

Messner, Michael (1987). "The Meaning of Success: The Athletic Experience and the Development of Male Identity." In Harry Brod (Ed.), *The Making of Masculinities: The New Men's Studies.* Boston: Allen & Unwin.

Messner, Michael (1997). *The Politics of Masculinity: Men in Movements.* Thousand Oaks, CA: Sage.

Meyers, Renee and David Seibold (1985). "Consumer Involvement as a Segmentation Approach for Studying Utilization of Health Organization Services." *Southern Communication Journal*, 50, 327–347.

Mitchell, Juliet (1975). *Psychoanalysis and Feminism.* New York: Vintage.

Mitka, Mike. (2000). "Some Men Who Take Viagra Die—Why?" *Journal of the American Medical Association*, 283, 5, 590, 593.

Moore, Henrietta (1987). *Space, Text, and Gender.* Cambridge, UK: Cambridge University Press.

Morris, David (1998). *Illness and Culture in the Postmodern Age,* Berkeley: University of California Press.

Morrisette, Alanis (1995). "Jagged Little Pill." *Jagged Little Pill.* Maverick.

Mosse, George (1985). *Nationalism and Sexuality: Respectability and Abnormal Sexuality in Modern Europe.* New York: Howard Fertig.

Moyer, Anne, Susan Greener, John Beauvais, and Peter Salovey (1995). "Accuracy of Health Research Reported in the Popular Press: Breast Cancer and Mammography." *Health Communication*, 7, 2, 147–161.

Moynihan, Ray (2003). "Urologist Recommends Daily Viagra to Prevent Impotence," *British Medical Journal*, 326, 7379, 9.

Mullaney, Jamie (1999). "Making It 'Count': Mental Weighing and Identity Attribution." *Symbolic Interaction*, 22, 3, 269–285.

Murphy, Peter (2001). *Studs, Tools, and Family Jewels.* Madison: University of Wisconsin Press.

Muschamp, Herbert (2002, March 12). "A Nation Challenged: A Critic's Notebook; In Lights at Ground Zero, Steps Toward Illumination." *New York Times,* A15.

National Institute of Health Consensus Development Panel on Impotence (1993). "Impotence," *Journal of the American Medical Association*, 270, 1, 83–90.

Nelkin, Dorothy (1995). *Selling Science: How the Press Covers Science and Technology.* New York: W. H. Freeman & Company.

Nelson, Dana (1998). *National Manhood: Capitalist Citizenship and the Imagined Fraternity of White Men.* Durham, NC: Duke University Press.

NOMAS: National Association of Men Against Sexism (1991). "Statement of Principles: The National Organization for Men Against Sexism." In Michael Kimmel and Michael Messner (Eds.), *Men's Lives.* Boston: Allyn & Bacon.

Ockman, Joan (1996). "Mirror Images: Technology, Consumption, and the Representation of Gender in American Architecture Since World War II." In Diana Agrest, Patricia Conway, and Leslie Kanes Weisman (Eds.), *The Sex of Architecture.* New York: Harry N. Abrams Publishers.

Ono, Kent and John Sloop (1992). "Commitment to Telos: A Sustained Critical Rhetoric." *Communication Monographs*, 59, 1, 48–60.

Parisi, Peter (1998). "The *New York Times* Looks at One Block in Harlem: Narratives of Race in Journalism." *Critical Studies in Mass Communication*,15, 3, 236–254.

Parker, Richard and Peter Aggleton (1999). *Culture, Society and Sexuality*. London: University College London Press.

Payne, David (1990). "Dramatistic Analysis." In Roderick Hart (Ed.), *Modern Rhetorical Criticism*. Glenview, IL: Scott Foresman/Little Brown.

Peck, M. Scott (1978). *The Road Less Traveled*. New York: Touchstone.

Philaretou, Andreas and Katherine Allen (2001). "Reconstructing Masculinity and Sexuality." *The Journal of Men's Studies*, 9, 3, 301.

Phillips, Helen (2001, May 12). "The Gender Police." *New Scientist*, 38–41.

Pleck, Joseph (1981). *The Myth of Masculinity*. Cambridge, MA: MIT Press.

Plummer, Ken (1995). *Telling Sexual Stories: Power, Change, and Social Worlds*. London: Routledge.

Pollock, Della (1995). "Performativity." In Cathy Davidson and Linda Wagner-Martin (Eds.), *The Oxford Companion to Women's Writing in the United States*. Oxford: Oxford University Press.

Potts, Annie (2000). "The Essence of the 'Hard On': Hegemonic Masculinity and the Cultural Construction of 'Erectile Dysfunction.'" *Men and Masculinities*, 3, 1, 85–103.

Potts, Annie, Nicola Garvey, Victoria Grace, and Tina Vares (2003). "The Downside of Viagra: Women's Experiences and Perspectives." *Sociology of Health and Illness*, 25, 7, 697–719.

Radway, Janice (1986). "Identifying Ideological Seams: Mass Culture, Analytical Method, and Political Practice." *Communication*, 9, 2, 93–123.

Ragsdale, J. Donald (1996). "Gender, Satisfaction Level, and the Use of Relational Maintenance Strategies in Marriage." *Communication Monographs*, 63, 354–369.

Real, Terrance (1997). *I Don't Want to Talk About It: Overcoming the Secret Legacy of Male Depression*. New York: Scribner.

Reinharz, Shulamith (1992). *Feminist Methods of Social Research*. New York: Oxford University Press.

Riley, Denise (1999). "Bodies, Identities, Feminisms." In Janet Price and Margrit Shildrick (Eds.), *Feminist Theory and the Body*. New York: Routledge.

Riska, Elianne (2002). "From Type A Man to Hardy Man: Masculinity and Health." *Sociology of Health and Illness*, 24, 3, 347–358.

Rose, Jacqueline (1986). *Sexuality in the Field of Vision*. London: Verso.

Rosen, Raymond, Alan Riley, Gorm Wagner, Ian Osterloh, John Kirkpatrick, and Avanish Mishra (1997). "The International Index of Erectile Dysfunction (IIEF): A Multidimensional Scale for Assessment of Erectile Dysfunction." *Urology*, 49, 6, 822–830.

Roth, Philip (2001). *The Human Stain*. New York: Vintage.

Rubin, Gayle (1975). "The Traffic in Women: Notes on the 'Political Economy' of Sex." In Rayna Reiter (Ed.), *Toward an Anthropology of Women*. New York: Monthly Review Press.

Rubin, Gayle (1984). "Thinking Sex: Notes for a Radical Theory of the Politics of Sexuality." In Carole Vance (Ed.), *Pleasure and Danger: Exploring Female Sexuality*. London: Routledge.

Sabo, Donald (1985). "Sports, Patriarchy, and Male Identity: New Questions About Men and Sport." *Arena Review,* 9, 2.

Sabo, Donald and David Gordon (1995). *Men's Health and Illness: Gender, Power, and the Body.* Thousand Oaks, CA: Sage.

Sanders, Joel (1996). *Stud: Architectures of Masculinity.* Princeton, NJ: Princeton University Press.

Savran, David (1998). *Taking It Like a Man: White Masculinity, Masochism, and Contemporary American Culture.* Princeton, NJ: Princeton University Press.

Sayre, Henry (1990). "Performance." In Frank Lentricchia and Thomas McLaughlin (Eds.), *Critical Terms for Literary Study.* Chicago: University of Chicago Press.

Schechner, Richard (2002). *Performance Studies.* London: Routledge.

Schiebinger, Londa (1989). *The Mind Has No Sex?: Women in the Origins of Modern Science.* Cambridge, MA: Harvard University Press.

Schofield, Toni, Robert Connell, and Linley Walker (2000). "Understanding Men's Health and Illness: A Gender-Relations Approach to Policy, Research, and Practice." *Journal of American College Health,* 48, 6, 247–256.

Schwartz, Pepper and Virginia Rutter (1998). *The Gender of Sexuality.* Thousand Oaks, CA: Sage.

Segal, Lynne (1990). *Slow Motion: Changing Masculinities, Changing Men.* New Brunswick, NJ: Rutgers University Press.

Segal, Lynne (1999). "Body Matters: Cultural Inscriptions." In Janet Price and Margrit Shildrick (Eds.), *Feminist Theory and the Body.* New York: Routledge.

Shapiro, Joan and Lee Kroeger (1991). "Is Life Just a Romantic Novel? The Relationship Between Attitudes About Intimate Relationships and the Popular Media." *American Journal of Family Therapy,* 19, 2, 226–236.

Shaw, Fiona (1998). "Foreword." In Lizbeth Goodman and Jane de Gay (Eds.), *The Routledge Reader in Gender and Performance.* London: Routledge.

Shaw, George Bernard (1919/1953). *Heartbreak House.* New York: Random House.

Sheehy, Gail (1999). *Understanding Men's Passages.* New York: Ballantine.

She Hate Me (2004). Spike Lee (director), Michael Genet and Spike Lee (screenplay). Forty Acres and a Mule Filmworks.

Silverman, David (2000). *Doing Qualitative Research.* London: Sage.

Silverman, Kaja (1992). "The Lacanian Phallus." *Differences,* 4, 1, 89.

Simon, William (1973). "The Social, the Erotic, and the Sensual: The Complexities of Sexual Scripts." In M. R. Jones (Ed.), *Nebraska Symposium on Motivation.* Lincoln: University of Nebraska Press.

Simon, William and John Gagnon (1984). "Sexual Scripts." *Society,* 22, 1.

Singer, Eleanor and Phyllis Endreny (1993). *Reporting on Risk.* New York: Russell Sage Foundation.

Sleeper (1973). Woody Allen (director and screenplay). MGM/United Artists.

Sloop, John (2000). "'A Van With a Bar and a Bed': Ritualized Gender Norms in the John/Joan Case." *Text and Performance Quarterly,* 20, 2, 130–149.

Snyder, C. R. and Timothy Smith (1982). "Symptoms as Self-handicapping Strategies: The Virtues of Old Wine in a New Bottle." In Gifford Weary and Herbert Mirels (Eds.), *Integration of Clinical and Social Psychology.* New York: Oxford University Press.

Solomon-Godeau, Abigail (1995). "Male Trouble." In Maurice Berger, Brian Wallis, and Simon Watson (Eds.), *Constructing Masculinity.* New York: Routledge.

Something's Gotta Give (2003). Nancy Meyers (director and screenplay). Columbia Pictures.

Staples, Robert (1995). "Health Among African-American Males." In Donald Sabo and David Gordon (Eds.), *Men's Health and Illness: Gender, Power, and the Body.* Thousand Oaks, CA: Sage.

Staples, Robert (1998). "Stereotypes of Black Male Sexuality: The Facts Behind the Myths." In Michael Kimmel and Michael Messner (Eds.), *Men's Lives.* Boston: Allyn & Bacon.

Stacks, Don and John Hocking (1992). *Essentials of Communication Research.* New York: HarperCollins.

States, Bert (1996). "Performance as Metaphor." *Theatre Journal,* 48, 1, 1–26.

Stewart, Charles, Craig Smith, and Robert Denton (1989). *Persuasion and Social Movements.* Prospect Heights, IL: Waveland Press.

Stroot, Phillipe (1997, November/December). "Health and the Media: Uneasy Partners?" *World Health,* 12–13.

Tannen, Deborah (1990). *You Just Don't Understand: Women and Men in Conversation.* New York: William Morrow.

Taylor, Charles (1992). *Ethics of Authenticity.* Cambridge, MA: Harvard University Press.

Tiefer, Leonore (1979). *Human Sexuality: Feelings and Functions.* New York: Harper & Row.

Tiefer, Leonore (1995). *Sex Is Not a Natural Act.* New York: Westview Press.

Tiger, Lionel (1969). *Men in Groups.* New York: Random House.

Tomkins, Calvin (2001, October 1). "Horizon Department: Towers of Light." *The New Yorker,* 27.

Tong, Rosemary (1998). *Feminist Thought* (2nd ed.). Boulder, CO: Westview Press.

Turner, Victor (1983). *From Ritual to Theatre: The Human Seriousness of Play.* New York: Performing Arts Publications Journal.

Turner, Victor (1988). *The Anthropology of Performance.* New York: Performing Arts Publications Journal.

Vance, Carole (1984). *Pleasure and Danger: Exploring Female Sexuality.* London: Routledge.

Vance, Carole (1991). "Anthropology Rediscovers Sexuality: A Theoretical Comment." *Social Science and Medicine,* 33, 8.

Vance, Carole (1995). "Social Construction Theory and Sexuality." In Maurice Berger, Brian Wallis, and Simon Watson (Eds.), *Constructing Masculinities.* New York: Routledge.

Vestergaard, Torben (1985). *The Language of Advertising.* London: Blackwell.

Waldron, Ingrid (1983). "Sex Differences in Illness Incidence, Prognosis, and Mortality." *Social Science and Medicine,* 17, 1107–1123.

Waldron, Ingrid (1991). "Effects of Labor Force Participation on Sex Differences in Mortality and Morbidity." In Marianne Frankenhaeuser, Ulf Lundberg, and Maragaret Chesney (Eds.), *Women, Work, and Health: Stress and Opportunities.* New York: Plenum.

Waldron, Ingrid (1995). "Contributions of Changing Gender Differences in Behavior and Social Roles to Changing Differences in Mortality." In Donald Sabo and David Gordon (Eds.), *Men's Health and Illness: Gender, Power, and the Body.* Thousand Oaks, CA: Sage.

Wallack, Lawrence (1990). "Improving Health Promotion: Media Advocacy and Social Marketing Approaches." In Charles Atkin and Lawrence Wallack (Eds.), *Mass*

Communication and Public Health: Complexities and Conflicts. Newbury Park, CA: Sage.

Watson, Jonathan (2000). *Male Bodies: Health, Culture, and Identity.* Buckingham, UK: Open University Press.

Weeks, Jeffrey (1977). *Coming Out: Homosexual Politics in Britain from the 19th Century to the Present.* London: Quartet.

West, Candace and Sarah Fenstermaker (1995). "Doing Difference." *Gender and Society,* 9, 1, 8–37.

West, Candace and Don Zimmerman (1987). "Doing Gender." *Gender and Society,* 1, 125–151.

Whitam, Frederick (1983). "Culturally Invariable Properties of Male Homosexuality: Tentative Conclusions From Cross-Cultural Research." *Archives of Sexual Behavior,* 12, 3, 207–226.

Williams, Raymond (1976). *Keywords: A Vocabulary of Culture and Society.* New York: Oxford.

Williamson, Judith (1978). *Decoding Advertisements: Ideology and Meaning in Advertising.* London: Marion Boyers.

Wood, Julia (1999). *Gendered Lives: Communication, Gender, and Culture* (3rd ed.). Belmont, CA: Wadsworth.

World Health Organization (1975). *Education and Treatment in Human Sexuality: The Training of Health Professionals.* Technical Report Series, No. 572. Geneva: World Health Organization.

Zilbergeld, Bernie (1999). *The New Male Sexuality* (revised ed.). New York: Bantam.

Index